Directory
of
Grants for Crafts
and

How to Write a Winning Proposal

James Dillehay

A Craft Business Book
from Warm Snow Publishers
Torreon, New Mexico

Other books by this author:

The Basic Guide to Selling Arts & Crafts
The Basic Guide to Selling Crafts on the Internet
The Basic Guide to Pricing Your Craftwork
Your Guide to Ebook Publishing Success
Overcoming the 7 Devils That Ruin Success

© 2007 by Warm Snow Publishers

First Edition

Published by:
Warm Snow Publishers
PO Box 75
Torreon NM 87061

ISBN: 0-9629923-4-8

Printed and bound in the United States of America
Printed on acid-free papers

Contents

Introduction 7
Chapter 1 Types of Grant Givers 9
Arts councils and arts agencies 9
Community foundations 9
Federal government giving programs 9
State government giving programs 11
Private foundations... 11
Corporate foundations 12
Individual givers 13
Artist in residency programs................................. 13
Microenterprise loans and assistance programs 14
Additional forms of assistance.............................. 15
Beginning research 16
Example of grant awards for crafts 17
How to find grants 18
Chapter 2 How to Write a Winning Proposal 19
What is your craft grant for? 19
Which grants do you go for? 20
Elements of a grant proposal 20
Cover letter 21
Tips to composing the proposal 21
Importance of the proposal summary.................... 23
Application forms 23
Letter of request 24
Common reasons why grant proposals fail 24
Grantsmanship workshops 28
Using a professional grant writer 29
Chapter 3 Catalog of Federal Domestic Assistance
Programs 31
Types of assistance 31
Government grant applications 33
Preparing to apply for a government grant 33
Developing ideas for the proposal 34
Community support 34
Identification of a funding resource....................... 35
Getting organized to write the proposal 36
Criticism 36
Signatures 36
Neatness 36

Mailing 36
Basic components of a federal grant proposal 37
Proposal summary: Outline of Project Goals 37
Introduction: Presenting Credibility 37
Problem Statement: Stating the Purpose at Hand ... 38
Project Objectives: Goals and Desired Outcome 39
Program Methods 39
Evaluation: Product and Process Analysis 40
Future Funding: Long-Term Project Planning 40
The Proposal Budget: Planning the Budget 41
Regional and federal depository libraries 41
**Chapter 4 How to Use a Computer and the Internet for
Grant Seeking** **42**
Word processor 42
Database programs 42
Internet grant links 42
Private Organizations 43
Government and Educational institutes 45
Internet resources for public art programs 47
Artist in residency programs 47
Miscellaneous fundraising sites 47
Grant writing tutorials 47
Appendixes - Directories **48**
Appendix I Directory of Craft Grants to Individuals 49
Appendix II Directory of Grants to Craft Organizations 64
Appendix III Directory of Community Foundations 68
Appendix IV Government Grants **69**
National Endowment for the Arts (NEA) 95
NEA grants to organizations 97
11.801 Native American Program 99
11.802 Minority Business Development 102
15.146 Ironworker Training Program 105
15.850 Indian Arts and Crafts Development 106
27.006 Federal Summer Employment 108
45.024 Grants to Organizations and Individuals ... 109
45.160 Promotion of the Humanities 115
45.161 Promotion of the Humanities--Research 118
45.201 Arts and Artifacts Indemnity 122
59.005 Assistance to Small Business 124
59.006 8(a) Business Development 125
59.007 Management and Technical Assistance for

Socially/Economically Disadvantaged Businesses . 128
64.116 For Disabled Veterans 130
82.015 Creative Arts Grants 133
82.032 Fund for U.S. Artists at International Festivals
and Exhibitions 136
84.170 Javits Fellowships 138
President's Committee on the Arts......................... 141
National Forest Service 142
U.S. Department of Agiculture 142
Rural Business Enterprise Grants........................... 143
Rural Business Opportunity Grants 145
Business and Industry Direct Loans 147
Business and Indutry Guaranteed Loans 148
Appendix V Funding for International Arts/Crafts 150
International Partnerships Office 150
The Fund for Artists at International Festivals 151
The US/Japan Creative Artists' Program 151
United States Information Agency 152
Appendix VI Directory of Arts Agencies..................... 153
National arts agencies 153
Statewide assemblies of arts agencies 154
Appendix VII Contacts for Public Art Programs 161
Appendix VIII Craft Artist in Residency Programs 168
Appendix IX Foundation Center Libraries 170
The Foundation Center... 170
The Foundation Center directories 180
**Appendix X Access points to Catalog of Federal
Domestic Assistance Programs 191**
Appendix XI Miscellaneous Resources 196
Helpful organizations.. 196
Periodicals 197
Bibliography 198
Glossary.. 199
Index 204

Introduction

Grant money for crafts is out there - in fact, millions of dollars are given away to craft artists every year. This book will show you where the money is and how to ask for it in a successful way.

Out of the 40,000+ foundations in the U.S. giving over $8 billion a year, there are over 5,000 grants giving away over $1 billion annually to arts related proposals. The trick is to match your project with those giving programs that seek to help people doing what you do.

This book will help you understand the different types of grant funding available and how to locate foundations and other sources who give money for arts and crafts.

If you were to start searching grant directories today, you would find little or no listings under the subject of "crafts." That doesn't mean money isn't given for crafts. Far from it. Hundreds of craft artisans receive grants for every kind of creative craft medium.

The trick to researching grants for crafts in the grant directories is to look under other subjects areas. The listings in this directory will save you many hours of research.

If you decide to research further, most of the listings which will be useful to you as a craft person will fall under subject headings like: arts, visual arts, folk arts, women, education, federated giving programs, Native Americans, small business, minorities, youth development, and grants to individuals.

I'll show you where and how to continue researching grants that offer additional types of support like continuing support, emergency funds, internships, matching grants, scholarships, fellowships, and seed money.

In addition to grants, this guide gives hundreds of organizations offering other kinds of assistance like national prize awards, funding for overseas exhibitions, payment for art in public places, low cost loans, technical assistance, training, and child care.

This book will be useful for both individuals seeking grant funding as well as nonprofit organizations in arts and crafts. Individuals will learn how to find and partner with larger organizations to achieve funding needs.

At first, you may find there are more grants than you think you have time to apply for. However, if you use this guide as an organizing tool for the grant application process, you will be able to build and maintain your own grant template which can be tailored for a specific grant.

If you use a computer, you will learn how to employ word processing and database software so that you can quickly put together numerous unique proposals to speed your grant seeking efforts.

Many foundations differ somewhat in the manner in which they wish to be approached. This guide will help you learn the most effective ways to approach all kinds of grant givers. And you'll find a standard grant application form that you can copy and modify to suit most granters' requirements.

The most effective means to successful grant seeking is to organize your approach through the following steps.

Identify which grant programs are appropriate for artists and craft persons. Many of the major grants for arts funding are listed in this directory. Also, included are ways to locate more sources of grants both in libraries and on the Internet.

Contact your list of prospective funders to get their guidelines and to identify who is the appropriate contact person in their organization. Get in touch with the contact person either by phone or interview to learn if there is a match between your project and their funding goals.

Gather and compose the elements that make up a funding proposal. This guide will help you create a standard proposal and instruct you how to recompose the proposal for different funders' guidelines.

The grant seeking process is time consuming. However, the rewards are worth the efforts. Check out the examples of craft persons who have received substantial amounts of money from various funding sources described in the first chapter.

Chapter 1 Types of Grant Givers

Grant money can come from several sources. The primary types of organizations that provide grants are arts agencies, the federal government, state governments, community foundations, corporate and private foundations and individual patrons.

It is important to learn as much as you can about each funding organization you wish to approach. The way you construct your proposal will differ somewhat according to the grant giver. Therefore it is important to understand the exact purpose each type of grant giver is trying to achieve. Simply applying for every grant as if they were all the same will waste your time and theirs.

Arts councils and arts agencies

There are over 4,000 local and regional arts agencies around the U.S.. Many of these councils provide a variety of services that support arts and crafts in their communities including grants and funding arts in public places.

I recommend that you begin your grant seeking with these organizations. Their mandate is to help local artists and craft persons without regard to race, sex or religion. At the end of this chapter, you can find examples of the grant awards by an arts council program in Massachusetts.

You can locate regional arts councils through the listings in the appendix of this book. For local and city councils, look in your phone book under "Arts Organizations" or "Arts Councils" or "Commission for the Arts"

Community foundations

After arts agencies, the next most accessible grant programs will come from community foundations. Community foundations are nonprofit, tax-exempt, and often considered public charities. They benefit local or regional area residents or organizations. They often receive funding from several sources including larger national foundations which they disburse in the form of grants to people or groups living in their community.

In addition to making grants available, these foundations often play a leadership role in their communities. They may serve as a resource for grant information for individuals and provide technical assistance for local nonprofits.

Federal government giving programs

The next most likely source for grant awards is one of the federal grant programs. The U.S. government annually gives away between $800 million and $1 billion in grants. Some of the money goes to organizations, some to individuals and the rest to states and local communities.

The most well known government grants program for craft artists is the National Endowment for the Arts. NEA grant winners have included craft workers in every area. The National Heritage Award gives the winning craft artist $10,000, national recognition and a presentation dinner at the White House.

To give you an idea of the variety of craft persons who have won this award, here is a partial list of past winners:

- George Lopez, Santos Woodcarver, Cordova, NM
- Elijah Pierce, Carver/Painter, Columbus, OH
- Georgeann Robinson, Osage Ribbonworker, Bartlesville, OK
- Duff Severe, Western Saddlemaker, Pendleton, OR
- Philip Simmons, Ornamental Ironworker, Charleston, SC
- Lanier Meaders, Potter, Cleveland, GA
- Ada Thomas, Basketmaker, Charenton, LA
- Lucinda Toomer, African-American Quilter, Columbus, GA
- Bertha Cook, Knotted Bedspread Maker, Boone, NC
- Albert Fahlbusch, Hammered Dulcimer Maker, Scottsbluff, NE
- Genevieve Mougin, Lace Maker, Bettendorf, IA
- Meali'i Kalama, Quilter, Honolulu, HI
- Jenny Thlunaut, Weaver, Haines, AK
- Emilio and Senaida Romero, Tin Embroidery, Santa Fe, NM
- Kepka Belton, Czech-American Egg Painter, Ellsworth, KS
- Amber Densmore, Quilter/Needleworker, Chelsea, VT
- Elmer Miller, Silversmith, Nampa, ID
- Lily Vorperian, Embroiderer, Glendale, CA
- Dolly Spencer, Dollmaker, Homer, AK
- Sophia "Sophie" George, Beadworker, Gresham, OR

For details on the National Heritage Award program see the description under the appendix for government grants.

Because of the size and number of government programs, they take more work to locate. We have included some grant programs that will be of interest to artists and craft persons in this book, but you will also want to check annual registers like the *Catalog of Federal Domestic Assistance,* described in more detail later.

Government giving programs differ widely in application procedure.

For whatever reasons, government procedures do not run as smoothly and uniformly as privately managed organizations.

Often, giving program application forms are more complex. Because government employees are taught to be obsessive about detail, you have to fill in every line of every form correctly or face being rejected.

However, the payoff for receiving a government grant can be worth the effort. Not only are the funds often larger than private grants, there is a certain amount of prestige that goes along with winning funding. For instance, my wife won an National Endowment for the Arts award for her work which she now includes with her list of credits and references.

Federal programs offer other forms of help like scholarships, fellowships, research grants, and technical help on specific projects to organizations and to individuals. The federal government is a better source for grants to individual craft persons than the private foundations. Also, because there are so many government giving programs, you should look into working with organizations who receive federal grant money directly.

Of all the federal assistance programs, support for small business is a major government activity. Small business financial health helps local and national economies. Small businesses create new jobs which stimulates growth and the amount of available spending money for families. In the directory on government grants, you'll find the different departments within the federal government which provide small business assistance like the Department of Commerce and the Small Business Administration.

State government giving programs

Many state grant programs derive funds from federal giving programs. State arts councils are a good example and are covered above. But there are other programs like funding for art in public places. You should locate and apply for all grants in your state and local community because those programs are intended for residents of that region which gives you an advantage over competing for a national grant.

Private foundations

Although most private foundations give to nonprofit organizations, some provide grants to individuals. A private foundation is a nonprofit organization that receives funding from a an individual, group, or a corporation with the purpose of disbursing the funds to help society in some way. Foundations act through charity, education and other means, usually in the form of paying grant money to organizations or individuals.

Foundation grant money for craft artists is designated for education, restoration, preservation or creative endeavor in crafts.

Examples of major private foundations that give grants for arts and crafts include: the John Simon Guggenheim Memorial Foundation, The Rockefeller Foundation, and the Ford Foundation,

There are many smaller foundations less well known, but important to know of for craft persons seeking grants. You will not be applying to most of the larger foundations because the number of them which fund craft art is limited. Included in the appendix of this guide is a directory list of foundation grants to individuals.

Some grants will be available through local community foundations, states or regional arts council organizations who have received large outside grants which they in turn, pass on to local applicants. Many of the examples of craft artists who won grants were from area giving programs. These types of giving programs are discussed later in this chapter.

Typically, a foundation has trustees or directors who oversee the organization of the foundation and which projects the foundation chooses to support. Foundations are often started as a philanthropic means of furthering the ideals of their founders and as an alternative to paying income or inheritance taxes.

Foundations are required by law to give away 5% of their assets in grants to charitable organizations every year. Foundations get tax breaks for giving away money to charitable organizations, not individual craft artists. Although there are sources of grants to individuals which we'll cover later, don't overlook the advantages of working with a nonprofit arts council or organization that receives outside funding from foundations.

Most larger foundations have a staff or a committee to handle day to day operations like sorting and arranging proposals to be considered. Smaller foundations may have only one or two persons who handle the routine work. The staff or committees report to the trustees or directors.

Corporate foundations

Corporations create grant giving programs in the form of corporate foundations. Often these grants are made to employees and families in geographical areas where the company has a presence so they may not be as likely a prospect for you as a craft artist. However, you may still benefit from programs for the local community or you may be eligible for such grants if you are your spouse or other family member are an employee of such a corporation.

Besides a tax benefit, corporate giving programs allow a company to receive public relations value from their contributions. For instance, you will often see Public Broadcasting Specials sponsored by a large foundation like the Ford Foundation or a grant from the Exxon Foundation.

When seeking funding from a corporation, ask yourself whether your project will result in a benefit for them. Examples include: improved corporate image, better reputation in the community, or creation of a more cultural or aesthetic environment for employees or residents. Your project should relate to their business, employees or environment.

Individual givers

Although there are individuals who give money to charitable or worthy causes, they are difficult to locate and approach. Unless you already know someone who gives funding and is willing to sponsor your project, you will have better results pursuing grants from the organizations mentioned above.

Artists have a history of attracting wealthy sponsors who support them through major purchases, money for continued work, or gallery exhibits. These funders are often referred to as patrons of the arts. The sponsor gains from being publicly associated with the fame of the artist. It works likewise for the artist who benefits from being recognized by someone with wealth and many connections.

Perhaps the biggest obstacle to getting grants from individuals is that they are not motivated to give to a nondeductible cause. Many of the above programs carry some tax benefits to the donors. Giving money to an artist or craft person doesn't save tax dollars for the giver, unless there is a nonprofit, charitable organization you are associated with who receives the funds directly.

Artist in residency programs

Artist in residency programs allow an artist or craft person a way to further their education in their chosen field. These programs resemble student fellowships in that they pay for tuition and basic living expenses for a specific period while the craft artist studies and develops their skills. You can find artist in residency programs around the world providing a broader experience of art and craft study.

Sources for artist in residence programs include:

• See the appendix of this book for artist in residency programs at craft schools

    • Universities or colleges with arts curriculum

    • State and local arts agencies

    • Art and craft schools

    • Internet search for "artist in residence" or "artist in residency."

See the chapter on using the Internet for a list of artist in residency web sites.

Microenterprise loans and assistance programs

Microenterprise is a term used to describe small unincorporated businesses with fewer than ten employees that do not have access to traditional bank financing. Most craft businesses would be described as microenterprises.

These programs offer several levels of help like technical and educational support, direct loans, and access to peer lending groups. Peer lending is when a group of business owners come together to guarantee loans made to members of the group. Often there is no collateral involved but group pressure is used to maintain loan payments. If a member defaults on a loan, the group loses its credit for borrowing.

Low-income individuals usually have trouble obtaining credit because of lack of loan collateral. They often have little or no experience in business. Low-income earning women need technical help, legal assistance, and child care to run their own business. Microenterprise programs were designed to help those with low incomes who wish to start their own business.

Microenterprise programs administer micro-loans, small loans made to low-income individuals to begin or expand their small business. Micro-loans are much smaller than loans made at banks, some starting at as low as $500 while banks often won't loan less than $10,000.

Microenterprise programs have become one of the most cost-effective ways to create new jobs and expand small businesses. These programs are especially helpful to women, who have often been discriminated against by commercial lenders.

Two examples of nonprofit lending agencies are ACCION International and Aid to Artisans.

In the United States, a three-year ACCION study of 849 clients released in April 1998 revealed that after two loans over 17 months, take-home income increased 38 percent or an average of $455 per month. ACCION borrowers with the lowest incomes saw take-home income jump 54 percent, an average of $515 monthly. As a group, the 849 borrowers realized a $228,000 increase in monthly business profits and contributed $215,000 more each month to their households than they did before entering ACCION-affiliated microlending programs. A subgroup of 312 clients who received three loans or more reported the cumulative net worth of their businesses grew by over $1 million. For more information on ACCION:

ACCION International
120 Beacon Street
Somerville, MA 02143 USA
Tel: (617) 492-4930
Fax: (617) 876-9509
Web site: http://www.accion.org

Aid to Artisans is a nonprofit organization that creates economic opportunities for craftspeople in communities around the world. ATA's design and business consultants and volunteers help establish handcraft-based businesses that can enter the global marketplace.

ATA provides design consultation, on-site workshops, business training, and the links to markets where craft products are sold. Through the efforts of ATA and their corporate and nonprofit associates, artisan groups are learning to help themselves and are becoming self-sustaining. For more information:

Aid to Artisans
14 Brick Walk Lane
Farmington, CT 06032 USA
Phone: (860)677-1649; FAX:(860)676-2170
Web site: http://www.aid2artisans.org

There are over 200 microenterprise programs across the U.S. with loan commitments of $44 million. Congress set aside $33 million to make micro-loans available to citizens through the Small Business Administration.

Microenterprise loans have a very high rate of repayment. The repayment rate in the U.S. is better than 90% with few defaults.

To locate a program local to you, consult the *Directory of U.S. Microenterprise Programs* ($15) available from The Aspen Institute, One Dupont Circle, NW #700, Washington DC 20036, Ph: (202)736-5800. If you have access to the Internet, do a search for "microenterprise program."

Additional forms of assistance

There are several kinds of government and private agencies that support small business with education, technical advice and research. In some cases, Women's Business Centers have programs that include child care. These organizations fall under the following headings:

Service Corps of Retired Executives (SCORE)
Web site: http://www.score.org

Small Business Association (SBA)
   Web site: http://www.sba.gov
Small Business Development Centers (SBDC)
   Web site: http://www.sba.gov/sbdc/
Women's Business Centers (WBC)
   Web site: http://www.onlinewbc.org/
Minority Business Development Centers (MBDC)
   Web site: http://www.mbda.gov/

To visit a center near you, consult your phone directory or contact the national office of the Small Business Administration at 1-800-8-ASK-SBA.

Beginning research

Now that you know the types of grants and assistance programs available, the next step is preparing for the application process. For non-grant support, contact the nearest program office in person.

For grants and fund-raising, begin by making a list of the grants and prospective funders. Use the listings provided in the appendixes of this book, grant sites on the Internet (see the chapter on Internet grant seeking), and other sources like The Foundation Center (see the appendix for a branch near you). The Foundation Center is a vital resource for grant seeking in any field.

You are going to be looking for granters that support arts, art in public places, small business, women, minorities, Native Americans, and any more subjects that your project might tie into. You will find few direct references to grants for crafts. That is because crafts are included under "arts" and "visual arts."

Don't waste your time listing every foundation out there. Target your search to match up some aspect of what you do with one of their giving purposes.

Get creative here. Perhaps you are a woman living in a rural area that meets the guidelines for a grant for women in business. The fact that your proposed business is selling handmade jewelry is not as important to the overall aims of the foundation or grant giver as their goal to support women starting a business.

On the other hand, don't apply for grants that have no obvious connection to what you do. If you see a grant award for research and study of parapsychology (yes, there is one) and you want money to create stained glass art, don't bother applying.

Learn the size and budget of each foundation's giving program. This information is almost always available in the listing where you first learn about a grant giving organization. Since foundation giving is a matter of public record, there is usually no difficulty uncovering annual spending history and current budgets.

After you have compiled a list of prospective grants, write to each and request their application guidelines. Strictly follow their submission guidelines.

Do not send your proposals first. It is inappropriate to approach private foundations as targets in a direct mail campaign. Even though you may be submitting proposals to many organizations at the same time, each approach will have to be targeted toward that foundation's interests.

When sending proposals, make sure you address them to the correct contact person for arts, crafts or the particular program you are applying to at each foundation. The guidelines will tell you who that person is. If not, call and ask for the contact person's name.

Example of grant awards for crafts

Grant awards come in all different forms and sizes. The following awards are examples of a grant program by an area arts council with giving programs for arts and crafts.

Massachusetts Cultural Council - The Artist Grants Program provides direct assistance to Massachusetts artists, to recognize exceptional work and to support the further development of their talents. Artist Grants give individuals the financial ability to hone and deepen their craft. They also provide artists with recognition and affirmation from their peers and the public.

Fellowship grants of $12,500 each and finalist grants of $1,000 each are offered in discipline categories which are reviewed every other year. Most artists who are legal residents of Massachusetts and 18 or older are eligible to apply. $361,000 was awarded in Artist Grants in 1999. In 1999, the following number of artists applied for and received Artist Grants.

Examples of community grant winners in arts and crafts

Category	Applicants	$7,500 Grants	$1,000 Awards
Crafts	143	8	5
Photography	230	7	6
Sculpture	228	12	3

Examples of craft and photography grant winners

Name	City	Grant
Maureen & Michael Banner	Monterey	$7,500
Cynthia Consentino	Northampton	$1,000
Henry S. Fox	Newburyport	$7,500
Michael M. Glancy	Rehoboth	$7,500
Christopher S. Gustin	South Dartmouth	$7,500
Nancy Clarke Hayes	New Bedford	$7,500
Judith Larzelere	Belmont	$1,000
Donna Rhae Marder	Winchester	$7,500
Michelle Samour	Acton	$1,000
Claire Sanford	Gloucester	$7,500
Photography		
Karl Baden	Cambridge	$7,500
Deborah Bright	Cambridge	$7,500
David Hilliard	Boston	$7,500
Jane Marsching	South Boston	$7,500
Mary Ann McQuillan	Somerville	$7,500
Daniel Ranalli	Cambridge	$1,000
Sonia Targontsidis	Brockton	$1,000

How to find grants

The first place to look for grants for craft artists is in the directories appendix of this book. Directories of foundations, government grants, arts councils and arts agencies, community foundations and their giving programs are provided.

For those with access to the Internet, there is a wealth of contact information online. See the chapter on using computers and the Internet for grant seeking.

For traditional resources for locating grants, the most accessible resource will be a cooperating collection branch of The Foundation Center library. These associate libraries will give you free access to their collection of directories which are the most comprehensive grant listings available. Locate a Foundation Center cooperating collection library near you by accessing the list in the appendix of this book.

Chapter 2 How to Write a Winning Proposal

A proposal is a written outline describing you, your project and how much money you are seeking. A proposal resembles a business plan in that it outlines your strategies for making use of capital to accomplish targeted goals.

The proposal is your main avenue for persuading a giver that your project is worth receiving funding. Therefore your proposal should be well thought out, professional in appearance, convincing, enthusiastic and positive.

The more powerful and well constructed your proposal, the better your chances of getting reviewed and awarded grant money. Allow time to devote to writing a convincing proposal. This is not a task you can throw together in one sitting and hope to win every grant you apply for.

First, ask yourself who will read your proposal? Foundations, corporations, individuals, and government agencies all have their own agendas and guidelines.

When applying to foundations, learn how your project fits their funding goals. Get a copy of their guidelines and application form, if any. Call and speak directly with the review or contact person.

Don't change your goal in order to match a funder's interest. If one foundation doesn't match closely enough, look elsewhere.

If you are writing proposals to individuals, do research into previous projects funded by the person and see how you can appeal to this person's interests.

Government grant applications have to be filled in meticulously without any omissions. See the next chapter for details on federal grant proposals.

There is no exact formula for every grant proposal. However, there is something close. You can get a head start by using the *Common Grant Proposal* (covered later in this chapter), which has been adopted by at least fifty major foundations, to create a template of your own proposal.

What is your craft grant for?

Before you can start to write a proposal, you have to have a clear picture of what you want to accomplish. Perhaps you are creating a large tapestry or a miniature city from wood carvings. Maybe you are publishing a book on a craft form that may soon be lost. Whatever your project is, write down a description. This will be your unique selling proposition or statement of purpose or mission statement. It is the first element of your grant proposal. After you know your mission, you can compare it with the giving criteria of foundations and government programs to learn which programs you should apply for.

Which grants do you go for?

In Chapter 1, we looked at the different types of grant and assistance programs. There will be many areas for you to look - private foundations, government grants, local arts agencies and more. Make a list of those whose criteria and goals match your project's goals.

Request proposal guidelines from each funder. Ask for a list of artists or craft persons they have funded previously. All grants are a matter of public record so don't hesitate to ask. Some "arts" grants go exclusively to support performing arts like theater or music. If so, you will not want to spend time applying to these funders.

When you have your list of prospective foundations that match your project, learn the size of the grants available. Will this grant be enough to complete your project? If not, maybe the foundation can point you to other programs. After all, the purpose of the foundations is to provide help.

You can even ask for help on how to write and present your proposal. Learn what you can about the foundation's review process. Whenever possible, meet the reviewers in person and develop relationships with as many of the staff as possible. This will help create interest in your project.

Elements of a grant proposal

There are several elements that will fit into every grant proposal. The following list will help you prepare. For some foundations, you may write the proposal from scratch. With others, you may fill in an application form that you get from the foundation.

Most grant programs will have a set of guidelines for applying which you can request from the foundation. Don't ignore these guidelines when submitting your proposal applications. Otherwise, your application will be rejected no matter how worthy you think your project is. Your project should match or coincide with the giving goals for the funder to whom you are applying.

When you have gathered the material for each point, you have the basic records to begin constructing a database from which to apply to multiple grant programs. We'll describe how to use a database and word processor software for speeding the grant writing process in the chapter on using computers and the Internet.

Since you will be working from the same basic material to recreate your next grant proposal, be sure to save each proposal even if it fails to win an award. You may need the information for future projects from the same foundation.

For most proposals, you will need:

• Cover letter, a short personal letter addressed to the contact person for the foundation you are applying to. Should be about three paragraphs that describe your proposal and how much funding you are seeking.

• Statement of purpose or what you intend to accomplish. Your project must coincide with the foundation's goals to get consideration. You may have several different statements prepared to match various grant awards.

• Resume or vitae summing up your previous work, awards, education, endorsements, reviews and testimonials. The resume should convince readers that you are qualified to accomplish the proposed task. When applying for multiple grants in different categories, you may want several variations of your resume on file to match each proposal.

• Timeline plan or schedule of how the project will develop through completion date. This is the outline of your project, your vision of what it looks like.

• Costs projection. Get estimates from suppliers, realtors, equipment dealers, and any other expenses to be involved in helping you complete the project. Include costs of hiring additional labor and location costs if any.

See also the example of the *Common Grant Application* form shown later in this chapter.

Cover letter

A cover letter will briefly describe the contents of the proposal without trying to substitute as a proposal itself. See the sample following.

Be sure to address your letter to a specific person at the foundation. If you don't know who that is, find out before sending your material. Make sure to spell their name correctly.

February 19, 2000

Ms. Juliet Pfunder
Arts Foundation
123 State St
New York NY 10001

Dear Ms. Pfunder,
        I am enclosing this formal request for a grant of
$17,500 from the Arts Foundation toward operating expenses
for one year.
        It is my hope that you will act favorably upon my
request for funding for my project which will help preserve the
craft of Ukranian egg painting.

                                        Sincerely

                                        Susan Oker

Tips to composing the proposal

A grant proposal is the first approach to getting funding from a foundation. An introductory proposal should be around three to ten pages typed or printed from a word processor.

• Compose an outline before you start writing to organize your thoughts and help plan your request

• Stress the benefits the funder will derive from funding your project more than the benefits you want to achieve. For instance, an arts foundation might want to promote craft development so you would emphasize how your work will benefit the community.

• Paint a vivid picture of how your project will look when finished. Avoid using negative wording. Strive to use active voice over passive voice.

• Stay focused on your mission.

• Proofread your proposal carefully and ask someone to check it for errors.

• Use brief paragraphs of about four to five sentences. Long text blocks are difficult to read.

• Print the proposal on good paper with black ink for the text.

• Make two copies, one to send to the foundation and one for your records. If using a computer, you will want to learn how to use a database to manage multiple grant proposals. More on databases later.

• Your proposal should be enthusiastic about your project. Avoid any negative comments about yourself or your previous work. When you make claims, back them with documented references. Don't assume that the granter knows about your work. Give them reasons to become interested.

• When describing a problem that matches the foundation's goals to alleviate, find evidence that supports how your project will help solve the situation. This is essential in applying for local grants which get their funding from larger national programs. Back up any claims you make with facts. Two or three references for any claim is sufficient.

• Avoid "begging" terminology or implying that the foundation "should" fund your project. Just keep the request simple and to the point.

Importance of the proposal summary

A summary of your proposal should appear at the start of your proposal but not in your cover letter. You probably won't write the summary until you have constructed the entire proposal. However, by the time you have written the complete proposal, you will be able to concisely sum up the important points effectively.

Your summary should tell who you are, your background as a craft artist, the purpose for which you are seeking funding, how you will spend the money, and the amount of funding you are seeking.

Some foundations receive so many proposals, that the reviewers only read the summaries to prequalify applicants. The summary is the first thing read, so you must create interest in the project if you want the reader to continue.

The summary helps provide the focus for the rest of your proposal, clarifying your intent for the reviewers. The summary should be two to three paragraphs and take up no more than half a typewritten page.

Application forms

Many organizations will have their own form or ask you to prepare a proposal based on their guidelines. There also exists a *Common Grant Application* program to standardize and simplify the application process. This form has been authored by the National Network of Grantmakers and is in use by about fifty major foundations. A sample of the forms follows.

CAUTION: Remember that grantmakers have different guidelines, priorities, timetables and deadlines. It is imperative to research and contact every potential funder. Please note: funders who accept the *Common Grant Application* format may still request additional information at any stage in the grantmaking process.

The *Common Grant Application* format is not a form. Just make your own text flow in the order under the designated headings and subheadings. Include all of the information you feel is important to your proposal. Remember to answer the questions or issues in every category.

The *Common Grant Application* offers you a lot of flexibility. It is designed to maximize your fund-raising efforts because it eliminates the need to rewrite and reorganize the same information for different foundations.

However, parts of your proposals will still need to be customized to address the specific goals of the foundations you are going after.

Always follow the guidelines of the foundation from whom you are seeking the grant.

Therefore: avoid the mass mailing of proposals. Personalize each request - particularly in the cover letter and executive summary - to appeal to the specific interests of each grantmaker.

You can photocopy and enlarge the sample shown here or you can download a full size version off the Internet at: http://www.nng.org/html/resources/cga_table.htm.

Whether the granter that you are applying to uses the standard form or not, you can use it as a template to create winning proposals.

Letter of request

Smaller foundations with little staff to review proposals will ask for a "letter of request" instead of a full proposal from grant seekers. This letter would be around two to three pages and summarize the main points made in a full proposal.

Begin with a paragraph describing your craft related project and how much money you are seeking. Then follow with a summary of how you plan to implement the project including how, when and where.

Describe yourself and previous accomplishments. Why should it be you who receives this money? Include a breakdown of how the money will be spent, shown as a budget.

In a letter of request, you are shrinking the full proposal down to a more concise letter.

Common reasons why grant proposals fail

• Failure to contact the right person within a funding source to

Example of a Common Grant Application form, page 1 of 3

---

1. COVER SHEET (Please use this format to create a one-page cover sheet.)

Organization Name:_____

Tax exempt status:____Year organization was founded:____Date of application:____

Address:_____

Telephone number:_____Fax number:_____

Director:_____

Contact person and title (if not director):_____

Grant request: _____Period grant will cover:_____

Type of request (general support, start-up, technical assistance, etc.):_____

Project title (if project funding is requested):_____

Total project budget (if request is for other than general support):_____

Total organizational budget (current year):_____

Starting date of fiscal year:_____

Summarize the organization's mission (2-3 sentences):_____

_____

Summary of project or grant request (2-3 sentences):_____

_____

11. NARRATIVE (Maximum of 5 pages.)
A._Introduction and Background of Organization_ (incorporating the following points:)
1. Briefly describe your organization's history,and major accomplishments.
2. Describe your current programs and activities.
3. Who is your constituency (be specific about demographics such as race, class, gender, ethnicity, age, sexual orientation, and people with disabilities)? How are they actively involved in your work and how do they benefit from this program and/or your organization?
4. If you are a grassroots group, describe your community. If you are a state, regional, or national organization, describe your work with local groups, if applicable, and how other regional and/or national organizations are involved.

B. _Describe Your Request_ (Incorporating the following points:)
1. Problem statement: what problems, needs, or issues does it address?
2. If other than general operating support, describe the program for which you seek funding, why you decided to pursue this project and whether it is a new or ongoing part of your organization.
3. What are the goals, objectives and activities/strategies involved in this request? Describe your specific activities/strategies using a timeline over the course of this request.
4. How does your work promote diversity and address inequality, oppression, and discrimination within your organization as well as the larger society?
5. Describe systemic or social change you are trying to achieve: How does your

Example of a Common Grant Application form, page 2 of 3

III. ATTACHMENTS/REQUIREMENTS (supply everything checked below by funder who prepared this copy.)

A. Evaluation
1. Briefly describe your plan for evaluating the success of the project or for your organization's work. What questions will be addressed? Who will be involved in evaluating this work -- staff, board, constituents, community, consultants? How will the evaluation results be used?

B. Organizational Structure/Administration
1. Briefly describe how your organization works: What are the responsibilities of board, staff, and volunteers? And if membership organization, define criteria for membership. Are there dues?
2. Who will be involved in carrying out the plans outlined in this request? Include a brief paragraph summarizing the qualifications of key individuals involved.
3. Provide a list of your board of directors with related demographic information.
4. How is the board selected, who selects them, and how often?
5. Include an organizational chart showing decision-making structure.

C. Finances
1. Most recent, completed full year organizational financial statement (expenses, revenue and balance sheet), audited, if available.
2. Organization's current annual operating budget (See attached budget format).
3. Current project budget, other than general support (See attached format).
4. Projected operating budget for upcoming year (See attached format).
5. List individually other funding sources for this request. Include amounts and whether received, committed, or projected/pending.
6. Describe your plans for future fund raising.
7. A copy of your IRS 501 (c)(3) letter. If you do not have 510(c)(3) status, check with the funder to see if they are willing to fund through your fiscal sponsor, or are willing to exercise expenditure responsibility. Additional information may be required to do so.
8. Other:_____

D. Other Supporting Material
1. Letters of support/commitment (up to three).
2. Recent newsletter, articles, newspaper clippings, evaluations, or reviews (up to 3).
3. Recent annual report.
4. Videos/cassettes are accepted ONLY if this box is checked.
5. Other:_____

Guidelines for applicants (completed by funder)
Send ___ number of complete copies: cover sheet, 5 page proposal, and attachments that are checked off.

Use a standard typeface no smaller than 10 points and no less than .25 in margins ___.
Proposals by fax are ___ are not ___ accepted.
Binders or folders are ___ are not ___ accepted.
Your proposal must be ___ double sided ___ single sided ___ no preference.

Please use the following paper ___ white/very light colored, ___ recycled, ___ 8.5xl 1 only, ___ no preference.

Si, aceptamos las solicitudes de fondos en espanol ___. Yes, we accept funding proposals in Spanish.
No aceptamos las solicitudes en espanol ___. No, we do not accept funding proposals in Spanish.

Example of a Common Grant Application form, page 3 of 3

IV. BUDGET

If you already prepare organizational and project budgets that approximate this format, please feel free to submit them in their original forms. You may reproduce this form on your computer, and/or submit separate pages for income and expenses.

Budget for the period:_____ to _____

EXPENSES			INCOME	
Item	Amount	FT/PT	Source	Amount
Salaries & wages (breakdown by individual position and indicate full or part time)	$_____	_____	Government grants & contracts (specify)	$_____
	_____	_____	Foundations (specify)	$_____
			Corporations	$_____
	_____	_____		
	_____	_____	Religious institutions	$_____
Fringe benefits & payroll taxes	$_____		United Way, Combined Federal Campaign & other federated campaigns	$_____
Consultants & professional fees	$_____		Individual contributions	$_____
Travel	$_____			
Equipment	$_____		Fundraising events & products	$_____
Supplies	$_____			
Training	$_____		Membership income	$_____
Printing & copying	$_____		In-kind support	$_____
Telephone & fax	$_____		Other (earned income, consulting fees, etc. Please specify)	$_____
Postage & delivery	$_____			
Rent & utilities	$_____		_____	_____
In-kind expense	$_____		_____	_____
Other (specify)	$_____		_____	_____
_____	$_____		_____	_____
TOTAL EXPENSE			TOTAL INCOME	$_____
			BALANCE	$_____

establish a relationship and learn more about the funder's goals.

• The application is not within the interests of the funding source. The person or group applying for the grant did not read the funder's limitations or did not understand the restrictions.

• The proposal is a bad idea.

• The proposal is a good idea but presented badly.

• The applicant lacks adequate credentials or experience.

• The applicant's previous accomplishments do not inspire confidence.

• The applicant's proposal relies too heavily on others without credentials or experience.

• The applicant tries to address too many issues instead of focusing on a central project.

• There are indications that other responsibilities would keep the applicant from applying sufficient time or attention to the project.

• With national foundations, the project does not address an issue of national significance.

• The project seems unfeasible from the budget proposed by the applicant. Funders are keen on financial responsibility and reporting.

• The funder has already funded a similar project.

• The funder's priorities and interests changed from the time you read their listing. Changes occur in the trends within society. There are periods of time when arts and crafts funding is more popular than others.

• Other projects reflect the funder's highest aims. Your proposal did not.

• Person or group applying has submitted a generic proposal to many funding sources at the same time. This is obvious to the funder looking for a match with the agency's priorities.

Grantsmanship workshops

For those who want more advanced training, consider attending a grantsmanship workshop. Here are some agencies who provide such training:

Polaris Grants Central
24 Kendal Green Drive
Greenville, SC, 29607-1509
Phone: 800-368-3775 or 864-271-3950
Fax 864-271-2882
Email at POLARISCO@aol.com or PolarisKat@aol.com
Web site: http://polarisgrantscentral.net/grantstraining.htm
Polaris workshops are held across the country annually on a variety

of grants topics.

David G. Bauer Associates
3171 Green Valley Road, Suite 322
Birmingham, AL 35243-5239
Phone: 800-836-0732, or 205-879-1457
Offers training programs annually on a variety of fundraising and grants topics.

The Grantsmanship Center
1125 West Sixth Street, Fifth Floor
PO Box 17220
Los Angeles, CA 90017
Phone: 213-482-9860 or 800-421-9512
The Grantsmanship Center offers grantsmanship workshops primarily through United Ways. They also offer numerous publications and resources for grant seekers. For $175, you can purchase a CD-ROM with 46 of the top ranked proposals that were actually funded by the National Endowment for the Arts and the National Endowment for the Humanities complete with application forms. This CD will be more useful to nonprofits than for individuals.

The Foundation Center
(see the appendix for contact information)

Nonprofit Management Development Center
1909 West Olney Avenue
Philadelphia, PA 19141-1199
Phone: 215-951-1701
Offers various programs on fundraising.

Local arts agencies and councils often sponsor grant writing workshops frequently through the year. Other sources for grants workshops include continuing education departments of colleges and universities, alternative educational courses like *The Learning Annex* and through searching for the phrase "grantsmanship workshops" on the Internet. See the chapter on using the Internet for grant seeking for online tutorials for grant writing.

Using a professional grant writer
There are professional grant writers who will create and submit

grant proposals for you. Typically they charge an upfront fee although some grant writers have been known to accept a portion of the grant award for their service. You can locate many grant writers on the Internet. Also, contact:

> National Grant Writers Association
> Research Associates
> Box 1755
> Irmo, SC 29063-1755
> Telephone (803) 750-9759 or Fax (803) 750-9366
> www.researchassociatesco.com

Their online directory lists over 1,000 professional grant writers by state who have to go through training and pass certification to be listed.

If you are a nonprofit organization looking for professional grant writing help, here are two national organizations with large directories:

> National Society of Fund Raising Executives
> 1101 King Street, Suite 700
> Alexandria, VA 22314
> Ph: (703)684-0410
> Web site: http://www.nsfre.org

> American Association of Fundraising Consultants, AAFRC
> Trust for Philanthropy
> P.O. Box 1020
> Sewickley, PA 15143-1020
> Ph: (412) 741-0609
> Web site: http://www.aafrc.org

Chapter 3 Catalog of Federal Domestic Assistance Programs

Developing and writing grant proposals for government grants differs from that of private foundations. This chapter gives you guidelines for successfully approaching government agencies and programs listed in the *Catalog of Federal Domestic Assistance Programs*. This application procedure is most helpful for an arts or crafts organization but can also be used by individuals.

You can search the Catalog online at: http://www.cfda.gov. A search for the keyword text "arts" brought a return of 43 programs.

You may also view the catalog at most public libraries and at Federal Depository Libraries around the U.S.. You can find the federal libraries listed in your Yellow Pages under "Government" and see the end of this chapter.

You will notice similarities to private foundation proposal writing in proposal writing for government grants. However, there are enough different steps that warrant studying this chapter before approaching government agencies.

Types of assistance

Currently, programs in the Catalog are being classified by General Services Administration into 15 types of assistance. Benefits and services of the programs are provided through seven financial types of assistance and eight nonfinancial types of assistance. The following list defines the types of assistance which are available through the programs.

Some of these types of assistance will be more useful than others to you as an artist or craft person. However, don't overlook the other programs as sources of additional kinds of support.

A. Formula Grants - Allocations of money to States or their subdivisions in accordance with a distribution formula prescribed by law or administrative regulation, for activities of a continuing nature not confined to a specific project.

B. Project Grants - The funding, for fixed or known periods, of specific projects or the delivery of specific services or products without liability for damages for failure to perform. Project grants include fellowships, scholarships, research grants, training grants, traineeships, experimental and demonstration grants, evaluation grants, planning grants, technical assistance grants, survey grants, construction grants, and unsolicited contractual agreements.

C. Direct Payments for Specified Use - Financial assistance from the Federal government provided directly to individuals, private firms, and other private institutions to encourage or subsidize a particular activity by conditioning the receipt of the assistance on a particular performance by the recipient. This does not include solicited contracts for the procurement of goods and services for the Federal government.

D. Direct Payments with Unrestricted Use - Financial assistance from the Federal government provided directly to beneficiaries who satisfy Federal eligibility requirements with no restrictions being imposed on the recipient as to how the money is spent. Included are payments under retirement, pension, and compensation programs.

E. Direct Loans - Financial assistance provided through the lending of Federal monies for a specific period of time, with a reasonable expectation of repayment. Such loans may or may not require the payment of interest.

F. Guaranteed/Insured Loans - Programs in which the Federal government makes an arrangement to indemnify a lender against part or all of any defaults by those responsible for repayment of loans.

G. Insurance - Financial assistance provided to assure reimbursement for losses sustained under specified conditions. Coverage may be provided directly by the Federal government or through private carriers and may or may not involve the payment of premiums.

H. Sale, Exchange, or Donation of Property and Goods - Programs which provide for the sale, exchange, or donation of Federal real property, personal property, commodities, and other goods including land, buildings, equipment, food and drugs. This does not include the loan of, use of, or access to Federal facilities or property.

I. Use of Property, Facilities, and Equipment - Programs which provide for the loan of, use of, or access to Federal facilities or property wherein the federally-owned facilities or property do not remain in the possession of the recipient of the assistance.

J. Provision of Specialized Services - Programs which provide Federal personnel to directly perform certain tasks for the benefit of communities or individuals. These services may be performed in conjunction with nonfederal personnel, but they involve more than consultation, advice, or counseling.

K. Advisory Services and Counseling - Programs which provide Federal specialists to consult, advise, or counsel communities or individuals, to include conferences, workshops, or personal contacts. This may involve the use of published information, but only in a secondary capacity.

L. Dissemination of Technical Information - Programs which provide for the publication and distribution of information or data of a specialized technical nature frequently through clearinghouses or libraries. This does not include conventional public information services designed for general public consumption.

M. Training - Programs which provide instructional activities conducted directly by a Federal agency for individuals not employed by the Federal government.

N. Investigation of Complaints - Federal administrative agency activities that are initiated in response to requests, either formal or informal, to examine or investigate claims of violations of Federal statutes, policy, or procedure. The origination of such claims must come from outside the Federal government.

O. Federal Employment - Programs which reflect the government-wide responsibilities of the Office of Personnel Management in the recruitment and hiring of Federal civilian agency personnel.

Government grant applications

For many government grants, the approach is often begun through application forms. Each agency will have its own forms and guidelines for submissions. Be sure to follow the guidelines exactly or your application will be rejected. Some government agencies use a score sheet for measuring the different areas of your application. You can request a copy of the score sheet when asking for the application.

Government applications usually have a place on the forms for including a summary of your proposal.

Preparing to apply for a government grant

A successful grant proposal is one that is well-prepared, thoughtfully planned, and concisely packaged. The potential applicant should become familiar with all of the pertinent program criteria related to the program from which assistance is sought.

Refer to the information contact person listed in the *Catalog of Federal Domestic Assistance* program description before developing a proposal to obtain information such as whether funding is available, when applicable deadlines occur, and the process used by the grantor agency for accepting applications.

Applicants should remember that the basic requirements,

application forms, information and procedures vary with the Federal agency making the grant award.

Developing ideas for the proposal

When developing an idea for a proposal it is important to determine if the idea has been considered in your locality or state. A careful check should be made with legislators and area government agencies and related public and private agencies which may currently have grant awards or contracts to do similar work.

If a similar program already exists, you may need to reconsider submitting the proposed project, particularly if duplication of effort is perceived. If significant differences or improvements in the proposed project's goals can be clearly established, it may be worthwhile to pursue Federal assistance.

Community support

If you are applying for a grant as a nonprofit organization, community support for most proposals is essential. Once proposal summary is developed, look for individuals or groups representing academic, political, professional, and lay organizations which may be willing to support the proposal in writing.

The type and caliber of community support is critical in the initial and following review phases. Numerous letters of support can be persuasive to a grantor agency. Do not overlook support from local government agencies and public officials. Letters of endorsement detailing exact areas of project commitment are often requested as part of a proposal to a Federal agency.

Several months may be required to develop letters of endorsement since something of value (e.g., buildings, staff, services) is sometimes negotiated between the parties involved.

Many agencies require, in writing, affiliation agreements (a mutual agreement to share services between agencies) and building space commitments prior to either grant approval or award. A useful method of generating community support may be to hold meetings with the top decision makers in the community who would be concerned with the subject matter of the proposal. The forum for discussion may include a query into the merits of the proposal, development of a contract of support for the proposal, to generate data in support of the proposal, or development of a strategy to create proposal support from a large number of community groups.

Identification of a funding resource

A review of the "Objectives and Uses" and "Use Restrictions" sections of the *Federal Catalog of Domestic Assistance* program description can point out which programs might provide funding for an idea.

Do not overlook the related programs as potential resources. Both the applicant and the grantor agency should have the same interests, intentions, and needs if a proposal is to be considered an acceptable candidate for funding.

Once a potential grantor agency is identified, call the contact telephone number identified in the "Information Contacts" and ask for a grant application kit. Later, get to know some of the grantor agency personnel. Ask for suggestions, criticisms, and advice about the proposed project.

In many cases, the more agency personnel know about the proposal, the better the chance of support and of an eventual favorable decision. Sometimes it is useful to send the proposal summary to a specific agency official in a separate cover letter, and ask for review and comment at the earliest possible convenience.

Always check with the Federal agency to determine its preference if this approach is under consideration. If the review is unfavorable and differences cannot be resolved, ask the examining agency (official) to suggest another department or agency which may be interested in the proposal. A personal visit to the agency's regional office or headquarters is also important. A visit not only establishes face-to-face contact, but also may bring out some essential details about the proposal or help secure literature and references from the agency's library.

Federal agencies are required to report funding information as funds are approved, increased or decreased among projects within a given State depending on the type of required reporting. Also, consider reviewing the Federal Budget (accessible online at http://w3.access.gpo.gov/usbudget/index.html) for the current and budget fiscal years to determine proposed dollar amounts for particular budget functions.

Carefully study the eligibility requirements for each Federal program under consideration (see the Applicant Eligibility section of the Catalog program description). Questions about eligibility should be discussed with the appropriate program officer.

Deadlines for submitting applications are often not negotiable. They are usually associated with strict timetables for agency review. Some programs have more than one application deadline during the fiscal year. Plan your proposal development around the established deadlines.

Getting organized to write the proposal

Throughout the proposal writing stage keep a notebook handy to write down ideas. Periodically, try to connect ideas by reviewing the notebook. Never throw away written ideas during the grant writing stage.

Maintain a file labeled "Ideas" or by some other convenient title and review the ideas from time to time. The file should be easily accessible. The gathering of documents such as articles of incorporation, tax exemption certificates, and bylaws should be completed, if possible, before the writing begins.

Criticism

After the first or second draft is completed, seek out a neutral third party to review the proposal working draft for continuity, clarity and reasoning. Ask for constructive criticism at this point, rather than wait for the Federal grantor agency to volunteer this information during the review cycle.

For example, have you made unsupported assumptions or used jargon or excessive language in the proposal?

Signatures

Most proposals are made to institutions rather than individuals. Often signatures of chief administrative officials are required. Check to make sure they are included in the proposal where appropriate.

Neatness

Proposals should be typed, collated, copied, and packaged correctly and neatly (according to agency instructions, if any). Each package should be inspected to ensure uniformity from cover to cover. Binding may require either clamps or hard covers.

Check with the Federal agency to determine its preference. A neat, organized, and attractive proposal package can leave a positive impression with the reader about the proposal contents.

Mailing

A cover letter should always accompany a proposal.

Standard U.S. Postal Service requirements apply unless otherwise indicated by the Federal agency. Make sure there is enough time for the proposals to reach their destinations. Otherwise, special arrangements may be necessary. Always coordinate such arrangements with the Federal grantor agency project office (the agency which will ultimately have the responsibility for the project), the grant office (the agency which will coordinate the grant review), and the contract office (the agency responsible for disbursement and grant award notices), if necessary.

Basic components of a federal grant proposal

There are eight basic components to creating a solid proposal package:

(1) the proposal summary
(2) introduction of organization
(3) the problem statement (or needs assessment)
(4) project objectives
(5) project methods or design
(6) project evaluation
(7) future funding
(8) the project budget

Proposal summary: Outline of Project Goals

The proposal summary outlines the proposed project and should appear at the beginning of the proposal. It could be in the form of a cover letter or a separate page, but should definitely be brief -- no longer than two or three paragraphs. The summary would be most useful if it were prepared after the proposal has been developed in order to encompass all the key summary points necessary to communicate the objectives of the project.

It is this document that becomes the cornerstone of your proposal, and the initial impression it gives will be critical to the success of your venture. In many cases, the summary will be the first part of the proposal package seen by agency officials and very possibly could be the only part of the package that is carefully reviewed before the decision is made to consider the project any further.

You must select a fundable project which can be supported in view of the local need. Alternatives, in the absence of Federal support, should be pointed out. The influence of the project both during and after the project period should be explained. The consequences of the project as a result of funding should be highlighted.

Introduction: Presenting Credibility

Gather data about yourself or your organization from all available sources. Most proposals require a description of an applicant's organization to describe its past and present operations. Some features to consider are:
  • A brief biography of board members and key staff members.
  • The organization's goals, philosophy, track record with other

grantors, and any success stories.

• The data should be relevant to the goals of the Federal grantor agency and should establish the applicant's credibility.

The Problem Statement: Stating the Purpose at Hand

The problem statement (or needs assessment) is a key element of a proposal that makes a clear, concise, and well-supported statement of the problem to be addressed. The best way to collect information about the problem is to conduct and document both a formal and informal needs assessment for a program in the target or service area.

The information provided should be both factual and directly related to the problem addressed by the proposal. Areas to document are:

• Purpose for developing the proposal.

• Beneficiaries -- who are they and how will they benefit.

• Social and economic costs to be affected.

• Nature of the problem (provide as much hard evidence as possible).

• How the applicant organization came to realize the problem exists, and what is currently being done about the problem.

• Remaining alternatives available when funding has been exhausted. Explain what will happen to the project and the impending implications.

• Most importantly, the specific manner through which problems might be solved.

• Review the resources needed, considering how they will be used and to what end.

There is a considerable body of literature on the exact assessment techniques to be used. Any local, regional, or State government planning office, or local university offering course work in planning and evaluation techniques should be able to provide excellent background references.

Types of data that may be collected include: historical, geographic, quantitative, factual, statistical, and philosophical information, as well as studies completed by colleges, and literature searches from public or university libraries.

Local colleges or universities which have a department or section related to the proposal topic may help determine if there is interest in developing a student or faculty project to conduct a needs assessment. It may be helpful to include examples of the findings for highlighting in the proposal.

Project Objectives: Goals and Desired Outcome

Program objectives refer to specific activities in a proposal. It is necessary to identify all objectives related to the goals to be reached, and the methods to be employed to achieve the stated objectives. Consider quantities or things measurable and refer to a problem statement and the outcome of proposed activities when developing a well-stated objective.

Figures used should be verifiable. Remember, if the proposal is funded, the stated objectives will probably be used to evaluate program progress, so be realistic. There is literature available to help identify and write program objectives.

Program Methods and Program Design: A Plan of Action

The program design refers to how the project is expected to work and solve the stated problem. Sketch out the following:

• The activities to occur along with the related resources and staff needed to operate the project (inputs).

• A flow chart of the organizational features of the project. Describe how the parts interrelate, where personnel will be needed, and what they are expected to do. Identify the kinds of facilities, transportation, and support services required (throughputs).

• Explain what will be achieved through 1 and 2 above (outputs); i.e., plan for measurable results. Project staff may be required to produce evidence of program performance through an examination of stated objectives during either a site visit by the Federal grantor agency and or grant reviews which may involve peer review committees. It may be useful to devise a diagram of the program design.

• Wherever possible, justify in the narrative the course of action taken. The most economical method should be used that does not compromise or sacrifice project quality. The financial expenses associated with performance of the project will later become points of negotiation with the Federal program staff. If everything is not carefully justified in writing in the proposal, after negotiation with the Federal grantor agencies, the approved project may resemble less of the original concept.

• Highlight the innovative features of the proposal which could be considered distinct from other proposals under consideration.

• Whenever possible, use appendices to provide details, supplementary data, references, and information requiring in-depth analysis. These types of data, although supportive of the proposal, if included in the body of the design, could detract from its readability. Appendices provide the proposal reader with immediate access to details if and when clarification of an idea, sequence or conclusion is required.

Time tables, work plans, schedules, activities, methodologies, legal papers, personal vitae, letters of support, and endorsements are examples of appendices.

Evaluation: Product and Process Analysis

The evaluation component is twofold: (1) product evaluation; and (2) process evaluation. Product evaluation addresses results that can be attributed to the project, as well as the extent to which the project has satisfied its desired objectives. Process evaluation addresses how the project was conducted, in terms of consistency with the stated plan of action and the effectiveness of the various activities within the plan.

Most Federal agencies now require some form of program evaluation among grantees. The requirements of the proposed project should be explored carefully. Evaluations may be conducted by an internal staff member, an evaluation firm or both. State the amount of time needed to evaluate, how the feedback will be distributed among the proposed staff, and a schedule for review and comment for this type of communication.

Evaluation designs may start at the beginning, middle or end of a project, but the applicant should specify a start-up time. Even if the evaluation design has to be revised as the project progresses, it is much easier and cheaper to modify a good design. If the problem is not well defined and carefully analyzed for cause and effect relationships then a good evaluation design may be difficult to achieve.

Evaluation requires both coordination and agreement among program decision makers (if known). Above all, the Federal grantor agency's requirements should be highlighted in the evaluation design. Also, Federal grantor agencies may require specific evaluation techniques such as designated data formats (an existing information collection system) or they may offer financial inducements for voluntary participation in a national evaluation study. The applicant should ask specifically about these points. Also, consult the *Criteria For Selecting Proposals* section of the Catalog program description to determine the exact evaluation methods to be required for the program if funded.

Future Funding: Long-Term Project Planning

Describe a plan for continuation beyond the grant period, and/or the availability of other resources necessary to implement the grant. Discuss maintenance and future program funding if program is for construction activity. Account for other needed expenditures if program includes purchase of equipment.

The Proposal Budget: Planning the Budget

Funding levels in Federal assistance programs change yearly. It is useful to review the appropriations over the past several years to try to project future funding levels (see Financial Information section of the Catalog program description).

However, it is safer to never anticipate that the income from the grant will be the sole support for the project. This consideration should be given to the overall budget requirements, and in particular, to budget line items most subject to inflationary pressures.

Restraint is important in determining inflationary cost projections (avoid padding budget line items), but attempt to anticipate possible future increases.

Some vulnerable budget areas are: utilities, rental of buildings and equipment, salary increases, food, telephones, insurance, and transportation. Budget adjustments are sometimes made after the grant award.

A well-prepared budget justifies all expenses and is consistent with the proposal narrative. Some areas in need of an evaluation for consistency are: (1) the salaries in the proposal in relation to those of the applicant organization should be similar; (2) if new staff persons are being hired, additional space and equipment should be considered, as necessary; (3) if the budget calls for an equipment purchase, it should be the type allowed by the grantor agency; (4) if additional space is rented, the increase in insurance should be supported; (5) if an indirect cost rate applies to the proposal, the division between direct and indirect costs should not be in conflict, and the aggregate budget totals should refer directly to the approved formula; and (6) if matching costs are required, the contributions to the matching fund should be taken out of the budget unless otherwise specified in the application instructions.

Regional and federal depository libraries

For accessing the *Federal Catalog of Domestic Assistance* programs, see your local library or one of the 1,350 Federal depository libraries throughout the U.S.. All provide free public access to a wide variety of Federal government information in both print and electronic formats, and have expert staff available to assist users. A list of depository and regional libraries is available by writing:

Chief, Library Division
Superintendent of Documents
Stop SLL
Washington, DC 20402

Chapter 4 How to Use a Computer and the Internet for Grant Seeking

For those who use computers, you can speed up your grant seeking tasks several times by using a few easy to learn software programs like a word processor and a database program.

Word processor

A word processor, like Microsoft Word or WordPerfect will allow you to create a template for your grant proposals and applications. You can then simply use the "save as" command and rename a file for each grant proposal you send. For instance, one proposal going to the J. Paul Getty Foundation which would be saved as "getty_proposal.doc." Another proposal going to the Dactyl Foundation might be named "dactyl_proposal.doc."

Word processors can speed your grant writing in other ways. Most programs include spell checkers which can replace misspelled words quickly. You can stylize the documents headings and titles to produce a uniform and professional appearing text.

Automatic page numbering, adjustment of margins, and footnotes are usually built-in features.

Database programs

Each proposal you write will have some material in common. Rather than reenter the same data again and again, you can store fields of information in a database program like Microsoft Access or FileMaker Pro.

Database software creates tables with fields of data. For instance, one field might contain dates, another names, a third your bio, a fourth your project summary and so on. You can then cut and paste the data from each field into your word processing document for quick composition of proposals.

Internet grant links

The Internet provides an excellent resource for the grant seeker. Many foundations and arts councils have web sites with descriptions of their grant programs. Some sites include guidelines and application forms.

If you don't yet have access to the Internet or need to change service providers, try Maktrix Internet at http://www.maktrix.com or call toll free 1-888-212-1363 to get details. Maktrix has fast connect times, no busy signals and no forced advertising like AOL.

The publishers of this guide have set up an ongoing Internet resource to keep you up to date on news and announcements for artists and craft persons seeking grant funding. You can access the site anytime at:

http://www.craftmarketer.com/grants_internet.htm

In compiling the listings below, we found many, many sites online for grant writing. Some web pages were written as early as 1995. The listings below represent the most current and most useful web sites for grant writing.

Check the listings for private foundations, community foundations and arts councils in the directory appendixes. Whenever an organization is known to have a web site, it's web address is included after the mailing address. Those organizations already listed in the appendix are generally not included again below.

Government grants are especially accessible online because the Internet originated as a way of government agencies and educational institutions to protect their information in case of emergencies.

Additional resources on the Internet help you look up specific information about a foundation or nonprofit organization. For instance, GuideStar described below allows you to pull up IRS information on 620,000 non-profits in the U.S..

The Foundation Center online searchable database allows you to search for foundations by name, location, types of support, fields of interest, or text word search. Their site offers many free services and a paid option for the online foundation directory search.

Private Organizations
Craftmarketer.com
Web site: http://www.craftmarketer.com/grants_internet.htm

This site is the online companion to this book. All of the links you see below will be found here plus updates and news of importance to grant seekers.

American Association of Fund-Raising Counsel
Web site: http://www.aafrc.org

AAFRC's annual "Giving USA" report gives an overall picture of U.S. giving from various sources.

Americans for the Arts

Web site: http://www.artsusa.org/

Provides links to state and local arts organizations who often post their grant giving programs and application forms on their web sites.

American Philanthropy Review

Web site: http://www.charitychannel.com

Reviews periodicals, books, and software on fund raising, written by volunteers from the fund-raising field. You can also locate email discussion forums on nonprofits and philanthropy.

Arts Grants Deadlines Newsletter

Web site: http://custwww.xensei.com/adl/

Newsletter which comes to you via email with deadline dates for grants in the arts and crafts fields.

Best of the Web for Grant Seekers

Web site: http://www.usc.edu/dept/source/grantsweb.htm

Many links to grant writing resources online.

The Foundation Center

Web site: http://www.fdncenter.org

Useful site for information for grantseekers and grantmakers.

Grantsmanship Center

Web site: http://www.tgci.com

This site lists new grant announcements daily from the federal government's online Federal Register.

GuideStar

Web site: http://www.guidestar.org

GuideStar is a searchable database of more than 620,000 nonprofit organizations in the United States. Type a name in the Charity Search box to find a charity. Includes IRS filings data on each nonprofit

Idealist

Web site: http://www.idealist.org

An online directory of over 10,000 nonprofit and community organizations working in 120 countries, with detailed information on their services, volunteer opportunities, materials, job listings and more.

Internet Prospector
Web site: http://www.internet-prospector.org
A nonprofit service to the prospect research fund-raising community.

National Society of Fund Raising Executives
Web site: http://www.nsfre.org
NSFRE Consultants' Directory, an annual listing of NSFRE members who provide fund-raising services on a consulting basis.

Nonprofit Center
Web site: http://www.nonprofits.org/
Lots of information on nonprofits around the country.

PhilanthropySearch
Web site: http://www.philanthropysearch.com
Search engine serving the nonprofit and philanthropic sector.

Proposal writing links from University of Wisconsin
Web site: http://www.library.wisc.edu/libraries/Memorial/grants/proposal.htm
Comprehensive collection of online links for proposal writing.

Government and Educational institutes

Amherst University
Web site: http://www.amherst.edu/~erreich/pcah_html/fundingguide.html
Reference directory to giving for artists and scholars

University of Michigan: Government Grant Resources
Web site: http://www.lib.umich.edu/libhome/Documents.center/fedgt.html
Great listing of government grant programs

National Endowment for the Arts
Web site: http://arts.endow.gov
Federal grantmaking agency that supports the arts.

The Catalog of Federal Domestic Assistance
Web site: http://www.cfda.gov/
Database of information on federal grant programs. Craft persons search for terms like arts, small business, minority business, women.

Arts Edge

Web site: http://artsedge.kennedy-center.org/artsedge.html

Contains information on federal grant resources and a listing of arts and education electronic newsletters.

U.S. Department of Education

Web site: http://www.ed.gov

Grant and funding information.

Federal Register

Web site: http://www.access.gpo.gov/su_docs/

FedWorld

Web site: http://www.fedworld.gov

Links to more than 100 government Web sites.

GrantsNet

Web site: http://www.os.dhhs.gov/progorg/grantsnet/index.html

Government grant information.

Grants Web

Web site: http://sra.rams.com/cws/sra/resource.htm

List of federal grant programs, discussion groups, online newsletters, and links to government sites.

National Endowment for the Humanities

Web site: http://www.neh.fed.us

Grants for projects in history, languages, philosophy, and other areas of the humanities.

Federal Web Locator

Web site: http://www.infoctr.edu/fwl/

Government web pages and other government-related resources.

Canadian Government Grants

Web site: http://www.governmentgrants.com

This site is a resource for Canadian residents seeking grants.

Canadian Community Foundations

Web site: http://www.community-fdn.ca/

Another site for Canadian residents seeking grants.

Internet resources for public art programs

Locate lists and web sites of public art programs online at the following sites:

http://www.arts.state.tx.us/public_art/public_art-l.htm
http://www.shu.ac.uk/services/lc/slidecol/weblinx.html
http://www.gsa.ac.uk/publicart/

http://www.artswire.org/ This site deserves special mention as you can get up-to-date announcements about new funding programs and news of interest to artists and craft persons.

Artist in residency programs

AboutCom Guide is an Internet site for artist in residency links. Many programs are summarized with links to their main web sites.

Web site: http://arttech.tqn.com/arts/arttech/msub2.htm

Alliance of Artists' Communities is a national service organization that supports the field of artists' communities and residency programs. It does this by encouraging collaboration among members of the field on field issues, raising the visibility of artists' communities, promoting philanthropy in the field, and generally encouraging programs that support the creation of art. Currently made up of about 80 leading, nonprofit artists' communities and 65 individuals.

Web site: http://www.teleport.com/~aac/index.html

Res Artis - A worldwide searchable database of artist in residency programs. Also links to helpful artist sites.

http://www.resartis.org

Miscellaneous fundraising sites

http://www.nonprofit-info.org/npofaq/
http://www.raise-funds.com/library.html
http://www.links2go.com/topic/Grants_and_Funding
http://www.gisd.k12.mi.us/gisd/Grants/GrantWritingTips.html - This site offers many links to grant writing resources online.

Grant writing tutorials

Online tutorials for grant writing:
http://www.cyberworkshops.com/
http://fdncenter.org/marketplace/training/proposal.html
http://granthelp.clarityconnect.com/
http://www.grantwriters.com/training.htm
http://ww2.hamptonu.edu/arts_edu/soc_behav/BehavSci/pdg/mdpdg.html

Appendixes · Directories

Appendix I Directory of Art & Craft Grants to Individuals

The following foundations and organizations give grants to individual artists and craft persons and in some cases to art/craft organizations, too. Note that some have regional limitations which appear in parenthesis to the right of the foundation name. Write or call for guidelines from each foundation.

A.C. Ratshesky Foundation   *(residents of Boston area)*
c/o GMA
77 Summer Street, 8th Floor
Boston, MA 02110
Ph:(617) 426-7172
Web site: http://www.agmconnect.org/ratshes1.html

Adolph and Esther Gottlieb Foundation
380 West Broadway
New York NY 10012
Ph: 212-226-0581

African-American Institute *(for women from southern Africa)*
833 United Nations Plaza
New York, NY 10017
Ph: 212-949-5666

Al J. Schneider Foundation
3720 7th St Rd
Louisville KY 40216

Alaska State Council on the Arts   *(residents of Alaska)*
411 W. 4th Ave., Suite 1E
Anchorage, AK 99501-2343
Telephone: (907) 269-6610
Fax: (907) 269-6601
E-mail: info@aksca.org
Web site: http://www.aksca.org/

Alberta Foundation for the Arts *(Alberta Canada)*
901 Standard Life Centre
10405 Jasper Avenue,
Edmonton, AB T5J 4R7
Reception: (780) 427-6315
Fax: (780) 422-9132
Website: www.affta.ab.ca

Alfred Juryzbowski Foundation *(Polish background)*
15 E. 65th St.
New York, NY 10021
Ph: 212-439-9628

American Academy and Institute of Arts and Letters
633 West 155th St.
New York, NY 10032
Ph: 212-368-5900

American Council of Learned Societies
228 E 45th St
New York NY 10017
Ph: 212-697-1505
Web site: http://www.acls.org

Americans For Indian Opportunity *(Native Americans)*
3508 Garfield St. NW
Washington, DC 20007
Ph: 202-338-8809

American National Heritage Association
Box 4827
Alexandria VA 22303
Ph: 730-960-6322

Arizona Commission on the Arts *(residents of Arizona)*
417 W. Roosevelt
Phoenix, AZ 85003
(602) 255-5882
email: general@ArizonaArts.org
Web site: http://az.arts.asu.edu/artscomm/artists/artists.html

Arlington Community Foundation *(residents of Arlington VA)*
2009 N. 14th St. # 103
Arlington, VA 22201
Ph: 703-243-4785

Art Matters
PO Box 1815, Chelsea Sta.
New York NY 10013
Ph: 212-929-7190

Artists Fellowship
C/O Salmagundi Club
47 Fifth Ave. 212-E
New York NY 10003

Arts Partnership of Greater Spartanburg *(residents of Spartanburg)*
385 S Spring St
Spartanburg SC 29306
Ph: 864-542-2787

Ashton Family Foundation   *(residents of Utah)*
261 E. 1200 S.
Orem, UT 84058
Phone: 801-226-1266

Asian Cultural Council
1290 Avenue of Americas Rm 3450
New York NY 10104
Ph: 212-373-4300
Web site: www.accny.org

ASTRAEA, National Lesbian Action Fund   *(for women in the arts)*
116 E 16th St 7th Flr
New York NY 10003
Ph: 212-529-8021
Web site: http://www.astraea.org

Atherton Family Foundation *(residents of Hawaii)*
PO Box 3170
Honolulu HI 96802
Ph: 808-537-6333 for grants
Ph: 808-536-8839 for scholarships

Aurora Foundation
111 West Downer Place #312
Aurora IL 60506-5136
Ph: 708-896-7800

Bagley Wright Fund *(residents of Seattle, WA)*
900 4th Avenue, #4114
Seattle WA 98164

Baltimore Community Fund
Latrobe Bldg.
Two E. Read St., 9th Fl
Baltimore. MD 21202
Ph: 301-332-4171

Bend Foundation
416 N.E. Greenwood
Bend OR 97708
Ph: 541-382-1662

Blanche E. Coleman Trust *(residents of New England)*
c/o Boston Safe Deposit & Trust Co.
One Boston Place
Boston, MA 02108

Blinken Foundation
466 Lexington Ave, 10th Floor
New York NY 10017

Bronx Council on the Arts *(Bronx area residents)*
1738 Howe Ave
Bronx NY 10461

Bush Foundation *(residents of WI, SD, MN)*
E-900 First National Bank Bldg,
332 Minnesota St.
St. Paul MN 55101
Ph: 612-227-5222

Central European University Foundation
C/O Open Society Institute
888 7th Ave 31st Fl
New York NY 10106
Ph: 212-548-0600

Charles G. & Rheta Kramer Foundation *(residents of Chicago, IL)*
C/O Lewis D. Ross
154 W Hubbard St #200
Chicago IL 60610
Ph: 312-527-4747

Chamiza Foundation *(limited to Pueblo Indian tribes of NM)*
State Farm Building
901 W Alameda
Santa Fe NM 87501
Ph: 505-986-5044

Chazen Foundation
PO Box 801
Nyack NY 10960
Contact: Dennis Fleming

Children's Foundation for the Arts
2000 Linwood Ave #8V
Fort Lee NY 07024
Ph: 201-504-6262
Contact: Deborah Baron

Christel DeHaan Family Foundation
1990 Market Tower
10 W Market St
Indianapolis IN 46204
Ph: 317-464-2378
Contact: Cheryl Wendling

CIRI Foundation
2600 Cordova St #206
Anchorage AK 99503
Ph: 907-274-8638

Cintas Foundation *(Cuban artist/craft persons living outside Cuba)*
Attn: William B. Warren
1301 Avenue of the Americas
New York NY 10019
Ph: 212-984-5370

Clark Foundation
1 Rockefeller Plaza 31st Flr
New York NY 10020
Ph: 212-977-6900

Community Foundation for Greater New Haven
70 Audubon St
New Haven CT 06510
Ph: 203-777-2386
Web site: http://www.cfgnh.org

Community Foundation of Boone County
PO Box 92
Zionsville IN 46077
Ph: 317-873-0210

Community Foundation of Cape Cod
PO Box 406
Yarmouth Port, MA 02675
Ph: 508-362-3040

Community College of Muncie and Delaware County
PO Box 807
Muncie IN 47308
Ph: 765-747-7181

Community Foundation of Santa Clara County
960 W. Hedding, No. 220
San Jose, CA 95126
Ph: 498-241-2666

Community Foundation of Southern Wisconsin
111 N Main St
Janesville WI 53545
Ph: 608-758-0883

Copolymer Foundation *(residents of Louisiana)*
PO Box 2591
Baton Rouge LA 70821
Ph: 504-267-3410

Creative Capital Foundation
65 Bleecker Street, 7th floor
New York, NY 10012
Ph: (212)598-9900   Fax: (212)598-4934
Web site: http://www.creative-capital.org/

Dactyl Foundation for the Arts and Humanities
64 Grand Street
New York, NY 10013
Ph: 212-219-2344
Web site: http://home.flash.net/~dactyl/menu.html

Derse Family Foundation   *(residents of Milwaukee, WI)*
14240 Heatherwood Ct
El Grove WI 53122

DuBose and Dorothy Heyward Memorial Fund
The Bank of New York
1 Wall Street, 28th Floor
New York NY 10286
Ph: 212-635-1622

Durfee Foundation
1453 Third Street Promenade Suite 312
Santa Monica, California 90401
Ph: (310) 899-5120

E.D. Foundation
C/O Randy Frischer, BDO Seidman
15 Columbus Cir
New York NY 10023

Echoing Green Foundation
800 3rd Ave #3702
New York NY 10022
Ph: 212-754-6080

Edward Bangs and Elsa Kelley Foundation
PO Drawer M
Hyannis MA 02106

Ella Lyman Cabot Trust
109 Rockland Street
Holliston, MA 01746
Ph: 508-420-8997

Emory and Ilona Ladanyi Foundation
12 Ranch Place
Merrick, NY 11566

Esther Foundation
1716 N Meadowlark Rd
Orem UT 84057

First Nations Development Institute *(Native Americans)*
69 Kelly Rd.
Falmouth, VA 22405
Ph: 703-371-5615

Fleishhacker Foundation *(northern California residents)*
One Maritime Plaza, Ste 830
San Francisco, CA 94111
Ph: 415-788-2909

Ford Foundation
320 E 43rd St
New York NY10017
Ph: 212-573-5000 Web site: http://www.fordfound.org

Foundation for Contemporary Performance Arts
151 E 63rd St
New York NY 10021
Ph: 212-308-6032

Foundation for Hellenic Culture
7 West 57th St #1
New York NY 10019
Ph: 212-308-6908

Foundation for Iranian Studies *(Iranian subjects)*
4343 Montgomery Ave #200
Bethesda MD 20814
Ph: 301-657-1990

GTE Foundation *(areas with employees of GTE)*
1 Stamford Forum
Stamford CT 06904
Ph: 203-965-3620

George T. Welch Testamentary Trust *(residents of Walla Walla)*
PO Box 1796
Walla Walla WA 99362
Ph: 509-525-2000

Geraldine C. and Emory M. Ford Foundation
C/O Beverly Holman
PO Box 548
Roseville MI 48066

Graham Foundation for Advanced Studies in the Arts
4 West Burton Place
Chicago IL 60610
Ph: 312-787-4071
Web site: http://www.grahamfoundation.org

Grand Haven Area Community Foundation
One South Harbor
Grand Rapids, MI 49417
Ph: 616-842-6278

Greater Tacoma Community Foundation
PO Box 1995
Tacoma WA 98401
Ph: 253-383-5622
Web site: http://www.gtcf.org

Gulf Coast Community Foundation *(southern counties in MS)*
PO Box 1899
Gulfport MS 39502
Ph: 601-868-1563

The Gunk Foundation
P.O. Box 333
Gardiner, NY 12525
Ph:(914) 255-8252
Web site: http://www.gunk.org

Hand Foundation *(residents of Tennessee)*
1800 Republic Ctr
633 Chestnut St
Chattanooga TN 37450
Ph: 423-756-2010

J. Paul Getty Trust
1200 Getty Center Drive #800
Los Angeles CA 90049
Ph: 310-440-7320
Web site: http://www.getty.edu/grant

Jewish Family & Children's Services of San Francisco
1600 Scott St
San Francisco, CA 94115
Ph: 415-561-1226

John and Elena Diaz Verson Amos Foundation
4 Bradley Park Ct.
Columbus, GA 31904

John Anson Kittredge Educational Fund
PO Box 1054
Augusta ME 04330

John D. and Catherine T. MacArthur Foundation
140 S. Dearborn Street
Chicago, IL 60603
Ph: 312/726-8000
Web site: http://www.macfdn.org/

John F. and Anna Lee Stacey Testamentary Trust
c/o Security Pacific National Bank
PO Box 3189, Terminal Annex
Los Angeles, CA 90051

John Simon Guggenheim Memorial Foundation
90 Park Avenue
New York, NY 10016
Phone: 212 687-4470   Fax: 212 697-3248
Web site: http://www.gf.org/

Joy Family Foundation
107-111 Goundry St
N Tonawanda NY 14120
Ph: 716-692-6665

Hawaiian Electric Industries Charitable Foundation
PO Box 730
Honolulu, HI 96808
Ph: 808-543-7356

Helene Wurlitzer Foundation of New Mexico
PO Box 545
Taos NM 87571
Ph: 505-758-2413

Honickman Foundation *(residents of NY and PA)*
210 W Rittenhouse Square #2201
Philadelphia PA 19103

Hudson-Webber Foundation *(residents of Detroit, MI)*
333 W Fort St #1310
Detroit MI 48226
Ph: 313-963-7777

J.Z. Knight Humanities Foundation
14507 Yelm Highway SE
Yelm WA 98597
Ph: 360-458-4492

James F. Lincoln Arc Welding Foundation *(arc welding grants)*
22801 St. Clair Ave.
Cleveland, OH 44117
Ph: 216-481-43400

Jerome Foundation
125 Park Square Court
400 Sibley Street
St. Paul, MN 55101
Ph: 651-224-9431 Web site: http://www.jeromefdn.org

Kentucky Foundation for Women *(women residents in KY, TN, WV, OH)*
Heyburn Building, #1215
332 West Broadway
Louisville KY 40202
Ph: 502-562-0045
Web site: http://www.kfw.org

Larry Aldrich Foundation
40 Central Park S
New York NY 10019

Leeway Foundation *(residents of Philadelphia, PA)*
123 South Broad St #2040
Philadelphia PA 19109
Ph: 215-545-4078
Web site: http://www.leeway.org

Lifebridge Foundation
Times Square Station
PO Box 793
New York NY 10108
Web site: http://www.lifebridge.org

Lorser and Helen Lundeburg Feitelson Arts Foundation
(southern California residents)
8307 West Third St.
Los Angeles CA 90048-3119
Ph: 213-655-3245

Louis Comfort Tiffany Foundation
C/O Sperone, Westwater and Fisher
142 Greene St
New York NY 10018
Ph: 212-431-9880

Lucy Daniels Foundation   *(residents of Raleigh, Chapel Hill, NC)*
9001 Weston Parkway
Cary NC 27513
Ph: 919-677-9888
Web site: http://ldf.org

Ludwig Vogelstein Foundation
PO Box 277
Hancock ME 04640

Marion D. and Maxine Hanks Foundation *(residents of Salt Lake City)*
Judge Building
8 East Broadway #405
Salt Lake City UT 84111
Ph: 801-364-7705

Martha Boschen Porter Fund (residents of NY, MA and CT)
White Hollow Rd.
Sharon CT 09606

McKnight Distinguished Artist Award   *(Minnesota residents)*
600 TCF Tower
121 South Eighth Street
Minneapolis, MN 55402
Tel: (612) 333-4220
Web site: http://www.mcknight.org/distart.htm

Melton Arts Foundation *(residents of Washington DC)*
2086 Hunters Crest Way
Vienna VA 22181

Merrill Ingram Foundation
PO Box 202
Village Station
New York, NY, 10014

Money for Women
Barbara Deming Memorial Fund *(feminists)*
PO Box 40-1043
Brooklyn NY 11240-1043

Murphy Foundation *(Arkansas & Louisiana residents)*
200 Jefferson
El Dorado, AR 71730
Ph: 501-862-6411

National Computer Systems Corporate Giving Program
11000 Prairie Lakes Dr
Eden Prairie MN 55344
Ph: 612-829-3000

National Foundation for Advancement in the Arts
800 Brickell Avenue Suite 500
Miami, Florida 33131
Toll free: 1-800-970-ARTS   Ph: 305-377-1147
Fax: 305-377-1149
Web site: http://www.nfaa.org/

National Sculpture Society
1177 Avenue of the Americas 15th Flr
New York, NY 10036
Ph: 212-764-5645

New England Biolabs Foundation
(residents of Suffolk and Essex counties in MA)
32 Tozer Rd
Beverly MA 01915
Ph: 508-927-2404
Web site: http://www.nebf.org

New England Foundation for the Arts   *(residents of New England)*
330 Congress St 6th Flr
Boston MA 02210
Ph: 617-951-0010
Web site: http://www.nefa.org

New York Foundation for the Arts
155 Avenue of the Americas, 14th Floor
New York, NY 10013-1507
Phone: 212-366-6900 Fax: 212-366-1778
Web site: http://www.nyfa.org/

Oshkosh Foundation *(residents of Wisconsin)*
PO Box 1726
Oshkosh WI 54902
Ph: 920-426-3993

Palmer Foundation *(residents of NY and PA)*
C/O Manchester Capital Corporation
635 Madison Ave 16th Flr
New York NY 10022
Ph: 212-832-3116

Peninsula Community Foundation
(residents of San Mateo County and north Santa Clara County)
PO Box 627
Burlingame CA 94402-3049
Ph: 415-358-9369

Penny McCall Foundation
136 E 64th St
New York NY 10021

Permanent Endowment Fund for Martha's Vineyard
(residents of Martha's Vineyard, MA)
47 Hatch Rd
RR2 Box 149
Vineyard Haven MA 02568
Ph: 508-693-0721

Pollack-Krasner Foundation
863 Park Ave.
New York, NY 10021
Ph: 212-517-5400
Web site: http://www.pkf.org

Porter Foundation *(residents of Grand Rapids, MI)*
PO Box 6484
Grand Rapids MI 49516
Ph: 616-459-9531

Presser Foundation
Presser Place
Bryn Mawr PA 19010
Ph: 610-525-4797

Puffin Foundation *(residents of New Jersey)*
20 East Oakdene Avenue
Teaneck NJ 07666
Ph: 201-836-8923
Web site: http://www.angelfire.com/nj/PuffinFoundation

R. J. McElroy Trust *(residents in Iowa)*
KWWL Building
500 E. Fourth St.
Waterloo IA 50703

Randall Tobias Foundation *(residents of Durham, IN)*
500 E 96th Street #110
Indianapolis IN 46240
Ph: 317-276-6327
Web site: http://www.rltfound.org

Richland County Foundation *(residents of Richland County, OH)*
24 West 3rd Street #100
Mansfield OH 44902
Ph: 419-525-3020

Robert G. Friedman Foundation *(residents of FL, OH, MI, WI)*
76 Isla Bahia Dr
Ft Lauderdale FL 33316

Robert Gore Rifkind Foundation
10100 Santa Monica Blvd #215
Los Angeles CA 90067
Ph: 310-552-0478

Robert and Patricia Schmidt Foundation *(residents of Kansas)*
PO Box 817
Hays KS 67601

Rockefeller Foundation
1133 Avenue of the Americas
New York NY 10036
Ph: 212-869-8500
Web site: http://www.rockfound.org

Sacramento Regional Foundation
1420 River Park Drive
Sacramento, CA 95815
Ph: 916-927-2241

Saint Paul Foundation *(residents of St. Paul MN area)*
600 Norwest Cir
St Paul MN 55101
Ph: 612-224-5463

Sarah Cora Gladish Endowment Fund *(residents in Missouri counties)*
Forest Hills Estate Apt. 11-C
Lexington MO 64067
Ph: 816-259-3643

Sequoia Trust Fund
555 California St. 36th Fl.
San Francisco, CA 94104
Ph: 415-393-8552

Shearwater Foundation
PO Box 335
Ft Lauderdale FL 33316

Shelby Foundation *(residents of Shelby, OH)*
C/O Poland Depler & Shepard
6 Water Street
Shelby OH 44875
Ph: 419-347-7421

Shifting Foundation
8000 Sears Tower
Chicago IL 60606

Sonoma County Foundation *(Sonoma County residents)*
1260 Dutton Ave. Ste 280
Santa Rosa CA 95401
Ph: 707-579-4073

Stockton Rush Bartol Foundation *(residents of counties in PA)*
The Belgravia, Suite 301
1811 Chestnut St
Philadelphia PA 19103
Ph: 215-557-7225

Susan Cook House Educational Trust *(residents of Sangamon County)*
Marine Bank of Springfield, Trust Dept.
One Old Capital Plaza E. Springfield, IL 62701
Ph: 217-525-9600

Target Foundation
*(Ask for a grant application at the Target store nearest you.
These grants are mostly for education in the arts.)*

Templeton Foundation
PO Box 563
Howell, NJ 07731

Thomas Family Foundation *(residents of Colorado and Rocky Mountains)*
7105 W 119th Pl
Broomfield CO 80020

Tompkins County Foundation *(residents of Tompkins County, NY)*
PO Box 97
Ithaca NY 14851

Wallace - Reader's Digest Foundation
2 Park Ave 23rd Flr
New York NY 10016
Ph: 212-251-9800
Web site: http://www.wallacefunds.org

Wendover Residence Program Application
The Center for Land Use Interpretation
9331 Venice Blvd.
Culver City CA 90232
Tel: (310) 839-5722
Web site: http://loft-gw.zone.org/clui/museum/wendapp.html

William C. Bannerman Fund
1405 N San Fernando Blvd., Ste 201
Burbank CA 91504

Women's Studio Workshop
P.O. Box 489
Rosendale, NY 12472
Ph: 914.658.9133
Web site: http://www.wsworkshop.org/

Appendix II Directory of Foundation Grants to Art/Craft Organizations

The listings here are some of the major foundations who provide grants and funding to non-profit organizations in the arts and crafts field. Although individuals can not apply, you can look at the recipient organizations for these grants, which changes every year. By working with a non-profit organization as a sponsor, you may be eligible to receive funding that originates from one of the following foundations. For more listings for foundations that give to nonprofit organizations in the arts, see The Foundation Center publication: *Grants for Arts, Culture and the Humanities* at your local Foundation Center library.

Andrew W. Mellon Foundation *(national organizations)*
140 East 62nd Street
New York, NY 10021
(212) 838-8400
Web site: http://www.mellon.org/

Arthur M. Blank Family Foundation
2455 Paces Ferry Road Suite C-22
Atlanta, Georgia 30339-4024
Web site: http://www.BlankFoundation.org/

ATT Foundation
32 Avenue of the Americas Room 2417
New York, NY 10013
Web site: http://www.att.com/foundation

Blandin Foundation *(organizations in Minnesota)*
100 N Pokegama Ave.
Grand Rapids MN 55744
Ph: (218) 326-0523
Web site: http://www.blandinfoundation.org/index.html

Boeing Company Charitable Trust
(limited to areas of company operations)
PO Box 3707
Seattle WA 98124
Ph: 206-655-6679

Boeing-McDonnell Foundation *(St. Louis MO organizations)*
PO Box 516
St Louis MO 63166

Dayton Hudson Foundation *(organizations in Minnesota)*
777 Nicollet Mall
Minneapolis MN 55402
Web site: http://www.dhc.com

DeWitt Wallace-Reader's Digest Fund
Two Park Avenue, 23rd Floor
New York, NY 10016
Web site: http://www.wallacefunds.org/

Eli Lilly and Company Foundation
Lilly Corporate Center D.C. 1627
Indianapolis, Indiana 46285
Web site: http://www.lilly.com/info/citizenship/philanthropy/apply.html

Exxon Education Foundation *(mostly educational organizations)*
5959 Las Colinas Blvd
Irving TX 75039
Ph: 972-444-1104

Flinn Foundation *(organizations in Arizona)*
1802 N. Central Avenue
Phoenix, AZ 85004-1506
Ph: (602) 744-6800
Web site: http://www.flinn.org/

Ford Foundation
320 East 43 Street
New York, N.Y. 10017
Web site: http://www.fordfound.org/

GE Fund
3135 Easton Turnpike
Fairfield CT 06431
Ph: 203-373-3216
Web site: http://www.ge.com/fund/

Geary, Division of Fairs & Expositions *(CA arts organizations)*
1010 Hurley Way, Suite 200
Sacramento, CA 95825
Ph: (916) 263-2946
email: ageary@cdfa.ca.gov

Geraldine R. Dodge Foundation *(organizations in New Jersey)*
163 Madison Avenue
P.O. Box 1239
Morristown, NJ 07962-1239
Ph: (973) 540-8442
Web site: http://www.grdodge.org/

Grants for the Arts *(organizations in the San Francisco area)*
San Francisco Hotel Tax Fund
401 Van Ness, Room 402
San Francisco, CA 94102
Web site: http://www.sfgfta.org

Gunk Foundation
P.O. Box 333
Gardiner, NY 12525
Ph:(914) 255-8252
Web site: http://www.gunk.org

Heinz Endowments   *(Pennsylvania organizations)*
30 CNG Tower
625 Liberty Avenue
Pittsburgh PA 15222
Web site: http://www.heinz.org/

Houston Endowment Inc.   *(Houston area organizations)*
600 Travis, Suite 6400
Houston, Texas 77002-3007
Ph: (713) 238-8100
Web site: http://www.hou-endow.org/

IBM International Foundation
Corporate Community Relations
590 Madison Avenue
New York, NY 10022
Web site: http://www.ibm.com/ibm/ibmgives/grant/

Independence Community Foundation
(New York City area organizations)
195 Montague Street, 12th Floor
Brooklyn, New York   11201
Ph: (718) 722-5952
Web site: http://www.icfny.org

Jessie Ball duPont Fund
First Union Bank Tower
225 Water Street, Suite 1200
Jacksonville, Florida 32202-5176
Ph: (904)353-0890
Web site: http://www.dupontfund.com/grant.html

John D. and Catherine T. MacArthur Foundation
Office of Grants Management
140 S. Dearborn Street
Chicago, IL 60603
Ph: 312/726-8000
Web site: http://www.macfdn.org/

The Nathan Cummings Foundation
1926 Broadway, Suite 600
New York, NY 10023-6915
Web site: http://www.ncf.org/

New York Foundation for the Arts
Tel: (212) 366--6900 x222
E-Mail: holoubek@nyfa.org
Web site: http://www.nyfa.org/asc_implementation/index.html

The Pew Charitable Trusts
2005 Market Street, Suite 1700
Philadelphia, PA 19103-7077
Telephone: (215) 575-9050
Web site: http://www.pewtrusts.com/

Philip Morris Companies
120 Park Avenue
New York, N.Y. 10017
Web site: http://www.philipmorris.com/pmcares/grantinfo.asp

Rockefeller Brothers Fund
437 Madison Avenue, 37th Floor
New York, New York 10022-7001
Ph: 212.812.4200
Web site: http://www.rbf.org/

Rockefeller Foundation
88 Kearny Street Suite 1850
San Francisco, CA 94108-5530
Web site: http://www.rockfound.org/

W. M. Keck Foundation
555 South Flower Street Suite 3230
Los Angeles, CA 90071
Ph: 213/680-3833
Web site: http://www.wmkeck.org/

Wallace Alexander Gerbode Foundation
(organizations around San Francisco and Hawaii)
470 Columbus Avenue, No. 209
San Francisco, CA 94133-3930
Tel: (415) 391-0911

William Bingham Foundation
20325 Center Ridge Road, Suite 629
Rocky River, OH 44116
Phone: (440) 331-6350
Web site: http://fdncenter.org/grantmaker/bingham/index.html

Appendix III Directory of Community Foundations

Many community foundations support arts and crafts. If you don't find a community foundation near you, check the list of state arts agencies for a referral. Although some community foundations only fund nonprofits, some provide grants for individual artists and craft persons. If a foundation near you only funds nonprofits, learn which organizations receive the funding and contact them about a prospective sponsoring relationship with you. Don't neglect to inquire about other grant programs like aid to women, small business, minority business, and public art.

Alaska

Alaska Community Foundation
701 W. 8th Avenue
Anchorage, AK 99510
Phone: (800) 483-3259
Fax: (907) 265-6122
E-mail: endowAK@pobox.alaska.net

Alaska Conservation Foundation
441 West Fifth Avenue Suite 402
Anchorage, AK 99501-2340
Phone: (907) 276-1917
Fax: (907) 274-4145

The Homer Foundation
3665 Ben Walters Lane Suite A
Homer, AK 99603-7738
Phone: (907) 235-5255
Fax: (907) 235-8126

Arizona

The Arizona Community Foundation
2122 E. Highland Suite 400
Phoenix, AZ 85016
Phone: (602) 381-1400
Fax: (602) 381-1575

Community Foundation for
Southern Arizona
6601 East Grant Road Suite 111
Tucson, AZ 85715
Phone: (520) 722-1707
Fax: (520) 722-0850
E-mail: CFSoAZ@aol.com

Arkansas

Arkansas Community Foundation
700 S. Rock Street
Little Rock, AR 72202
Phone: (501) 372-1116
Fax: (501) 372-1166

Union County Community Foundation
P. O. Box 148
El Dorado, AR 71731
Phone: (870) 862-8223
Fax: (870) 862-8254
E-mail: uccf@ipa.net

California

Anaheim Community Foundation
200 S. Anaheim Blvd., Suite 433
Anaheim, California   92805-3820
Phone: (714) 254-5160

Berkeley Community Fund
2041 Bancroft Way, Suite 204
Berkeley, California 94704
Phone: (510) 843-5202
Fax: (510) 843-4421
Email: bcf@berkfund.org

California Community Foundation
445 S. Figueroa Street Suite 3400
Los Angeles, CA 90071-1638
Phone: (213) 413-4130
Fax: (213) 383-2046
E-mail: jshakely@ccf-la.org

Claremont Community Foundation
205 Yale Avenue
Claremont, CA 91711
Phone: (909) 398-1060
Fax: (909) 624-6629
E-mail: claremontfoundation.org

Coastal Community Foundation
P.O. Box 230415
Encinitas, California   92023-0415
Phone: (760) 942-9245

East Bay Community Foundation
501 Wickson Avenue
Oakland, CA 94610-2727
Phone: (510) 836-3223
Fax: (510) 836-3287
E-mail: nhowe@eastbaycf.org

El Dorado Community Foundation
P.O. Box 1388
Placerville, CA 95667
Phone: (530) 622-5621
Fax: (530) 626-7100
E-mail: edcomfnd innercite.com

Fresno Regional Foundation
1999 Tuolumne Suite 650
Fresno, CA 93721
Phone: (209) 233-2016
Fax: (209) 233-2078

Glendale Community Foundation
P.O. Box 313
327 W. Arden, Suite 201
Glendale, CA 91209-0313
Phone: (818) 241-8040
Fax: (818) 241-8045
E-mail: gcfndn@earthlink.net

The Humboldt Area Foundation
P.O. Box 99
Bayside, CA 95524-0099
Phone: (707) 442-2993
Fax: (707) 442-3811
E-mail: Peter@hafoundation.org

International Community Foundation
1420 Kettner Blvd. Suite 500
San Diego, CA 92101
Phone: (619) 235-2300
Fax: (619) 239-1710

Marin Community Foundation
17 E. Sir Francis Drake Blvd. #200
Larkspur, CA 94939-1708
Phone: (415) 461-3333
Fax: (415) 464-2555

Mendocino County Community
Foundation
605 S. State Street
Ukiah, CA 95482-4912
Phone: (707) 468-9882
Fax: (707) 468-5529
E-mail: mccf@pacific.net

Community Foundation for Monterey
County
Heritage Harbor, #155-A 99 Pacific St
Monterey, CA 93940
Phone: (831) 375-9712
Fax: (831) 375-4731
E-mail: lueders@commfdnmc.org

Community Foundation of Napa Valley
3295 Claremont Way Suite 5
Napa, CA 94558
Phone: (707) 254-9565
Fax: (707) 254-7955
E-mail: patricia@interx.net

North Valley Community Foundation
660 Manzanita Court Suite Four
Chico, CA 95926
Phone: (530) 891-1150
Fax: (530) 891-1502

Orange County Community Foundation
2081 Business Center Drive Suite 100
Irvine, CA 92612-1101
Phone: (949) 553-4202
Fax: (949) 553-4211

Pasadena Foundation
16 North Marengo Avenue Room 300
Pasadena, CA 91101
Phone: (626) 796-2097
Fax: (626) 583-4738

Peninsula Community Foundation
1700 South El Camino Real Suite 300
San Mateo, CA 94402-3049
Phone: (650) 358-9369
E-mail: sterling@pcf.org

Riverside Community Foundation
3800 Orange Street, Suite 230
Riverside, California   92501-3622
Phone: (909) 684-4194

Rancho Santa Fe Foundation
P.O. Box 811
Rancho Santa Fe, CA 92067
Phone: (858) 756-6557
Fax: (858) 756-6561

Sacramento Regional Foundation
555 Capitol Mall Suite 747
Sacramento, CA 95814
Phone: (916) 492-6510
E-mail: srf@sacregfoundation.org

The San Diego Foundation
1420 Kettner Blvd. Suite 500
San Diego, CA 92101
Phone: (619) 235-2300
Fax: (619) 239-1710
E-mail: bob@sdcf.org

The San Francisco Foundation
225 Bush Street Suite 500
San Francisco, CA 94104
Phone: (415) 733-8500
Fax: (415) 477-2783
E-mail: srh@sff.org

San Luis Obispo County Community
Foundation, Inc.
P. O. Box 1580
San Luis Obispo, CA 93403-1580
Phone: (805) 543-2323
Fax: (805) 781-3825
E-mail: strategiem@fix.net

Santa Barbara Foundation
15 East Carrillo Street
Santa Barbara, CA 93101
Phone: (805) 963-1873
Fax: (805) 966-2345
E-mail: cslosser@sbfoundation.org

The Community Foundation of Santa
Cruz County
2425 Porter Street Suite 16
Soquel, CA 95073
Phone: (831) 477-0800
E-mail: lance@cfscc.org

Community Foundation Silicon Valley
60 S Market Street Suite 1000
San Jose, CA 95113-2336
Phone: (408) 278-0270
Fax: (408) 278-0280
E-mail: phero@cfsv.org

Sonoma County Community Foundation
250 D Street Suite 205
Santa Rosa, CA 95404-4773
Phone: (707) 579-4073
Fax: (707) 579-4801
E-mail: sccfkay@metro.net

Sonora Area Foundation
Box 577
Sonora, CA 95370-0577
Phone: (209) 533-2596
Fax: (209) 533-2412
E-mail: acorn@sonora.area.org

Streams in the Desert Foundation
15030 Genesee Road
Apple Valley, CA 92307
Phone: (760) 242-4887
Fax: (760) 946-1243

Truckee Tahoe Community Foundation
P. O. Box 366
Truckee, CA 96160
Phone: (530) 587-1776
Fax: (530) 587-1316
E-mail: ldobey@ix.netcom.com

Ventura County Community Foundation
1317 Del Norte Road Suite 150
Camarillo, CA 93010-8504
Phone: (805) 988-0196
E-mail: kmclean@vccf.org

Colorado
Aspen Valley Foundation
110 East Hallam Street Suite 126
Aspen, CO 81611
Phone: (970) 925-9300

Community Foundation Serving
Boulder County
2060 Broadway Suite 255
Boulder, CO 80302-5218
Phone: (303) 442-0436
Fax: (303) 415-1542

Broomfield Community Foundation
P.O. Box 2040
Broomfield, CO 80038-2040
Phone: (303) 469-7208
Fax: (303) 410-1733
E-mail: BCF2040@aol.com

Community Foundation of Northern
Colorado
The Nicol Building
528 South College Avenue
Fort Collins, CO 80524
Phone: (970) 224-3462
Fax: (970) 224-5153

Denver Foundation
950 S. Cherry Street Suite 200
Denver, CO 80246
Phone: (303) 300-1790
Fax: (303) 300-6547
E-mail: denverfoundation@aol.com

Community Foundation of Greeley
801 Eighth Street Suite 230
Greeley, CO 80631
Phone: (970) 304-9970
Fax: (970) 352-8761
E-mail: rrbond@bentley.unco.edu

Pikes Peak Community Foundation
P.O. Box 1443
Colorado Springs, CO 80901
Phone: (719) 389-1251
Fax: (719) 389-1252

Southern Colorado Community
Foundation
207 W. 6th Street
Pueblo, CO 81003
Phone: (719) 583-4546
Fax: (719) 583-4574
E-mail: sscf@lex.net

Community Foundation of Southwest
Colorado
P.O. Box 1673
Durango, CO 81302
Phone: (970) 382-8208
Fax: (970) 382-8208
E-mail: mdi@frontier.net

Western Colorado Community
Foundation
P.O. Box 4334
Grand Junction, CO 81502-4334
Phone: (970) 243-3767
Fax: (970) 243-3767

Yampa Valley Community Foundation
P.O. Box 774965
Steamboat Springs, CO 80477
Phone: (970) 879-8632
Fax: (970) 871-0431
E-mail: donate@yvcf.org

Connecticut
Greater Bridgeport Area Foundation
940 Broad Street
Bridgeport, CT 06604-4813
Phone: (203) 334-7511
Fax: (203) 333-4652

Fairfield County Foundation
523 Danbury Road
Wilton, CT 06897
Phone: (203) 834-9393
Fax: (203) 834-9996

Hartford Foundation for Public Giving
85 Gillett Street
Hartford, CT 06105
Phone: (860) 548-1888
Fax: (860) 524-8346

Main Street Community Foundation
P.O. Box 2702
Bristol, CT 06011-2702
Phone: (860) 583-6363
Fax: (860) 589-1252

Meriden Foundation
C/O Webster Trust Co., N.A.
346 Main Street
Kensington, CT 06037
Phone: (203) 235-4456
Fax: (203) 639-6530

Middlesex County Community
Foundation
P.O. Box 25
Middletown, CT 06457-0025
Phone: (860) 347-0025
E-mail: middlesexcounty.@snet.net

New Britain Foundation
29 Russell Street
New Britain, CT 06052
Phone: (860) 229-6018
Fax: (860) 229-2641
E-mail: mepowell@nbfoundation.org

New Canaan Community Foundation
P.O. Box 1285
New Canaan, CT 06840
Phone: (203) 966-0231

Community Foundation for Greater New
Haven
70 Audubon Street
New Haven, CT 06510
Phone: (203) 777-2386
Fax: (203) 787-6584
E-mail: nhadley@cfgnh.org

Community Foundation of Southeastern
Connecticut
One Union Plaza   P.O. Box 769
New London, CT 06320
Phone: (860) 442-3572
Fax: (860) 442-0584

Waterbury Foundation
156 West Main Street
Waterbury, CT 06702-1216
Phone: (203) 753-1315
Fax: (203) 756-3054
E-mail: info@waterburyfoundation.org

Delaware
Delaware Community Foundation
P.O. Box 1636
Wilmington, DE 19899
Phone: (302) 571-8004
Fax: (302) 571-1553

District of Columbia
Community Foundation for The
National Capital Region
1112 16th Street, N.W. Suite 340
Washington, DC 20036
Phone: (202) 955-5890
Fax: (202) 955-8084
E-mail: cfncrtfreeman@erols.com

Florida
Community Foundation of Brevard
700 S. Babcock Street Suite 102
Melbourne, FL 32901
Phone: (407) 724-6133
Fax: (407) 724-2740

Community Foundation of Broward
800 East Broward Blvd. Suite 610
Fort Lauderdale, FL 33301
Phone: (954) 761-9503
Fax: (954) 761-7102
E-mail: lcarter@cfbroward.org

Community Foundation of Central
Florida
P.O. Box 2071
Orlando, FL 32802
Phone: (407) 872-3050
Fax: (407) 425-2990

Community Foundation of Collier
County
2400 Tammiami Trail North Suite 300
Naples, FL 34103
Phone: (941) 649-5000
Fax: (941) 649-5337

Coral Gables Community Foundation
1825 Ponce De Leon Blvd. P M B 447
Coral Gables, FL 33134-4418
Phone: (305) 446-9670
Fax: (305) 446-9608
E-mail: gburns@coralgables.net

Dade Community Foundation
200 South Biscayne Blvd Suite 2780
Miami, FL 33131-2343
Phone: (305) 371-2711
Fax: (305) 371-5342

Community Foundation of Florida Keys
1300 Tropical Avenue
Key West, FL 33040
Phone: (305) 292-1502
Fax: (305) 294-2675

Gainesville Community Foundation
5346 S.W. 91st Terrace
Gainesville, FL 32608
Phone: (352) 367-0060
E-mail: tillman@post.harvard.edu

Jacksonville Community Foundation
112 West Adams Street Suite 1414
Jacksonville, FL 32202
Phone: (904) 356-4483
Fax: (904) 356-7910
E-mail: jfound@bellsouth.net

Manatee Community Foundation
P.O. Box 14152
Bradenton, FL 34280
Phone: (941) 761-9560
Fax: (941) 761-9641

Community Foundation for Palm Beach
& Martin Counties
324 Datura Street, Suite 340
West Palm Beach, FL 33401-5431
Phone: (561) 659-6800
Fax: (561) 832-6542
E-mail: cfpbmc@aol.com

Pinellas County Community Foundation
P.O. Box 205
Clearwater, FL 33757-0205
Phone: (727) 446-0058

Community Foundation of Sarasota Cty
P.O. Box 49587
Sarasota, FL 34230-6587
Phone: (941) 955-3000

Southwest Florida Community
Foundation
Unit 72 12734 Kenwood Lane
Fort Myers, FL 33907
Phone: (941) 274-5900

Community Foundation of Tampa Bay
4950 West Kennedy Blvd. Suite 250
Tampa, FL 33609-1837
Phone: (813) 282-1975

Georgia

Community Foundation for Greater
Atlanta
50 Hurt Plaza - Suite 449 The Hurt
Building
Atlanta, GA 30303
Phone: (404) 688-5525
Fax: (404) 688-3060

Community Foundation of Central
Georgia
277 Martin Luther King Jr. Blvd. Suite
303
Macon, GA 31201-3489
Phone: (912) 750-9338
Fax: (912) 738-9214

Gwinnett Foundation
1770 Indian Trail Road Suite 160
Norcross, GA 30093
Phone: (770) 564-3451
Fax: (770) 564-0010

North Georgia Community Foundation
P.O. Box 1583
Gainesville, GA 30503
Phone: (770) 535-7880
Fax: (770) 535-0554
E-mail: jmathis@ngcf.org

Community Foundation of Northwest
Georgia
P.O. Box 942
Dalton, GA 30722
Phone: (706) 275-9117

Savannah Foundation
428 Bull Street
Savannah, GA 31401
Phone: (912) 238-3288
Fax: (912) 231-8082

Community Foundation of Southwest
Georgia
P.O. Box 2654 135 N. Broad Street
Thomasville, GA 31799
Phone: (912) 228-5088
Fax: (912) 228-0848

Hawaii

The Hawaii Community Foundation
900 Fort Street Mall Suite 1300
Honolulu, HI 96813-3714
Phone: (808) 537-6333

Idaho

Idaho Community Foundation
101 S. Capitol Blvd., Suite 1700
Boise, ID 83702-5958
Phone: (208) 342-3535

Iowa

The Greater Cedar Rapids Foundation
101 Second Street, S.E. Suite 506
Cedar Rapids, IA 52401
Phone: (319) 366-2862
E-mail: gcrfdr@fyiowa.infi.net

Decorah Area Community Foundation
P.O. Box 450
Decorah, IA 52101
Phone: (319) 382-2959

The Greater Des Moines Foundation
601 Locust Street Suite 1051
Des Moines, IA 50309-3738
Phone: (515) 245-3766
Fax: (515) 247-2255

Community Foundation of The Great
River Bend
111 East Third Street Suite 710
Davenport, IA 52801
Phone: (319) 326-2840
Fax: (319) 326-2870

The Greater Jefferson County
Foundation
P.O. Box 1325
Fairfield, IA 52556-1325
Phone: (515) 472-0758
Fax: (515) 472-1521

Siouxland Foundation
P.O. Box 2014
Sioux City, IA 51104
Phone: (712) 239-3303

Community Foundation of Waterloo &
Northeast Iowa
500 East Fourth St., Suite 316 P.O. Box
1176
Waterloo, IA 50704-1176
Phone: (319) 291-1202

Illinois

The Aurora Foundation
111 West Downer Place Suite 312
Aurora, IL 60506
Phone: (630) 896-7800
Fax: (630) 896-7811

Community Foundation of Champaign
County
404 West Church Street
Champaign, IL 61820
Phone: (217) 359-0125
Fax: (217) 352-6494
E-mail: jdniles@net66.com

The Chicago Community Trust
222 North LaSalle St. Suite 1400
Chicago, IL 60601
Phone: (312) 372-3356
Fax: (312) 580-7411

DeKalb County Community Foundation
2225 Gateway Drive
Sycamore, IL 60178
Phone: (815) 748-5383
Fax: (815) 748-5873

The Dupage Community Foundation
110 North Cross Street
Wheaton, IL 60187-5318
Phone: (630) 665-5556
Fax: (630) 665-9861

Evanston Community Foundation
828 Davis Street Suite 300
Evanston, IL 60201
Phone: (847) 475-2402
Fax: (847) 475-2469

Highland Park Community Foundation
P. O. Box 398
Highland Park, IL 60035
Phone: (847) 433-4100
Fax: (847) 509-9196
E-mail: fugitwlv@aol.com

Oak Park River Forest Community
Foundation
1042 Pleasant
Oak Park, IL 60302
Phone: (708) 209-1560
Fax: (708) 386-4886
E-mail: Advisors@oprfcommfd.org

Peoria Area Community Foundation
124 SW Adams Street Suite M-1
Peoria, IL 61602
Phone: (309) 674-8730

Quincy Area Community Foundation
P.O. Box 741
Quincy, IL 62306
Phone: (217) 222-1237
Fax: (217) 223-4138

The Rockford Community Foundation
321 West State Street Suite 1300
Rockford, IL 61101
Phone: (815) 962-2110
Fax: (815) 962-2116

Indiana
Central Indiana Community Foundation
615 North Alabama Street, Suite 119
Indianapolis, IN 46204
Tel: 317-634-CICF
Web Site: www.cicf.org

Community Foundation of Boone
County
P.O. Box 92
Zionsville, IN 46077
Phone: (317) 873-0210
Fax: (317) 873-0219
E-mail: cfbc@in-motion.net

Community Foundation Alliance
123 N.W. 4th Street Suite 322
Evansville, IN 47708-1712
Phone: (812) 429-1191

Dekalb County Community Foundation
P. O. Box 285
704 W. Seventh Street
Auburn, IN 46706
Phone: (219) 925-0311

Elkhart County Community Foundation
Key Bank Building 301 S. Main, P.O.
Box 279
Elkhart, IN 46515-0279
Phone: (219) 295-8761
Fax: (219) 295-2882
E-mail: elkcommfdn@aol.com

Fort Wayne Community Foundation
701 S. Clinton Street Suite 324
Fort Wayne, IN 46802
Phone: (219) 426-4083
Fax: (219) 424-0114

Community Foundation of Grant County
505 West Third Street
Marion, IN 46952
Phone: (317) 662-0065
Fax: (317) 662-1438
E-mail: comfdn@nxco.com

Hancock County Commmunity
Foundation, Inc.
One Courthouse Plaza
Greenfield, IN 46140
Phone: (317) 462-8870
Fax: (317) 462-8871

Henry County Community Foundation
P.O. Box 6006
New Castle, IN 47362
Phone: (317) 529-2235
Fax: (317) 529-2284
E-mail: hccfound@nltc.net

Heritage Fund of Bartholomew County
P.O. Box 1547
Columbus, IN 47202-1547
Phone: (812) 376-7772
Fax: (812) 376-0051

Community Foundation of Howard
County
202 N. Main
Kokomo, IN 46901
Phone: (765) 454-7298
Fax: (765) 868-4123
E-mail: ron@inkokomo.com

Indianapolis Foundation
119 English Foundation Bldg. 615
North Alabama Street
Indianapolis, IN 46204
Phone: (317) 634-7497
Fax: (317) 684-0943
E-mail: keng@cicf.org

Community Foundation of Jackson
County
P.O. Box 1231
Seymour, IN 47274
Phone: (812) 523-4483
Fax: (812) 524-8176
E-mail: vccf@hsonline.net

Greater Johnson County Community
Foundation
18 West Jefferson Street
Franklin, IN 46131
Phone: (317) 738-2213
Fax: (317) 736-7220

Koscuisko County Foundation
117 W. Center St. Suite B
Warsaw, IN 46580
Ph: 219-267-1901
Email: kcfoundation@waveone.net

Greater Lafayette Community
Foundation
1114 State Street P.O. Box 677
Lafayette, IN 47902-0677
Phone: (765) 742-9078
Fax: (765) 742-9079
E-mail: jklusman@glcf.lafayette.in.us

Lawrence County Community
Foundation
P.O. Box 1235
Bedford, IN 47421
Phone: (812) 279-2215
Fax: (812) 279-1984

Legacy Fund of Hamilton County
650 East Carmel Drive Suite 490
Carmel, IN 46032
Phone: (317) 843-2479
Fax: (317) 848-5463
E-mail: meganw@cicf.org

Community Foundation of Madison and
Jefferson County
P.O. Box 306
Madison, IN 47250-0306
Phone: (812) 265-3327
Fax: (812) 273-0181
E-mail: cfmjc@cfmjc.org

Madison County Community
Foundation
32 West Tenth Street
Anderson, IN 46016
Phone: (765) 644-0002
Fax: (765) 644-3392
E-mail: mccf-in@ecicnet.org

Montgomery County Community
Foundation
118 East Main Street P.O. Box 334
Crawfordsville, IN 47933
Phone: (765) 362-1267
Fax: (765) 361-0562
E-mail: lann@tctc.com

Community Foundation of Muncie &
Delaware County
P.O. Box 807
Muncie, IN 47308
Phone: (765) 747-7181
Fax: (765) 289-7770
E-mail: cfmd@ecicnet.org

Noble County Community Foundation
2092 North State Road 9
Albion, IN 46701
Phone: (219) 636-3436
Fax: (219) 636-3922

Ohio County Community Foundation
P. O. Box 199
Rising Sun, IN 47040
Phone: (812) 438-4490
Fax: (812) 438-4503

Putnam County Foundation
P.O. Box 514
Greencastle, IN 46135
Phone: (765) 653-4978
Fax: (765) 653-6385

Community Foundation of Southern
Indiana
4104 Charlestown Road
New Albany, IN 47150-9538
Phone: (812) 948-4662

Community Foundation of St. Joseph
County
P.O. Box 837
South Bend, IN 46624
Phone: (219) 232-0041
Fax: (219) 233-1906

Steuben County Community Foundation
207 S. Wayne Street Suite A
Angola, IN 46703-1936
Phone: (219) 665-6656
Fax: (219) 665-8420

Unity Foundation of LaPorte County
P.O. Box 527
Michigan City, IN 46361
Phone: (219) 879-0327
Fax: (219) 873-2416
E-mail: unity@niia.net

Community Foundation of Wabash Cty
PO Box 98
North Manchester, IN 46962
Phone: (219) 982-4824
Fax: (219) 982-4824

Wabash Valley Community Foundation
2901 Ohio Boulevard Suite #153
Terre Haute, IN 47803
Phone: (812) 232-2234
Fax: (812) 234-4853
E-mail: beth@wvcf.com

Washington County Community
Foundation
P.O. Box 50
Salem, IN 47167
Phone: (812) 883-8803
Fax: (812) 883-1467
E-mail: dmahuron@blueriver.net

Wayne County, Indiana Foundation
33 South Seventh Street Suite One
Richmond, IN 47374
Phone: (765) 962-1638

The White Lick Heritage Community
Foundation
P.O. Box 501
Danville, IN 46168
Phone: (317) 718-1200
Fax: (317) 718-1033

Kansas
Abilene Community Foundation
P.O. Box 735
Abilene, KS 67410
Phone: (785) 263-1863

Dodge City Area Community
Foundation
P. O. Box 1313
Dodge City, KS 67801-1313
Phone: (316) 225-0959

Hutchinson Community Foundation
P. O. Box 298
Hutchinson, KS 67504-0298
Phone: (316) 663-5293
Fax: (316) 663-9277

Legacy Community Foundation
P.O. Box 312
Winfield, KS 67156
Phone: (316) 221-2750
Fax: (316) 221-2810
E-mail: jhnpkn@kanokla.net

South Central Community Foundation
348 N.E. State Road 61
Pratt, KS 67124
Phone: (316) 672-5936
Fax: (316) 672-5288
E-mail: dbryan@prmc.org

Topeka Community Foundation
P.O. Box 4525
Topeka, KS 66604
Phone: (785) 272-4804
Fax: (785) 273-2467

Western Kansas Community
Foundation
P. O. Box 1452
Garden City, KS 67846
Phone: (316) 271-9484
E-mail: wkcf@pld.com

Wichita Community Foundation
151 N. Main, Suite 140
Wichita, KS 67202
Phone: (316) 264-4880
Fax: (316) 264-7592

Kentucky
Blue Grass Community Foundation
200 West Vine Street Suite 305
Lexington, KY 40507-1620
Phone: (606) 225-3343
Fax: (606) 243-0770
E-mail: screek@bgcf.org

Community Foundation of Louisville
Waterfront Plaza, Suite 1110
325 West Main Street
Louisville, KY 40202
Phone: (502) 585-4649

Paducah Area Community Foundation
P.O. Box 7901
Paducah, KY 42002-7901
Phone: (502) 575-5892
Fax: (502) 575-5726

Foundation for the Tri-State
Community
P.O. Box 2096
Ashland, KY 41105-2096
Phone: (606) 324-3888
Fax: (606) 324-5961

Louisiana
Baton Rouge Area Foundation
406 N. Fourth Street
Baton Rouge, LA 70802
Phone: (225) 387-6126
Fax: (225) 387-6153

Central Louisiana Community
Foundation
201 Johnston Street Suite 600
Alexandria, LA 71301
Phone: (318) 445-7702
Fax: (318) 445-1283
E-mail: moranch@aol.com

Greater New Orleans Foundation
1055 St. Charles Avenue Suite 100
New Orleans, LA 70130-3941
Phone: (504) 598-4663
Fax: (504) 598-4676
E-mail: benj@gnof.org

Community Foundation of Shreveport-
Bossier
401 Edwards Street Suite 1111
Shreveport, LA 71101
Phone: (318) 221-0582
Fax: (318) 221-7463
E-mail: gwin@comfoundsb.org

Maine
Maine Community Foundation
245 Main Street
Ellsworth, ME 04605
Phone: (207) 667-9735
Fax: (207) 667-0447
E-mail: mkane@maincf.org

Maryland
The Baltimore Community Foundation
2 East Read Street Ninth Floor
Baltimore, MD 21202
Phone: (410) 332-4171
Fax: (410) 837-4701
E-mail: tdarmbrust@aol.com

Chesapeake Community Foundation
521 First Street
Annapolis, MD 21403
Phone: (410) 268-7245
Fax: (410) 268-8860
E-mail: chcommunityfdn@juno.com

Columbia Foundation
10221 Wincopin Circle Suite 100
Columbia, MD 21044
Phone: (410) 730-7840
Fax: (410) 715-3043

Community Foundation of the Eastern
Shore
P.O. Box 152
Salisbury, MD 21803-0156
Phone: (410) 742-9911
Fax: (410) 742-6638

Mid Shore Community Foundation
300 Talbot Street
Easton, MD 21601
Phone: (410) 819-3695
Fax: (410) 819-3706

Community Foundation of Washington
County
14606 Pennslyvania Avenue
Hagerstown, MD 21742
Phone: (301) 745-5210
Fax: (301) 791-5752

Massachussetts
Berkshire Taconic Community
Foundation
271 Main Street
Great Barrington, MA 01230
Phone: (800) 969-2823
Fax: (413) 528-8158
E-mail: btcf@bcn.net

Boston Foundation
One Boston Place 24th Floor
Boston, MA 02108
Phone: (617) 723-7415

Cambridge Community Foundation
99 Bishop Richard Allen Drive
Cambridge, MA 02139
Phone: (617) 576-9966
Fax: (617) 876-8187

Community Foundation of Cape Cod
P.O. Box 406
Yarmouthport, MA 02675
Phone: (508) 362-3040
Fax: (508) 362-4069
E-mail: comfndcc@capecod.net

Crossroads Community Foundation
20 Main Street Suite 301
Natick, MA 01760
Phone: (508) 647-2260
Fax: (508) 647-2288
E-mail: ccfdn@acunet.net

Greater Lowell Community Foundation
P.O. Box 9193 11 Kearney Square, 4th
Floor
Lowell, MA 01853
Phone: (978) 970-1600
Fax: (978) 454-7637
E-mail: glcf@gis.net

Old Colony Charitable Foundation
P.O. Box 9477
Boston, MA 02205
Phone: (617) 434-5669
Fax: (617) 434-7567

Permanent Endowment Fund for
Martha's Vineyard
RR 2, Box 149
Vineyard Haven, MA 02568-9774
Phone: (508) 693-0721

Community Foundation of Southeastern
Massachusetts
227 Union Street Suite 609
New Bedford, MA 02740
Phone: (508) 996-8253
Fax: (508) 996-8254

Community Foundation of Western
Massachusetts
P.O. Box 15769
Springfield, MA 01115
Phone: (413) 732-2858
Fax: (413) 733-8565

Greater Worcester Community
Foundation
44 Front Street, Suite 530
Worcester, MA 01608-1782
Phone: (508) 755-0980
Fax: (508) 755-3406
E-mail: atlisi@greaterworcester.org

Michigan

Albion Community Foundation
203 S. Superior P.O. Box 156
Albion, MI 49224
Phone: (517) 629-3349
Fax: (517) 629-8027
E-mail: execdir@albionfoundation.org

The Ann Arbor Area Community
Foundation
201 South Main, Suite 801
Ann Arbor, MI 48104-2113
Phone: (734) 663-0401
Fax: (734) 663-3514

Battle Creek Community Foundation
One Riverwalk Centre
34 West Jackson Street
Battle Creek, MI 49017-3505
Phone: (616) 962-2181
Fax: (616) 962-2182
E-mail: brenda@bccfoundation.org

Bay Area Community Foundation
703 Washington Avenue
Bay City, MI 48708
Phone: (800) 926-3217
Fax: (517) 893-4448

The Community Foundation of Greater
Birmingham
2027 First Avenue North Suite 410
Birmingham, MI 35203
Phone: (205) 328-8641
Fax: (205) 328-6576

Calhoun County Community
Foundation
1000 Quintard Avenue Suite 307
Anniston, MI 36202
Phone: (256) 231-5160
Fax: (256) 231-5161
E-mail: cccf@cybrtyme.com

Capital Region Community Foundation
300 N. Washington Square Suite 104
Lansing, MI 48933-1233
Phone: (517) 485-1630
Fax: (517) 485-1636
E-mail: crcf1@mindspring.com

Central Alabama Community
Foundation
P.O. Box 11587
Montgomery, MI 36111
Phone: (334) 264-6223
Fax: (334) 263-6225
E-mail: macf@mindspring.com

Charlevoix County Community
Foundation
507 Water Street, Suite 6 P.O. Box 718
East Jordan, MI 49727
Phone: (616) 536-2440
Fax: (616) 536-2640
E-mail: cccf@freeway.net

Community Foundation of Southeast
Alabama Cty
P. O. Box 1422
Dothan, MI 36302-1422
Phone: (334) 792-4792
Fax: (334) 671-7036

Community Foundation of Greater Flint
502 Church Street
Flint, MI 48502-1206
Phone: (810) 767-8270
Fax: (810) 767-0496
E-mail: commfdn@tir.com

The Fremont Area Foundation
4424 W. 48Th Street P.O. Box B
Fremont, MI 49412
Phone: (616) 924-5350
Fax: (616) 924-5391
E-mail: lcherin@tfaf.org

Grand Haven Area Community
Foundation
One S. Harbor Drive
Grand Haven, MI 49417
Phone: (616) 842-6378
Fax: (616) 842-9518

The Grand Rapids Foundation
161 Ottawa, N.W. Suite 209-C
Grand Rapids, MI 49503-2757
Phone: (616) 454-1751
Fax: (616) 454-6455
E-mail: dsieger@grfoundation.org

The Jackson Community Foundation
230 W. Michigan Avenue
Jackson, MI 49201
Phone: (517) 787-1321
Fax: (517) 787-4333
E-mail: nmdelaney@jacksoncf.org

Kalamazoo Foundation
151 South Rose Street Suite 332
Kalamazoo, MI 49007
Phone: (616) 381-4416
Fax: (616) 381-3146

Midland Foundation
812 West Main St. P. O. Box 289
Midland, MI 48640
Phone: (517) 839-9661
Fax: (517) 832-8842

Community Foundation For Muskegon
County
Suite 200 425 W. Western Avenue
Muskegon, MI 49440
Phone: (616) 722-4538

Petoskey-Harbor Springs Area
Community Foundation
616 Petoskey Street Suite 100
Petoskey, MI 49770
Phone: (616) 348-5820
Fax: (616) 348-5883

Saginaw Community Foundation
100 S. Jefferson Suite 501
Saginaw, MI 48607
Phone: (517) 755-0545
Fax: (517) 755-6524

The Community Foundation of South
Alabama
P.O. Box 990
Mobile, MI 36601-0990
Phone: (334) 438-5591
Fax: (334) 438-5592

Community Foundation for
Southeastern Michigan
333 West Fort Street Suite 2010
Detroit, MI 48226
Phone: (313) 961-6675
Fax: (313) 961-2886

Southfield Community Foundation
26080 Berg Road
Southfield, MI 48034
Phone: (248) 351-1320
Fax: (248) 208-8185
E-mail: scfdn@aol.com

Community Foundation of St. Clair
County
Michigan National Bank Bldg.
800 Military, Suite 309
Port Huron, MI 48060
Phone: (810) 984-4761
Fax: (810) 984-3394

Minnesota
Central Minnesota Community
Foundation
Suite 200 101 South Seventh Avenue
Saint Cloud, MN 56301
Phone: (320) 253-4380
Fax: (320) 240-9215

Duluth-Superior Area Community
Foundation
227 West First Street
618 Missabe Building
Duluth, MN 55802
Phone: (218) 726-0232
Fax: (218) 726-0257
E-mail: dsacf@cp.duluth.mn.us

Grand Rapids Area Community
Foundation
504 N.W. First Avenue
Grand Rapids, MN 55744
Phone: (218) 327-9677

Initiative Foundation
70 S.E. First Avenue
Little Falls, MN 56345
Phone: (320) 632-9255
Fax: (320) 632-9258

Minneapolis Foundation
A200 Foshay Tower
821 Marquette Avenue South
Minneapolis, MN 55402
Phone: (612) 339-7343
Fax: (612) 672-3868

Northwest Minnesota Foundation
4225 Technology Drive N W
Bemidji, MN 56601-5118
Phone: (218) 759-2057
Fax: (218) 759-2328

Rochester Area Foundation
21 First Street, S.W. Suite 350
Rochester, MN 55902
Phone: (507) 282-0203
Fax: (507) 282-4938
E-mail: rafmn@aol.com

Saint Paul Foundation
600 Norwest Center
St. Paul, MN 55101-1797
Phone: (651) 224-5463
Fax: (651) 224-8123
E-mail: pav@tspf.org

Greater Winona Area Community
Foundation
1705 Wilkie Drive
Winona, MN 55987
Phone: (507) 454-6511
Fax: (507) 452-2964

Mississippi
Create
P.O. Box 1053
Tupelo, MS 38802
Phone: (601) 844-8989
Fax: (601) 844-8149

Gulf Coast Community Foundation
P.O. Box 1899
Gulfport, MS 39502
Phone: (228) 868-1563

Greater Jackson Foundation
4500 I-55 North Suite 258
Jackson, MS 39211
Phone: (601) 981-4572
Fax: (601) 981-4258

Foundation for the Mid South
308 E. Pearl Street, 2Nd Floor
Jackson, MS 39201
Phone: (601) 355-8167
Fax: (601) 355-6499
E-mail: gpenick@fdnmidsouth.org

Missouri
Greater Kansas City Community
Foundation
1055 Broadway Suite 130
Kansas City, MO 64105
Phone: (816) 842-0944
Fax: (816) 842-8079
E-mail: president@gkccf.org

Community Foundation of the Ozarks
901 St. Louis Street Suite 701
Springfield, MO 65806
Phone: (417) 864-6199
Fax: (417) 864-8344
E-mail: jancf@getonthenet.

St. Louis Community Foundation
319 North Fourth Street Suite 501
St. Louis, MO 63102
Phone: (314) 588-8200
Fax: (314) 588-8088

Montana
Lower Flathead Valley Community
Foundation
P.O. Box 379
Pablo, MT 59855-0379
Phone: (406) 675-4300
Fax: (406) 675-4969

Montana Community Foundation
101 No. Last Chance Gulch Suite 211
Helena, MT 59601
Phone: (406) 443-8313
Fax: (406) 442-0482
E-mail: mtcf@mt.net

Nebraska
Fremont Area Community Foundation
P.O. Box 182
Fremont, NE 68026
Phone: (231) 721-4252
Fax: (231) 721-9359

Grand Island Community Foundation
231 South Locust Suite 214
Grand Island, NE 68801
Phone: (308) 381-7767
Fax: (308) 389-3789

Hastings Community Foundation
P.O. Box 703
Hastings, NE 68901
Phone: (402) 462-5152
Fax: (402) 462-5152

Kearney Area Community Foundation
P.O. Box 607
Kearney, NE 68848
Phone: (308) 237-3114
Fax: (308) 236-8785

Lincoln Community Foundation
215 Centennial Mall South Room 200
Lincoln, NE 68508
Phone: (402) 474-2345
Fax: (402) 476-8532
E-mail: dowty@lcf.org

Merrick Foundation
1530 17Th Avenue
Central City, NE 68826
Phone: (308) 946-3707
Fax: (308) 946-3707

Mid-Nebraska Community Foundation
106 S. Vine
North Platte, NE 69103
Phone: (308) 534-3315
Fax: (308) 534-6117

Nebraska Community Foundation
The Atrium, Suite 610
1200 N Street
Lincoln, NE 68508-2022
Phone: (402) 471-6009
Fax: (402) 471-8690

Omaha Community Foundation
1623 Farnam Street Suite 600
Omaha, NE 68102
Phone: (402) 342-3458
Fax: (402) 342-3582

Oregon Trail Community Foundation
115 Railway Plaza
Scottsbluff, NE 69361
Phone: (308) 635-3393
Fax: (308) 635-3393

Phelps County Community Foundation
701 Fourth Avenue 2A
Holdrege, NE 68949
Phone: (308) 995-6847
Fax: (308) 995-2146

New Hampshire
New Hampshire Charitable Foundation
37 Pleasant Street
Concord, NH 03301-4005
Phone: (603) 225-6641
Fax: (603) 225-1700
E-mail: lf@nhcf.org

New Jersey
Community Foundation of New Jersey
P.O. Box 317
Morristown, NJ 07963-0317
Phone: (973) 267-5533
Fax: (973) 267-2903
E-mail: CFNJ@bellatlantic.net

Princeton Area Community Foundation
188 Tamarack Circle
Skillman, NJ 08558
Phone: (609) 688-0300

Westfield Foundation
P.O. Box 2295
Westfield, NJ 07091
Phone: (908) 233-9787

New Mexico
Albuquerque Community Foundation
P.O. Box 36960
Albuquerque, NM 87176-6960
Phone: (505) 883-6240
Fax: (505) 883-3629
E-mail: albcfdn@swcp.com

Carlsbad Foundation
116 S. Canyon
Carlsbad, NM 88220
Phone: (505) 887-1131

New Mexico Community Foundation
1227 Paseo De Peralta
Santa Fe, NM 87501
Phone: (505) 820-6860
Fax: (505) 820-7860

New Mexico Women's Foundation
1030 San Pedro NE
Albuquerque, New Mexico 87110
Web site: http://www.worldplaces.com/
nmwf/

Santa Fe Community Foundation
P.O. Box 1827
Santa Fe, NM 87504-1827
Phone: (505) 988-9715
Fax: (505) 988-1829
E-mail: foundtion@santafecf.org

Taos Community Foundation
P.O. Box 1925
Taos, NM 87571
Phone: (505) 758-9272
Fax: (505) 758-7811

New York
Adirondack Community Trust
c/o J.S. Lansing Crestview Plaza
Lake Placid, NY 12946
Phone: (518) 523-4433
Fax: (518) 523-4434
E-mail: jslansing@compuserve.com

Community Foundation for Greater
Buffalo
712 Main Street
Buffalo, NY 14202-1720
Phone: (716) 852-2857
Fax: (716) 852-2861

Community Foundation for the Capital
Region
Executive Park Drive
Albany, NY 12203
Phone: (518) 446-9638
Fax: (518) 446-9708

Central New York Community
Foundation
500 South Salina Street Suite 428
Syracuse, NY 13202-3302
Phone: (315) 422-9538
Fax: (315) 471-6031
E-mail: peggy@cnycf.org

Northern Chautauqua Community
Foundation
212 Lake Shore Drive, West
Dunkirk, NY 14048
Phone: (716) 366-4892
Fax: (716) 366-4276
E-mail: nccf@netsync.net

Chautauqua Region Community
Foundation
21 East 3rd Street Suite 301
Jamestown, NY 14701
Phone: (716) 661-3390
Fax: (716) 488-0387
E-mail: crcf@netsync.net

Community Foundation of Dutchess
County
80 Washington Street Suite 201
Poughkeepsie, NY 12601-2304
Phone: (914) 452-3077
Fax: (914) 452-3083

Community Foundation of the Elmira-
Corning Area
307 B East Water Street
Elmira, NY 14901
Phone: (607) 734-6412
Fax: (607) 734-7335

Glens Falls Foundation
P. O. Box 318
Glens Falls, NY 12801
Phone: (518) 792-1151
Fax: (518) 743-0261

Community Foundation of Herkimer
and Oneida Counties
270 Genesee Street
Utica, NY 13502
Phone: (315) 735-8212
Fax: (315) 735-9363
E-mail: commfdn@borg.com

New York Community Trust
2 Park Avenue 24th Floor
New York, NY 10016-9385
Phone: (212) 686-0010
Fax: (212) 532-8528
E-mail: las@nyct-cfi.org

Northern New York Community
Foundation
H. S. B. C. Building
120 Washington Street
Watertown, NY 13601
Phone: (315) 782-7110
Fax: (315) 782-0047

Rochester Area Community Foundation
500 East Avenue
Rochester, NY 14607-1912
Phone: (716) 271-4100
Fax: (716) 271-4292
E-mail: jleonard@racf.org

Nevada
Lake Tahoe Community Trust
Box 9281
Incline Village, NV 89452
Phone: (702) 334-5846
Fax: (702) 831-8892
E-mail: hessda@wellsfargo.com

Nevada Community Foundation
1660 East Flamingo Road
Las Vegas, NV 89119
Phone: (702) 892-2326
Fax: (702) 892-8580

The Parasol Foundation of Incline
Village
P.O. Box 5206
Incline Village, NV 89450
Phone: (702) 831-3083
Fax: (702) 831-3050

Community Foundation of Western
Nevada
165 W. Liberty Street Suite 220
Reno, NV 89501
Phone: (775) 333-0360
Fax: (775) 333-0366

North Carolina

Cape Fear Community Foundation
P.O. Box 119
Wilmington, NC 28402
Phone: (910) 251-3911
Fax: (910) 251-1040

Foundation for the Carolinas
P.O. Box 34769
Charlotte, NC 28234-4769
Phone: (704) 376-9541
Fax: (704) 376-1243

Cumberland Community Foundation
P.O. Box 2171 308 Green Street
Fayetteville, NC 28302-2171
Phone: (910) 483-4449
Fax: (910) 483-2905
E-mail: ccfnd@fayettevillenc.com

Community Foundation of Greater
Greensboro
100 S. Elm Street Suite 307
Greensboro, NC 27401-2641
Phone: (336) 379-9100
Fax: (336) 378-0725

Community Foundation of Henderson
County
P.O. Box 1108
Hendersonville, NC 28793
Phone: (828) 697-6224
Fax: (828) 696-4026
E-mail: cfhc@ioa.com

North Carolina Community Foundation
333 Corporate Plaza Suite 1410
Raleigh, NC 27601
Phone: (919) 828-4387

Outer Banks Community Foundation
P.O. Box 1100
Kill Devil Hills, NC 27948-1100
Phone: (252) 261-8839

Polk County Community Foundation
505 North Trade St.
Tryon, NC 28782
Phone: (828) 859-5314
Fax: (828) 859-6122
E-mail: scooper@polkcf.org

Triangle Community Foundation
P.O. Box 12834
Research Triangle Park, NC 27709
Phone: (919) 549-9840
Fax: (919) 990-9066
E-mail: sstjohn@trianglecf.org

Community Foundation of Western
North Carolina
P. O. Box 1888
Asheville, NC 28802
Phone: (828) 254-4960
Fax: (828) 251-2258

Winston-Salem Foundation
860 West Fifth Street
Winston-Salem, NC 27101-2506
Phone: (336) 725-2382
Fax: (336) 727-0581
E-mail: swierman@wsfoundation.org

North Dakota

Fargo-Moorhead Area Foundation
609 1/2 First Avenue North Suite 205
Fargo, ND 58102
Phone: (701) 234-0756
Fax: (701) 234-9724
E-mail: fmaf@rrnet.com

North Dakota Community Foundation
1025 North 3rd Street P.O. Box 387
Bismarck, ND 58502-0387
Phone: (701) 222-8349
Fax: (701) 222-8257

Ohio

Akron Community Foundation
345 West Cedar Street
Akron, OH 44307-2407
Phone: (330) 376-8522

The Foundation for Appalachian Ohio
P. O. Box 787
Athens, OH 45701
Phone: (937) 767-7355

Ashland County Community
Foundation
P.O. Box 733
Ashland, OH 44805
Phone: (419) 281-4733

The Greater Cincinnati Foundation
300 West Fourth Street Suite 200
Cincinnati, OH 45202
Phone: (513) 241-2880
Fax: (513) 852-6886

The Cleveland Foundation
1422 Euclid Avenue Suite 1400
Cleveland, OH 44115-2001
Phone: (216) 861-3810
Fax: (216) 589-9039
E-mail: sminter@clevefdn.org

The Columbus Foundation & Affiliated
Organizations
1234 East Broad Street
Columbus, OH 43205-1463
Phone: (614) 251-4000
Fax: (614) 251-4009
E-mail: info@columbusfoundation.com

Coshocton Foundation
P.O. Box 55
Coshocton, OH 43812-0055
Phone: (740) 622-0010
Fax: (740) 622-1660
E-mail: wbreon@compuserve.comm

Hamilton Community Foundation
319 North Third Street
Hamilton, OH 45011
Phone: (513) 863-1389
Fax: (513) 863-2868

The Community Foundation of Greater
Lorain County
1865 North Ridge Road East Suite A
Lorain, OH 44055
Phone: (440) 277-0142

Marietta Community Foundation
P.O. Box 77
Marietta, OH 45750
Phone: (614) 376-4380
Fax: (614) 376-4509

Middletown Community Foundation
29 City Centre Plaza United Way Bldg
Middletown, OH 45042
Phone: (513) 424-7369
Fax: (513) 423-0005

The Muskingum County Community
Foundation
220 North Fifth Street PO Box 3042
Zanesville, OH 43702-3042
Phone: (614) 453-5192
Fax: (740) 453-5734

Portage Foundation
143 Gougler Avenue
Kent, OH 44240-2401
Phone: (330) 676-1110
Fax: (303) 676-1106
E-mail: portagefound.@mindspring.com

Richland County Foundation of
Mansfield
24 West Third Street Suite 100
Mansfield, OH 44902-1209
Phone: (419) 525-3020
Fax: (419) 525-1590

Sandusky/Erie County Community
Foundation
165 E. Washington Row Suite 304
Sandusky, OH 44870
Phone: (419) 621-9690
Fax: (419) 621-9691

Springfield Foundation
4 West Main Street Suite 425
Springfield, OH 45502-1323
Phone: (937) 324-8773
Fax: (937) 324-1836

Stark Community Foundation
The Saxton House
331 Market Avenue South
Canton, OH 44702-2107
Phone: (330) 454-3426

Toledo Community Foundation
608 Madison Avenue Suite 1540
Toledo, OH 43604-1151
Phone: (419) 241-5049
Fax: (419) 242-5549

Troy Foundation
C/O Firstar Bank
Troy 910 West Main Street
Troy, OH 45373
Phone: (937) 335-8513

Community Foundation of Union Cnty
P.O. Box 608
Marysville, OH 43040-0608
Phone: (937) 642-9618
Fax: (937) 644-4390

Warren County Foundation
P.O. Box 495 118 E. Main Street
Lebanon, OH 45036-0495
Phone: (513) 934-1001
Fax: (513) 934-3001

Greater Wayne County Foundation
P.O. Box 201
Wooster, OH 44691
Phone: (330) 262-3877
Fax: (330) 262-8057

Youngstown Foundation
P.O. Box 1162
Youngstown, OH 44501
Phone: (330) 744-0320
Fax: (330) 742-4290

Oklahoma

Oklahoma City Community Foundation
P.O. Box 1146
Oklahoma City, OK 73101-1146
Phone: (405) 235-5603
Fax: (405) 235-5612
E-mail: nanthony@occf.org

Tulsa Community Foundation
7010 S. Yale Suite 110
Tulsa, OK 74136
Phone: (918) 494-8823
Fax: (918) 491-4694

Oregon

Oregon Community Foundation
621 Southwest Morrison Street #725
Portland, OR 97205
Phone: (503) 227-6846
Fax: (503) 274-7771

Pennsylvania

Beaver County Foundation
P.O. Box 569
Beaver, PA 15009
Phone: (412) 847-6614
Fax: (412) 847-5017

Community Foundation of Bedford,
Cambria & Somerset Counties
216 Franklin Street Suite 606
Johnstown, PA 15901
Phone: (814) 536-7741
Fax: (814) 536-5859
E-mail: CFdnBCS@aol.com

Berks County Community Foundation
P.O. Box 212
Reading, PA 19601
Phone: (610) 685-2223
Fax: (610) 685-2240
E-mail: kevinm@bccf.org

Blair County Community Endowment
1216 11Th Avenue Suite 315
Altoona, PA 16601
Phone: (814) 944-6102
Fax: (814) 944-6102
E-mail: cessna@bcce.org

Centre County Community Foundation
P.O. Box 824
State College, PA 16804-0824
Phone: (814) 237-6229
Fax: (814) 237-4296
E-mail: cccf@shas.com

Chester County Community Foundation
The Lincoln Building
28 W. Market Street
West Chester, PA 19382
Phone: (610) 696-8211

Erie Community Foundation
127 West Sixth Street
Erie, PA 16501-1001
Phone: (814) 454-0843
Fax: (814) 456-4965

Greater Harrisburg Foundation
200 N. Third Street P.O. Box 678
Harrisburg, PA 17108-0678
Phone: (717) 236-5040

Lancaster County Foundation
29 East King Street Suite 221
Lancaster, PA 17602
Phone: (717) 397-1629
Fax: (717) 397-6877

Lehigh Valley Community Foundation
961 Marcon Boulevard Suite300
Allentown, PA 18103-9521
Phone: (610) 266-4284
Fax: (610) 266-4285

Luzerne Foundation
613 Baltimore Drive
Wilkes-Barre, PA 18702
Phone: (570) 822-5420
Fax: (570) 208-9145
E-mail: luzernefdn@aol.com

Philadelphia Foundation
1234 Market Street Suite 1800
Philadelphia, PA 19107-3794
Phone: (215) 563-6417
Fax: (215) 563-6882
E-mail: rswinney@philafound.org

Pittsburgh Foundation
One PPG Place 30th Floor
Pittsburgh, PA 15222-5401
Phone: (412) 391-5122
Fax: (412) 391-7259

Schuylkill Area Community Foundation
816 Center Street
Ashland, PA 17921
Phone: (570) 875-3740
Fax: (570) 875-1424

Scranton Area Foundation
321 Spruce Street Bank Towers, #608
Scranton, PA 18503-1409
Phone: (570) 347-6203
Fax: (570) 347-7587

Shenango Valley Foundation
41 Chestnut Street
Sharon, PA 16146
Phone: (724) 981-5882
Fax: (724) 981-5480

Washington County Community
Foundation
77 South Main Street
Washington, PA 15301
Phone: (724) 222-6330
Fax: (724) 223-4167

Wayne County Community Foundation
C/O W.B. McAllister
214 9th Street, #201
Honesdale, PA 18431-1911
Phone: (570) 253-5005
Fax: (570) 253-9396
E-mail: rlhesg@postoffice.ptd.net

Williamsport-Lycoming Foundation
220 West Fourth St., Suite C, 3rd Floor
Williamsport, PA 17701-6102
Phone: (570) 321-1500
Fax: (570) 321-6434

York Foundation
20 West Market Street First Floor
York, PA 17401-1203
Phone: (717) 848-3733
Fax: (717) 854-7231
E-mail: info@yorkfoundation.org

Puerto Rico
Puerto Rico Community Foundation
P.O. Box 70362
San Juan, PR 00936-8362
Phone: (787) 721-1037
Fax: (787) 721-1673
E-mail: EthelRB@compuserve.com

Rhode Island
Rhode Island Community Foundation
One Union Station
Providence, RI 02903
Phone: (401) 274-4564
Fax: (401) 528-1143
E-mail: rgallo@prodigy.com

South Carolina
Central Carolina Community
Foundation
P.O. Box 11222
Columbia, SC 29211
Phone: (803) 254-5601
Fax: (803) 799-6663

Community Foundation Serving Coastal
South Carolina
456 King Street
Charleston, SC 29403
Phone: (843) 723-3635
Fax: (843) 577-3671

Community Foundation of Greater
Greenville
27 Cleveland Street, Suite 101
Greenville, SC 29601
Phone: (864) 233-5925
Fax: (864) 242-9292

Hilton Head Island Foundation
P.O. Box 23019
Hilton Head Island, SC 29925-3019
Phone: (843) 681-9100

Spartanburg County Foundation
320 East Main Street
Spartanburg, SC 29302-1943
Phone: (864) 582-0138

South Dakota
Sioux Falls Area Foundation
1000 N. West Avenue Suite 200
Sioux Falls, SD 57104-1314
Phone: (605) 336-7055
Fax: (605) 336-0038

South Dakota Community Foundation
207 East Capitol Box 296
Pierre, SD 57501
Phone: (605) 224-1025
Fax: (605) 224-5364

Watertown Community Foundation
P.O. Box 116
Watertown, SD 57201-0116
Phone: (605) 882-3731
Fax: (605) 886-5957

Tennessee
Community Foundation of Greater
Chattanooga
1270 Market Street
Chattanooga, TN 37402
Phone: (423) 265-0586
Fax: (423) 265-0587
E-mail: pcooper@cfgc.org

East Tennessee Foundation
550 NationsBank Center
550 W. Main Street
Knoxville, TN 37902
Phone: (423) 524-1223
Fax: (423) 637-6039

Community Foundation of Greater
Memphis
1900 Union Avenue
Memphis, TN 38104
Phone: (901) 728-4600
Fax: (901) 722-0010
E-mail: gsmith@cfgm.org

Community Foundation of Middle
Tennessee
210 23rd Avenue North
Nashville, TN 37203-1502
Phone: (615) 321-4939
Fax: (615) 327-2746

Texas
Community Foundation of Abilene
P.O. Box 1001
Abilene, TX 79604
Phone: (915) 676-3883
Fax: (915) 676-4206
E-mail: cfa@abilene.com

Austin Community Foundation for the
Capital Area
P. O. Box 5159
Austin, TX 78763
Phone: (512) 472-4483
Fax: (512) 472-4486
E-mail: auscomfdn@aol.com

Brownsville Community Foundation
275 Jose Marti Blvd. Suite B
Brownsville, TX 78521
Phone: (956) 546-8787
Fax: (956) 546-8262
E-mail: comfound@chiline.net

Coastal Bend Community Foundation
860 Mercantile Tower - MT 276
615 North Upper Broadway
Corpus Christi, TX 78477
Phone: (361) 882-9745
Fax: (361) 882-2865

Dallas Foundation
900 Jackson Street Suite 150
Dallas, TX 75202
Phone: (214) 741-9898
Fax: (214) 741-9848

East Texas Communities Foundation
P.O. Box 1432
Tyler, TX 75710
Phone: (903) 533-0208
Fax: (903) 533-0258

El Paso Community Foundation
P. O. Box 272
El Paso, TX 79943-0272
Phone: (915) 533-4020
Fax: (915) 532-0716

Foundation for Southeast Texas
P.O. Box 3092
Beaumont, TX 77704
Phone: (409) 833-5775
Fax: (409) 833-7885

Heart of Texas Community Foundation
700 Jefferson
Kerrville, TX 78028
Phone: (830) 792-3048
Fax: (830) 792-3045

Greater Houston Community
Foundation
4550 Post Oak Place Suite 317
Houston, TX 77027-3106
Phone: (713) 960-1990
Fax: (713) 960-1944
E-mail: jfr@ghcf.com

Lubbock Area Foundation
1655 Main Street Suite 209
Lubbock, TX 79401
Phone: (806) 762-8061
Fax: (806) 762-8551

Permian Basin Area Foundation
P.O. Box 10424
Midland, TX 79702
Phone: (915) 682-4704
Fax: (915) 498-8999
E-mail: jswallow@mo.quik.com

San Antonio Area Foundation
PO Box 120366
San Antonio, TX 78212-9566
Phone: (210) 225-2243
Fax: (210) 225-1980

Communities Foundation of Texas
4605 Live Oak Street
Dallas, TX 75204-7099
Phone: (214) 826-5231
Fax: (214) 823-7737
E-mail: efjordbak@cftexas.org

Community Foundation Of North Texas
306 West Seventh Street Suite 702
Fort Worth, TX 76102
Phone: (817) 877-0702
Fax: (817) 877-1215

Community Foundation Of The Texas
Hill Country
P.O. Box 291354
Kerrville, TX 78029-1354
Phone: (830) 896-8811
Fax: (830) 792-5956
E-mail: info@kact.org

Waco Foundation
900 Austin Avenue #1000
Waco, TX 76701-1933
Phone: (254) 754-3404
Fax: (254) 753-2887
E-mail: info@wacofdn.org

Utah
Salt Lake Foundation
10 E. South Temple Suite 900
Salt Lake City, UT 84133
Phone: (801) 883-0941
Fax: (801) 582-2937

Vermont
Vermont Community Foundation
Three Court Street P.O. Box 30
Middlebury, VT 05753
Phone: (802) 388-3355
Fax: (802) 388-3398
E-mail: vcf@vermontcf.org

Virginia
Arlington Community Foundation
2250 Clarendon Blvd. Suite J
Arlington, VA 22201
Phone: (703) 243-4785
Fax: (703) 243-4796
E-mail: arlcf@erols.com

Charlottesville-Albemarle Community
Foundation
P.O. Box 1767
Charlottesville, VA 22902
Phone: (804) 296-1024
Fax: (804) 296-2503

Greater Lynchburg Community Trust
P.O. Box 714
Lynchburg, VA 24505
Phone: (804) 845-6500
Fax: (804) 845-6530
E-mail: gltc@inmind.net

Norfolk Foundation
One Commercial Place Suite 1410
Norfolk, VA 23510-2113
Phone: (757) 622-7951
Fax: (757) 622-1751

Northern Virginia Community
Foundation
8283 Greensboro Drive
McLean, VA 22102
Phone: (703) 917-2600
Fax: (703) 902-3564

Portsmouth Community Foundation &
Trust
P.O. Box 1394
Portsmouth, VA 23705-1394
Phone: (757) 397-5424
Fax: (757) 391-0004

Community Foundation of
Rappahannock River Region
P.O. Box 208
Fredericksburg, VA 22404-0208
Phone: (540) 899-2474
Fax: (540) 899-2478
E-mail: cfrrr@erols.com

Community Foundation of Richmond &
Central Virginia
7325 Beaufont Springs Drive Suite 210
Richmond, VA 23225-5546
Phone: (804) 330-7400
Fax: (804) 330-5992
E-mail: doman@tcfrichmond.org

Foundation for Roanoke Valley
P.O. Box 1159
Roanoke, VA 24006
Phone: (540) 985-0204
Fax: (540) 982-8175

Virginia Beach Foundation
P.O. Box 4629
Virginia Beach, VA 23454
Phone: (757) 422-5249
Fax: (757) 422-1849

Virgin Islands
St. Croix Foundation for Community
Development
P.O. Box 1128
Suite 202, Chandler's Wharf
St. Croix, VI 00821-1128
Phone: (340) 773-9898
Fax: (340) 773-8727
E-mail: stxfound@att.net

Community Foundation of the Virgin
Islands
P.O. Box 11790
St. Thomas, VI 00801
Phone: (340) 774-6031
Fax: (340) 774-3852

Washington
Columbia Basin Foundation
P.O. Box 1623
Moses Lake, WA 98837
Phone: (509) 766-5808

The Community Foundation
505 West Fourth Avenue Suite A
Olympia, WA 98501
Phone: (360) 705-3340

Foundation Northwest
421 W. Riverside Suite 555
Spokane, WA 99201-0403
Phone: (509) 624-2606
Fax: (509) 624-2608

Grays Harbor Community Foundation
P.O. Box 63 630 Seafirst Building
Aberdeen, WA 98520
Phone: (360) 532-6873
Fax: (360) 532-6882

Orcas Island Community Foundation
P. O. Box 1496
Eastsound, WA 98245
Phone: (360) 376-2450
Fax: (360) 376-5924
E-mail: rwlorcas@rockisland.com

The Seattle Foundation
425 Pike Street Suite 510
Seattle, WA 98101
Phone: (206) 622-2294
Fax: (206) 622-7673
E-mail: afarrell@seafound.org

The Skagit Community Foundation
P.O. Box 705
Anacortes, WA 98221
Phone: (360) 419-3181

Community Foundation for Southwest
Washington
703 Broadway Suite 610
Vancouver, WA 98660
Phone: (360) 694-2550
Fax: (360) 737-6335

The Greater Tacoma Community
Foundation
P.O. Box 1995
Tacoma, WA 98401-1995
Phone: (253) 383-5622
Fax: (253) 272-8099
E-mail: margy@gtcf.org

Greater Wenatchee Community
Foundation
P.O. Box 3332
Wenatchee, WA 98807-3332
Phone: (509) 663-7716

Whatcom Community Foundation
119 Grand Avenue Suite A
Bellingham, WA 98225
Phone: (360) 671-6463

West Virginia
Barbour County Community Foundation
304 Brown Avenue
Belington, WV 26250
Phone: (304) 823-3101
Fax: (304) 823-3101

Beckley Area Foundation
129 Main Street P.O. Box 1092
Beckley, WV 25801-1092
Phone: (304) 253-3806

Bluefield Area Foundation
P.O. Box 4127
Bluefield, WV 24701
Phone: (304) 324-0222

Greater Kanawha Valley Foundation
P.O. Box 3041
Charleston, WV 25331
Phone: (304) 346-3620

Community Foundation for Ohio Valley
Post Office Box 1233
Wheeling, WV 26003
Phone: (304) 242-3144

Parkersburg Area Community
Foundation
Post Office Box 1762
Parkersburg, WV 26102-1762
Phone: (304) 428-4438

Wisconsin
Greater Beloit Community Foundation
159 W. Grand Avenue
Beloit, WI 53511-6245
Phone: (608) 362-4228

Eau Claire Area Foundation
P. O. Box 511
Eau Claire, WI 54702
Phone: (715) 832-5138

Fond du Lac Area Foundation
104 South Main Street Suite 302
Fond Du Lac, WI 54935
Phone: (920) 921-2215

Community Foundation for the Fox
Valley Region
P.O. Box 563
Appleton, WI 54912
Phone: (920) 830-1290

Greater Green Bay Community
Foundation
302 N Adams Street #100
Green Bay, WI 54301-5144
Phone: (920) 432-0800

Greater Kenosha Area Foundation
P.O. Box 1829
Kenosha, WI 53141
Phone: (414) 654-2412

La Crosse Community Foundation
319 Main Street Suite 301
La Crosse, WI 54601-0708
Phone: (608) 782-3223

Madison Community Foundation
P.O. Box 5010
Madison, WI 53705-0010
Phone: (608) 232-1763

Marshfield Area Community
Foundation
P.O. Box 456
Marshfield, WI 54449
Phone: (715) 384-9029

Milwaukee Foundation
1020 North Broadway Suite 112
Milwaukee, WI 53202
Phone: (414) 272-5805
Fax: (414) 272-6235

Oshkosh Community Foundation
P.O. Box 1726
Oshkosh, WI 54903
Phone: (920) 426-3993
Fax: (920) 426-6997

Community Foundation of Portage
County
P.O. Box 968
Stevens Point, WI 54481
Phone: (715) 342-4454
Fax: (715) 345-5219

Racine Community Foundation
818 Sixth Street Suite 201
Racine, WI 53403
Phone: (414) 632-8474
Fax: (414) 632-3739
E-mail: racinecf@execpc.com

Community Foundation of S Wood Cty
P.O. Box 444
Wisconsin Rapids, WI 54495-0444
Phone: (715) 423-3863

St. Croix Valley Community Foundation
P. O. Box 530
Somerset, WI 54025
Phone: (715) 247-4600
Fax: (715) 247-4610
E-mail: linda.jacobson@pressenter.com

Wausau Area Community Foundation
500 Third Street Suite 310
Wausau, WI 54403
Phone: (715) 845-9555
Fax: (715) 845-5423
E-mail: jeant@dware.org

Community Foundation of Southern
Wisconsin
111 N. Main Street
Janesville, WI 53545
Phone: (608) 758-0883
Fax: (608) 758-8551
E-mail: cfsw@jvlnet.com

Wyoming
Community Foundation of Jackson Hole
P.O. Box 574
Jackson, WY 83001
Phone: (307) 739-1026
Fax: (307) 734-2841

Wyoming Community Foundation
221 Ivinson Avenue Suite 202
Laramie, WY 82070
Phone: (307) 721-8300
Fax: (307) 721-8333
E-mail: jfreeman@vcn.com

For a list of Canadian community
foundations, see this web site:
http://www.community-fdn.ca/

Appendix IV Directory of Federal Government Grants

For most artists and craft persons, the National Endowment for the Arts (NEA) will be the starting place for government grants. The NEA has several types of assistance programs which head the list below.

Following the NEA grants are examples of federal government grants listed as they appear in the *Catalog of Federal Domestic Assistance*. The number and title assigned to each program is in bold, followed by the government agency and a description. Many programs can be applied to by individuals and local nonprofit arts agencies. Be sure to read the limitations section to learn which grants you qualify for.

Included are grants on a wide range of topics that might apply to artists and craft persons, including minority business development, small business assistance, women in business, and disadvantaged business. However, this is a list of the grants available most likely to benefit you. For more grants, see the *Catalog of Federal Domestic Assistance Programs*.

National Endowment for the Arts (NEA)
National Heritage Fellowships in the Folk & Traditional Arts

As part of its efforts to honor, assist, encourage, and present those artists and forms of artistic expression and practice that reflect the many cultural traditions that make up our nation, the National Endowment for the Arts annually provides up to twelve one-time-only National Heritage Fellowships for master folk and traditional artists. These fellowships are intended to recognize the recipients' artistic excellence and support their continuing contributions to our nation's traditional arts heritage.

The selection criteria are authenticity, excellence, and significance within the particular artistic tradition. The individuals who are nominated should be worthy of national recognition; they should have a record of continuing artistic accomplishment and must be actively participating in their art form, either as practitioners or teachers.

In addition, one National Heritage Fellowship per year may be awarded to an individual whose achievements have had major and positive impact on the excellence, vitality, and public appreciation of the folk & traditional arts. Keepers of the folk & traditional arts who will be recognized by this fellowship might include artists/documentarians who have preserved important traditional repertoires and maintained their practice, artists who through passing on their skills have greatly benefited their art form, or arts organizers/producers whose efforts have comprehensively increased opportunities for and public visibility of traditional arts and artists.

The selection criteria are demonstrated achievements in fostering excellence, ensuring vitality, preserving important repertoires, and promoting public appreciation of the folk & traditional arts. Individuals nominated should be worthy of national recognition and must be actively engaged in preserving the folk & traditional arts.

This fellowship category is not open to application. Fellowships are awarded on the basis of nominations from the public. Nominations may be for individuals or a group of individuals (e.g., a duo). The recipients must be citizens or permanent residents of the United States.

Each fellowship award is $10,000, subject to annual Congressional appropriations and the availability of funds.

How to Submit a Nomination

Nominations may be made by submitting a letter that details the reasons that the nominee(s) should receive a National Heritage Fellowship. Describe the nominee's contributions to his or her particular artistic tradition and explain why this individual or group deserves national recognition. No one may nominate him/herself.

Wherever possible and appropriate, include the following items with your nomination letter:

• A resume or a short biography that outlines the career of the nominee(s).

• Clearly labeled samples of the work of the artist(s). Visual artists must be represented by slides; musicians and storytellers by videotapes or sound recordings; and dancers by film or videotape samples. Other documentation may be added as desired. +

• References to articles written about the nominee(s), or copies of the articles themselves.

• A list of major public appearances or exhibitions by the nominee(s) and the titles of published works, if appropriate.

• A maximum of five letters that demonstrate expert and/or community support for this nomination.

• For keepers of the folk & traditional arts, a detailed statement demonstrating the nominee's achievements in fostering the excellence, vitality, and public appreciation of traditional arts and artists.

Deadline for Nominations: October

Send your nomination to:

National Heritage Fellowships in the Folk & Traditional Arts
National Endowment for the Arts
Nancy Hanks Center
1100 Pennsylvania Avenue, N.W. Room 720
Washington, DC 20506-0001
Phone: 202/682-5428

NOTE: Support material such as slides and tapes will not be returned except under the most special circumstances. Please do not send the only copy. You can submit additional material in support of your nomination at any time. If the review process for this round of fellowships has started, the staff will retain this material for consideration in future years.

Review of Nominations

Once a nomination has been submitted to the Arts Endowment, it is reviewed by an advisory panel of folk & traditional arts experts and at least one knowledgeable layperson. Panel recommendations are forwarded to the National Council on the Arts. The Council sends to the Chairman of the National Endowment for the Arts those nominations that it recommends for funding. Nominations remain active for five years. The nominee(s) will be reviewed annually during this period.

11.801 Native American Program

FEDERAL AGENCY:

MINORITY BUSINESS DEVELOPMENT AGENCY, DEPARTMENT OF COMMERCE

OBJECTIVES:

To provide business development service to Native Americans interested in entering, expanding or improving their efforts in the marketplace. To help Native American business development centers and Native American business consultants to provide a wide range of services to Native American clients, from initial consultation to the identification and resolution of specific business problems.

TYPES OF ASSISTANCE:

Project Grants.

USES AND USE RESTRICTIONS:

The Minority Business Development Agency (MBDA) competitively selects and funds eight Native American Business Development Centers (NABDC's) to provide management and technical assistance to Native Americans located throughout the country. Recipients of NAP funds provide clients with advice and counseling in such areas as preparing financial packages, business counseling, business information and management, accounting guidance, marketing, business/industrial site analysis, production, engineering, construction assistance, procurement and identification of potential business opportunities. MBDA does not have the authority to make loans to Native American firms. Program funds are restricted to providing management and technical assistance.

ELIGIBILITY REQUIREMENTS:

Applicant Eligibility: There are no eligibility restrictions for this program. Eligible applicants may include individuals, nonprofit organizations, for-profit firms, local and State governments, Native American Tribes, and educational institutions.

Beneficiary Eligibility: Native Americans will benefit. Award recipients must provide assistance to Native Americans interested in starting, expanding, or maintaining a business. Assistance emphasis is on Native Americans.

APPLICATION AND AWARD PROCESS:

Preapplication Coordination: Preapplication conferences may be scheduled for NAP projects. The conferences will be announced in the Federal Register. This program is excluded from coverage under E.O. 12372.

Application Procedure: The standard application forms as furnished by the Federal agency and required by 15 CFR Part 24 must be used for this program. This program is subject to the provisions of OMB Circular No. A-110.

Award Procedure: The application package will advise the applicant where to submit the application. Each application will be reviewed and evaluated by MBDA. Name checks, verification of academic credentials and pre-award audits may be required from applicants.

Deadlines: Deadlines for formal competitive awards are outlined in the Federal Register and Commerce Business Daily.

Range of Approval/Disapproval Time: From 4 to 6 months. Successful and unsuccessful applicants shall be notified in writing at the same time.

Renewals: NAP awards are made for a period of one year with the possibility of renewal for up to two more years or a total of three years. Performance evaluations will be conducted, and funding levels will be established for each of three budget periods. The NAP recipient will receive continued funding after the initial competitive year at the discretion of MBDA based upon the availability of funds, the recipients performance, and agency priorities.

ASSISTANCE CONSIDERATIONS:

Length and Time Phasing of Assistance: Awards may be granted for 1 to 3 years.

POST ASSISTANCE REQUIREMENTS:

Reports: Financial (quarterly and annually); narrative (quarterly and annually); statistical reports on each client are required.

Audits: "In accordance with the provisions of OMB Circular No. A- 133 (Revised, June 24, 1997), recipients that are States, Local Governments, Nonprofits Organizations (to include Hospitals), and Institutions of Higher Learning shall be subject to the audit requirements contained in the Single Audit Act Amendments of 1996 (31 U.S.C. 7501-7501). Commercial organizations shall be subject to the audit requirements as stipulated in the award document."

Records: Documents, papers and financial records relating to the NAP are required to remain available to the Federal government for 3 years from the date of submission of the final financial status report.

FINANCIAL INFORMATION:

Account Identification: 13-0201-0-1-376.

Obligations: (Cooperative Agreements) FY 98 $693,250; FY 99 est $1,701,500; and FY 00 est $1,701,500.

Range and Average of Financial Assistance: $169,125 to $310,575; $187,230.

PROGRAM ACCOMPLISHMENTS:

In fiscal year 1998, MBDA funded Native American business development centers in approximately 8 locations that provided management and technical assistance to minority business enterprise clients, of the 1,237 clients who received assistance in fiscal year 1998, 852 represented actual operating business enterprise clients. Clients obtained $26.3 million in financial packages and $37.9 million in procurement contracts.

INFORMATION CONTACTS:

Regional or Local Office: Contact the nearest Minority Business Development Agency Regional Office listed in Appendix IV of the Catalog.

Headquarters Office: Juanita E. Berry, Chief, Field Coordination Division, Room 5079, Minority Business Development Agency, Department of Commerce, 14th and Constitution Avenue, NW., Washington, DC 20230. Telephone: (202) 482-6022.

EXAMPLES OF FUNDED PROJECTS:

An NABDC located in Arizona received a $197,825 award to provide one-to-one management and technical assistance to eligible Native American clients to develop business plans and promote the development and operation of businesses.

CRITERIA FOR SELECTING PROPOSALS:

Competitive awards for the NAP are made based upon a panel evaluation of the applications. This evaluation includes such factors as capability and experience of staff assigned to the project, techniques, methodology, resources and costs.

11.802 Minority Business Development

FEDERAL AGENCY:

MINORITY BUSINESS DEVELOPMENT AGENCY, DEPARTMENT OF COMMERCE

OBJECTIVES:

The resource development activity provides for the indirect business assistance programs conducted by MBDA. These programs encourage minority business development by identifying and developing private markets and capital sources; expanding business information and business services through trade associations; promoting and supporting the mobilization of resources of Federal agencies and State and local governments at the local level; and assisting minorities in entering new and growing markets.

TYPES OF ASSISTANCE:

Project Grants.

USES AND USE RESTRICTIONS:

Funds will be used in support of the MBDA policy statement on funding business Development programs. MBDA is charged under Executive Order 11625 with fostering new minority business enterprises and maintaining and strengthening existing firms to increase their opportunities to participate and receive the benefits of our economic system. MBDA uses a portion of its program funds to award contracts, grants, and cooperative agreements to public and private sector entities which have the greatest potential for developing access to capital, market, and other opportunities on behalf of minority business. The performance of each funded recipient is evaluated on a scheduled basis. Renewals are based on Agency priorities and performance of recipients.

ELIGIBILITY REQUIREMENTS:

Applicant Eligibility: Applicants for this program are established businesses, professional organizations, individuals, trade associations and chambers of commerce.

Beneficiary Eligibility: Beneficiaries of this program are minority business persons/firms.

APPLICATION AND AWARD PROCESS:

Preapplication Coordination: A preapplication conference may be scheduled for resource development projects. Conferences will be announced in the Federal Register. This program is excluded from coverage under E.O. 12372.

Application Procedure: The standard application forms as furnished by the Department of Commerce must be used for this program. Recipients are subject to the administrative requirements contained in OMB Circular No. A-110.

Award Procedure: The application package will advise the applicant where to submit the application. Each application will be reviewed and evaluated by MBDA. Name checks, verification of academic credentials and pre-award audits may be required from applicants.

Deadlines: Deadlines for formal competitive awards are outlined in the Federal Register and Commerce Business Daily.

Range of Approval/Disapproval Time: 4 to 6 months. Successful and unsuccessful applicants shall be notified in writing at the same time.

Appeals: All decisions are final. There are no administrative appeals.

Renewals: Business development awards may be renewed after the successful completion of the initial competitive project award, at the discretion of the agency for two additional years without undergoing formal competition for participating in this program, subject to the availability of funds and the satisfactory performance of the recipient.

ASSISTANCE CONSIDERATIONS:

Formula and Matching Requirements: Projects may require a minimum amount of cost-sharing in the form of in-kind contributions and cash.

Length and Time Phasing of Assistance: For 1 to 3 years depending on the requirements of the projects.

POST ASSISTANCE REQUIREMENTS:

Reports: Financial (quarterly and annually), narrative (quarterly and annually); statistical reports are required.

Audits: In accordance with the provisions of OMB Circular No. A- 133 (Revised, June 24, 1997), recipients that are States, Local Governments, Non-Profit Organizations (to include Hospitals), and Institutions of Higher Learning shall be subject to the audit requirements contained in the Single Audit Act Amendments of 1996 (31 U.S.C. 7501-7507). Commercial organizations shall be subject to the audit requirements as stipulated in the award document.

Records: Documents, papers and financial records relating to the resource development program are required to remain available to the Federal Government for 3 years from the date of submission of the final financial status report. All financial and programmatic records, supporting documents, statistical reports, and other records of funded recipients are required to be maintained by the terms of the award document. The recipient must retain records for 3 years after completion of the project or submission of the final financial report, whichever is later, and be readily available for inspection and audit.

FINANCIAL INFORMATION:

Account Identification: 13-0201-0-1-376.

Obligations: (Cooperative Agreements/Contracts) FY 98 $1,452,572; FY 99 est $1,721,730; and FY 00 est $1,721,730.

Range and Average of Financial Assistance: $5,000 to $550,000; $101,664.

PROGRAM ACCOMPLISHMENTS:

In fiscal year 1998, MBDA began implementing a program that will allow the agency to deliver program services through line telecommunications. This vehicle will enable the agency to provide management and technical assistance to business owners who lack access to a MBDC. MBDA has a home page on the World Wide Web through which it will disseminate business information.

INFORMATION CONTACTS:

Regional or Local Office: Contact the nearest Minority Business Development Agency Regional Office listed in Appendix IV of the Catalog.

Headquarters Office: Juanita E. Berry, Chief, Field Coordination Division, Room 5079, Minority Business Development Agency, Department of Commerce, 14th and Constitution Avenue, NW., Washington, DC 20230. Telephone: (202) 482-6022.

EXAMPLES OF FUNDED PROJECTS:

In FY 1998, MBDA used a variety of delivery mechanisms to deliver services, including the Minority Business Opportunity Committees (MBOCs). MBOC is a program strategy, that is designed to partner MBDA resources with Federal, State, local and quasi governmental entities to create and stimulate business economic opportunities for minority entrepreneurs. As an example of this approach, the Los Angeles MBOC's strategic outreach efforts can account for $1.1 billion in minority contracting, over 21,000 new jobs and will pave the way for future competitive efforts to stimulate growth in a challenged economy.

CRITERIA FOR SELECTING PROPOSALS:

Competitive awards for the resource development program are made based on a panel evaluation of the applications. This evaluation includes such factors as capability and experience of staff assigned to the project; techniques and methodology resources and costs.

15.146 Ironworker Training Program

FEDERAL AGENCY: BUREAU OF INDIAN AFFAIRS, DEPARTMENT OF THE INTERIOR

OBJECTIVES:

To provide ironworker vocational training, apprenticeships, and job placement to eligible American Indians through the National Ironworkers Training Program, located in Broadview, Illinois.

TYPES OF ASSISTANCE:

Project Grants.

USES AND USE RESTRICTIONS:

Eligible American Indians who reside on or near an Indian reservation may receive vocational training in ironworking and assistance with job placement upon completion of the program.

ELIGIBILITY REQUIREMENTS:

Applicant Eligibility: Applicants must be an American Indian who is a member of a Federally Recognized Indian Tribe, at least 20 years old, possess a high school diploma or General Equivalency Development (GED) Certificate, be in good physical health, and reside on or near an Indian reservation under the jurisdiction of the Bureau of Indian Affairs.

Beneficiary Eligibility: Must be an American Indian who is a member of a Federally Recognized Indian Tribal Government, at least 20 years old, possess a high school diploma or General Equivalency Development (GED) Certificate, be in good physical health, and reside on or near an Indian reservation under the jurisdiction of the Bureau of Indian Affairs. Complete information on beneficiary eligibility is found in 25 CFR, Parts 26 and 27.

APPLICATION AND AWARD PROCESS:

Application Procedure: Applicants should apply for program services on Bureau of Indian Affairs Form BIA-8205 at the nearest Bureau Employment Assistance office or tribal government offices.

Award Procedure: Individual applications are processed at the Bureau agency or tribal contract offices to determine eligibility.

Range of Approval/Disapproval Time: 1 to 90 days.

ASSISTANCE CONSIDERATIONS:

Length and Time Phasing of Assistance: Assistance for Ironworker training is not to exceed 12 weeks. Payments for subsistence and related training costs are released as required by beneficiary. Job placement assistance is provided upon completion of training.

FINANCIAL INFORMATION:

Account Identification: 14-2100-0-1-452.

Obligations: (Grants) FY 98 $524,000; FY 99 est $524,000; and

FY 00 est $0.

Range and Average of Financial Assistance: Students receive $175 per week for the duration of the program for room and board and miscellaneous expenses. Work clothes and tools are also provided.

PROGRAM ACCOMPLISHMENTS:

In fiscal year 1998, 120 individuals participated in this program; 82 completed their training and 62 of these individuals were subsequently employed as ironworkers.

INFORMATION CONTACTS:

Regional or Local Office: Applications may be filed with the local Bureau of Indian Affairs agency office. For direct contact: Mr. Robert Mitacek, Director, National Ironworkers Training Program for American Indians, 1819 Beach Street, Broadview, Illinois 60153. Telephone (708) 345-2344.

Headquarters Office: Office of Economic Development, Division of Job Placement and Training, Bureau of Indian Affairs, 1849 C Street, NW., MS-4640 MIB, Washington, DC 20240. Contact: Deano Poleahla. Telephone: (202) 208-2671.

EXAMPLES OF FUNDED PROJECTS:

This program provides vocational training and job placement in ironworking to individuals.

CRITERIA FOR SELECTING PROPOSALS:

Applications are received for both vocational training and direct employment participants. Final determination to fund an application is based on the individual's eligibility.

15.850 Indian Arts and Crafts Development

FEDERAL AGENCY: INDIAN ARTS AND CRAFTS BOARD, DEPARTMENT OF THE INTERIOR

OBJECTIVES:

To encourage and promote the development of American Indian and Alaska Native arts and crafts.

TYPES OF ASSISTANCE:

Use of Property, Facilities, and Equipment; Advisory Services and Counseling; Investigation of Complaints.

USES AND USE RESTRICTIONS:

Program planning assistance, such as the development of innovative educational, production, promotion, and economic concepts related to Native culture. Complaints about imitation American Indian arts and crafts that are misrepresented as genuine handcrafts are referred to appropriate Federal or local authorities for action. The three museums operated by the Board serve Indians and the general public: the Sioux Indian Museum, in Rapid City, South Dakota; the Museum of the Plains Indian, in Browning, Montana; and the Southern Plains Indian Museum, in Anadarko, Oklahoma.

ELIGIBILITY REQUIREMENTS:

Applicant Eligibility: American Indian and Alaska Native individuals and organizations, federally recognized Indian tribal governments, State and local governments, and nonprofit organizations.

Beneficiary Eligibility: American Indian and Alaska Native individuals and organizations, federally recognized Indian tribal governments, State and local governments, and nonprofit organizations.

APPLICATION AND AWARD PROCESS:

Application Procedure: Submit request to headquarters office.

Range of Approval/Disapproval Time: Acknowledgment usually in 14 days.

FINANCIAL INFORMATION:

Account Identification: 14-2100-0-1-999.

Obligations: (Salaries and expenses) FY 98 $967,000; FY 99 est $974,000; and FY 00 est $1,164,000.

PROGRAM ACCOMPLISHMENTS:

In fiscal year 1998, advisory and other services were extended to the general public and to an estimated 6,500 Native artists and craftsmen on a continuing basis. In addition, the operation of three Indian museums provided professional museum services to over 200,000 individuals.

REGULATIONS, GUIDELINES, AND LITERATURE:

25 CFR 301, 304, 307, 308, 309, 310. "Fact Sheet: General Information about the Activities of the Indian Arts and Crafts Board," free.

INFORMATION CONTACTS:

Director, Indian Arts and Crafts Board
Room 4004-Main Interior Building
Washington, DC 20240
Contact: Meridith Z. Stanton, Acting Director
Telephone: (202) 208-3773

EXAMPLES OF FUNDED PROJECTS:

(Note: Advisory assistance only; no grants or other direct financial assistance is offered.) Assistance to an Indian craftsmen's cooperative to plan a series of exhibitions to recognize and promote outstanding work by its members; assistance to an Indian tribe to plan fund-raising to operate a new museum facility; assistance to an Indian craftsman to locate a grant to set aside time for creative experimentation; assistance to an Indian artist to organize, publicize, and professionally install a one-person sales exhibition at an Indian Arts and Crafts Board museum; assistance to an Indian nonprofit organization to develop a comprehensive plan for a multi-facility cultural center.

CRITERIA FOR SELECTING PROPOSALS:

All requests receive a response. The depth and extent of assistance offered depend on: relevance to agency objectives; extent to which American Indians and Alaska Natives have had and will have control over any decision-making involved; artistic and/or professional quality and feasibility of the proposed project; anticipated benefits to American Indian and Alaska Native artists and craftsmen.

27.006 Federal Summer Employment (Summer Jobs in Federal Agencies)

FEDERAL AGENCY: OFFICE OF PERSONNEL MANAGEMENT

OBJECTIVES:

To provide summer employment primarily for college students and high school students.

TYPES OF ASSISTANCE:

Federal Employment.

USES AND USE RESTRICTIONS:

Most Federal agencies employ individuals during summer vacation periods. The jobs may be clerical, crafts and trades, administrative or subprofessional related to career interests. Employees are paid at the regular Federal pay rate for the position.

ELIGIBILITY REQUIREMENTS:

Applicant Eligibility: Any U.S. citizen may apply. The minimum age requirement is 16 years at time of appointment. Summer jobs are filled through agency staffing plans.

Beneficiary Eligibility: U.S. Citizens, 16 years old at time of appointment.

APPLICATION AND AWARD PROCESS:

Deadlines: Applicants apply directly to agencies. Deadlines vary by agency and job location.

FINANCIAL INFORMATION:

Account Identification: Funded by accounts of numerous participating Federal agencies.

Obligations: Program is coordinated by OPM, but is carried out by numerous Federal agencies. Obligations devoted to administration are not separately identifiable.

REGULATIONS, GUIDELINES, AND LITERATURE:

Information about open examinations and/or Job Vacancy Announcements are available from sources listed below under "Headquarters Office."

INFORMATION CONTACTS:

Regional or Local Office: Information may be obtained from Federal agency personnel offices or through the National Job Information sources listed below.

Headquarters Office: Federal employment information is available nationwide from the following sources: USAJOBS - OPM's Web site: www.usajobs.opm.gov; Federal Job Opportunities Board (FJOB): Telephone: (912) 757-3100; Touch Screen Computer Kiosks: Located in OPM offices and Federal buildings throughout the country. USAJOBS by Telephone Listing System: Atlanta, GA, (404) 331-4315; Chicago, IL, (312) 353- 6192; Dayton, OH, (937) 225-2720; Denver, CO, (303) 969-7050; Detroit, MI, (313) 226-6950; Honolulu, HI, (808) 541-2791; Huntsville, AL, (205) 837-0894; Kansas City, MO, (816) 426-5702; Norfolk, VA, (757) 441-3355; Philadelphia, PA, (215) 597-7440; Raleigh, NC, (919) 790-2822; San Antonio, TX, (210) 805-2402; San Francisco, CA, (415) 744-5627; Seattle, WA, (206) 553-0888; Twin Cities, MN, (612) 725-3430; Washington, DC, (202) 606-2700; Nationwide, (912) 757-3000; and TDD Service, (912) 744- 2299.

45.024 Promotion of the Arts--Grants to Organizations and Individuals

FEDERAL AGENCY: NATIONAL ENDOWMENT FOR THE ARTS, NATIONAL FOUNDATION ON THE ARTS AND THE HUMANITIES

OBJECTIVES:

The National Endowment for the Arts, an investment in America's living cultural heritage, serves the public good by nurturing the expression of human creativity, supporting the cultivation of community spirit, and fostering the recognition and appreciation of the excellence and diversity of our nation's artistic accomplishments. This mission is accomplished through: 1) Support to the visual, literary, media, design, and performing arts to the benefit of all Americans through project grants to organizations in five categories: creation and presentation, planning and stabilization (services to the field), heritage and preservation, access, and education;

and 2) assistance to published creative writers and literary translators of exceptional talent through individual fellowships. Joining with the White House Millennium Council to "honor the past and imagine the future" at the turn of the Millennium, the Endowment welcomes applications for projects with a Millennium focus within the regular grants to organizations categories.

TYPES OF ASSISTANCE:

Project Grants.

USES AND USE RESTRICTIONS:

Grants to Organizations: All grants will be awarded for specific projects that address one or more of the Endowment's five categories. A project may include aspects of more than one category; however, the organization must apply to the category most relevant to its project goals. A project may consist of one or more specific events or activities. It must possess some characteristic or unifying principle distinguishing it from the applicant's entire season or overall operations. The Endowment is interested in projects, regardless of size or type of applicant organization, that are of national, regional, or field-wide significance, including local projects of potentially profound effect within their community or likely to serve as models to a field. Significance can be measured by excellence or creativity, not by budget size, organizational longevity, or numbers of people or areas reached. In FY 2000, endowments and cash reserves will not be funded through the Planning and Stabilization category.

Grants to Individuals: Literature fellowships: Fellowships for Creative Writers are awarded to writers of poetry, fiction, and creative nonfiction to allow them to devote time to writing, research, travel, and to advance their writing careers. Fellowships for translators are awarded to writers for specific projects to translate into English works by creative writers insufficiently represented in the language. Awards in the genres of poetry and prose will alternate each year. In fiscal years 1999 and 2001, fellowships will be awarded to writers and translators of poetry; in fiscal year 2000, they will be awarded to writers and translators of prose.

ELIGIBILITY REQUIREMENTS:

Applicant Eligibility: Grants to Organizations: Nonprofit tax-exempt organizations meeting the following conditions may apply: 1) No part of any earnings may benefit a private stockholder or individual, and 2) donations to the organization qualify as charitable deductions under Section 170(c) of the Internal Revenue Code. Examples of eligible organizations are arts institutions, arts service organizations, local arts agencies, official units of State and local governments, federally recognized tribal communities and Indian tribes. Consortia of such organizations also may apply. Generally an organization may submit, on its own behalf, one application for a single project under one of the five category deadlines. The 56 designated State arts agencies and their regional arts organizations may serve as fiscal agents or as consortium members and participants, including consortium lead applicants. However, all grant funds must be passed on to the sponsored organization or to other consortium members.

Grants to individuals: Individuals who are U.S. citizens or permanent residents and who, according to Public Law 89-209, Section 5(c), must demonstrate exceptional talent. Literature fellowships: Applicants must be published writers. Writers who have received from the Arts Endowment 1) two or more Creative Writing or Translation Fellowships or 2) any Creative Writing or Translation Fellowship since October 1, 1990, are ineligible. An individual may submit only one application per two-year cycle.

Beneficiary Eligibility: Grants to Organizations: Nonprofit organizations, local governments, and local arts agencies, federally recognized tribal communities and Indian tribes, and through activities and services supported, the general public.

Grants to Individuals: Literature fellowships: Individual literary artists.

APPLICATION AND AWARD PROCESS:

Preapplication Coordination: Grants to Organizations: Applicants must use standard application forms in Grants to Organizations Guidelines. This program is excluded from coverage under E.O.12372, "Intergovernmental Review of Federal Programs. "Grants to Individuals: Literature fellowship applicants must use standard application forms provided in Literature Fellowships Guidelines.

Application Procedure: Grants to Organizations: Applicants must obtain fiscal year 2000 Grants to Organizations Guidelines from Endowment. Additional supplemental materials may be required. (See guidelines for special requirements.) This program is subject to provisions of OMB Circular No. A-110, "Uniform Administrative Requirements for Grants and Agreements with Institutions of Higher Education, Hospitals, and Other Non-Profit Organizations." It is also subject to the provisions of OMB Circular No. A-102, "Grants and Cooperative Agreements with State and Local Governments." Grants to Individuals: Literature fellowship applicants must obtain fiscal year 2000/01 Literature Fellowships Guidelines from the Endowment. A manuscript of the applicant's own work in the genre in which eligibility is established must be submitted as part of application.

Award Procedure: Grants to Organizations: Applications are reviewed in closed session by advisory panelists. Each panel comprises a diverse group of arts experts and other individuals with broad knowledge in related areas, including at least one knowledgeable layperson. Panel funding recommendations are reviewed in open session by the National Council on the Arts, the advisory body to the Endowment. The Council's decision not to fund an application is final. All applications the Council has recommended for funding are then considered by the Endowment's Chairman, who makes the final award decisions. Grants to Individuals: Literature fellowships: Applications are reviewed in closed session by advisory panelists from the literature field. Each panel comprises a diverse group of arts experts, as well as a knowledgeable layperson. Panel funding recommendations are reviewed by the National Council on the Arts in open session. The Council's decision not to fund an application is final. All applications the Council has recommended for funding are then considered by the Endowment's Chairman, who makes the final award decisions.

Deadlines: Grants to Organizations: application deadlines for categories: Creation and Presentation - March 29, 1999; Planning and Stabilization - March 29, 1999; Heritage and Preservation - August 16, 1999; Access - August 16, 1999; Education - August 16, 1999. Grants to Individuals: Literature Fellowships: Creative Writing Fellowships for Fiction and Creative Nonfiction and for Translation Projects in Prose - March 15, 1999. Creative Writing Fellowships for Poetry and Translation Projects in Poetry - March 14, 2000.

Range of Approval/Disapproval Time: Dependent on meetings of the National Council on the Arts.

ASSISTANCE CONSIDERATIONS:

Formula and Matching Requirements: Grants to Organizations: Matching requirements for all five categories: at least 1:1 Some grants may require higher match. (See guidelines for details). All matches must be made with non-Federal funds. Grants to Individuals: None.

Length and Time Phasing of Assistance: Grants to Organizations: Grant period is generally up to two years. Projects may begin any time after following earliest project start dates: for Creation and Presentation and Planning and Stabilization - December 1, 1999; for Heritage and Preservation, Access, and Education - April 1, 2000. Literature Fellowships: FY 2000 prose projects must begin any time between February 1, 2000 and February 1, 2001, and may extend up to two years. FY 2001 poetry projects must begin any time between February 1, 2001 and February 1, 2002, and may extend up to two years. Timing of fund disbursements will vary according to the project. Generally, requests for payment to cover immediate project expenses may be received at any time.

POST ASSISTANCE REQUIREMENTS:

Reports: Grants to Organizations: Progress reports are required for all grants, and must be submitted at the time the cumulative amount requested exceeds two-thirds of the grant amount. Final reports, comprising financial and narrative components, are required for all grants within 90 days of the end of the grant period. In some instances, products of grant projects also may be required as part of the final report. Grantees also must report on geographic location of grant activity within 30 days of award receipt. Grants to Individuals: Final reports, comprising financial and narrative components, are required from all literature fellowship recipients within 90 days of the end of the grant period.

Audits: Grants to Organizations: Regarding applicant and grantee-initiated audits: All grantees must comply with audit requirements mandated by OMB Circular No. A-133, "Audits of States, Local Governments, and Non-profit Organizations." Nonprofit institutions expending $300,000 or more a year in Federal awards shall have an audit made in accordance with A-133's provisions. Local governments expending $300,000 or more in Federal awards within the State's fiscal year shall have an audit made for that year in accordance with A-133's provisions. Grants to Individuals: None.

Records: Grant-related records must be retained by grantee for three years following submission of the final financial status report.

FINANCIAL INFORMATION:

Account Identification: 59-0100-0-1-503.

Obligations: (Grants) Grants to Organizations: FY 98 $38,649,673; FY 99 est $38,780,480; and FY 00 est not separately identifiable. Grants to Individuals: Literature Fellowships: FY 98 $705,000; FY 99 est $895,000; and FY 00 est not separately identifiable.

Range and Average of Financial Assistance: Grants to Organizations: generally $5,000 to $200,000. Grants to Individuals: Literature Fellowships - $20,000.

PROGRAM ACCOMPLISHMENTS:

Grants to Organizations: Fiscal 1998 applications: 236 in Heritage and Preservation, 488 in Education and Access, 353 in Planning and Stabilization, and 997 in Creation and Presentation. Fiscal 1998 grants awarded: 140 in Heritage and Preservation, 265 in Education and Access, 613 in Creation and Presentation, and 154 in Planning and

Stabilization. Grants to Individuals: Literature Fellowships: Fiscal 1998 (prose), 588 applications were received and 32 awards made.

REGULATIONS, GUIDELINES, AND LITERATURE:

For fiscal year 2000 Grants to Organizations Guidelines and fiscal year 2000/01 Literature Fellowships Guidelines, contact the Office of Communications, National Endowment for the Arts, Washington, DC 20506-0001, or visit the Endowment website at http://arts.endow.gov for guidelines in downloadable format.

INFORMATION CONTACTS:

National Endowment for the Arts
1100 Pennsylvania Avenue, NW
Washington, DC 20506-0001
Website: http://arts.endow.gov
Telephone: (202) 682-5400

Grants to Organizations: For information about discipline or field appropriate to your project, telephone: Arts Education (pre-K through 12): (202) 682-5563. Dance: (202) 682-5452. Design: (202) 682-5452. Folk and Traditional Arts: (202) 682-5678, 682-5724, or 682-5726. Literature: (202) 682-5787 or 682-5771. Local Arts Agencies: (202) 682-5581 or 682-5586. Media Arts: (202) 682-5452. Multidisciplinary: (202) 682- 5658. Museums: (202) 682-5452. Music: (202) 682-5590 or 682-5487. Musical Theater: (202) 682-5509. Opera: (202) 682-5438 or 682-5600. Presenting: (202) 682-5591. Theater: (202) 682-5509, 682-5511 or 682-5020. Visual Arts: (202) 682-5452. Grants to Individuals: For information about Literature Fellowships, telephone: (202) 682-5428. Individuals who are deaf or hard of hearing should call Voice/T.T.: Telephone: (202) 682-5496. Individuals unable to read conventional print should contact the Endowment's Office for Accessibility. Telephone: (202) 682-5532 for help in acquiring a cassette recording of guidelines.

EXAMPLES OF FUNDED PROJECTS:

Projects supported by fiscal 1998 Grants to Organizations: Heritage and Preservation: 1) conservation of Thomas Hart Benton's 1933 epic murals in Indiana; 2) national radio series documenting the history of rhythm and blues; 3) several major U.S. orchestras' showcasing of works by African-American composers. Education. and Access: 1) travel by Artrain, a mobile museum exhibiting worldclass artworks, and offering lectures, residencies, and print making workshops to 36 communities in 18 states; 2) expansion of Poetry in Motion, a program of poetry on posters in buses, trains, and trolleys which now reaches more than a million viewers; 3) multi-state tours by dance companies, including professional performances and artist residencies. Creation and Presentation: 1) presentation of 15th annual Chicago International Children's Film Festival; 2) artist residencies at Seattle's Pilchuk Glass School and Omaha's Bemis Center for Contemporary Arts; 3) expanding a dance company's performance of modern choreography in North Carolina. Planning and Stabilization: 1) rebuilding of flood- damaged art museum in North Dakota; 2) bolstering Native arts through consortium of Native American cultural organizations in Arizona, Minnesota, Montana, North Carolina, and New York; and 3) a new Louisiana regional arts center's enhanced programming and services for area artists and arts presenters.

CRITERIA FOR SELECTING PROPOSALS:

Primary criteria by which all applications are assessed are artistic excellence and artistic merit. (See Grants to Organization Guidelines for specifications to meet these criteria under each category.) For literature fellowships, applicant's manuscript is the sole indicator of artistic excellence and artistic merit considered by the panel. (See Literature Fellowships Guidelines for specifications to meet additional criteria for translation projects.)

45.160 Promotion of the Humanities--Fellowships and Stipends

FEDERAL AGENCY: NATIONAL ENDOWMENT OF THE HUMANITIES, NATIONAL FOUNDATION ON THE ARTS AND THE HUMANITIES

OBJECTIVES:

Fellowships and Summer Stipends provide support for scholars to undertake full-time independent research and writing in the humanities. Grants are available for 6 to 12-month fellowships and two months of summer study. Faculty Graduate Study grants provide 9 to 12 months of support for teachers at Historically Black Colleges and Universities to work toward completion of a doctoral degree in the humanities.

TYPES OF ASSISTANCE:

Project Grants.

USES AND USE RESTRICTIONS:

Fellowships and Summer Stipends: Projects may contribute to scholarly knowledge or to the general public's understanding of the humanities. The proposed study or research may be completed during the grant period or it may be part of a longer project. Applications to plan institutional curricula, educational research projects, work in the creative or performing arts, and studies that lack humanities content or methodology are not eligible. Faculty Graduate Study: Applicants must be employed at a Historically Black College or University and they must be graduate students in a humanities discipline. Graduate study leading to a doctorate in education is ineligible.

ELIGIBILITY REQUIREMENTS:

Applicant Eligibility: All applicants must be U.S. citizens, native residents of U.S. jurisdictions, or foreign nationals who have been legal residents in the U.S. or its jurisdictions for at least the three years immediately preceding the application deadline. Fellowships: Faculty members at colleges and universities, individuals affiliated with other institutions, independent scholars, and others who work in the humanities are eligible. Applicants need not have advanced degrees, but they must have completed their professional training. Active candidates for degrees and persons seeking support for work leading to degrees are not eligible. Summer Stipends: University and college faculty members normally must be nominated by their academic institutions. Faculty members with terminating appointments and all other applicants are exempt from nomination and may apply directly. Faculty Graduate Study: Applicants must submit a written statement from the chief administrator of the institution certifying their faculty status at a Historically Black College or University. Applicants must have completed at least one year of graduate work and an official of the graduate school must certify the applicant's graduate status.

Beneficiary Eligibility: Fellowships and Stipends: College and university faculty and staff, individuals affiliated with institutions other than colleges and universities, and scholars and writers working independently. Faculty Graduate Study grants: faculty at Historically Black Colleges or Universities who are working toward the Ph.D. degree.

APPLICATION AND AWARD PROCESS:

Application Procedure: Application materials are available from, and submitted to, the headquarters office listed below. This program is excluded from coverage under OMB Circular No. A-110.

Award Procedure: Applications are reviewed by panels of scholars and other appropriate individuals. Awards are made by the Chairman of the National Endowment for the Humanities after advice from the National Council on the Humanities.

Deadlines: Fellowships: Annual deadline of May 1, for projects beginning after January 1, of the following year. Summer Stipends: annual deadline of October 1, for projects beginning after May 1, of the following year. Faculty Graduate Study: Annual deadline of March 15, for the following academic year.

Range of Approval/Disapproval Time: Six to seven months.

ASSISTANCE CONSIDERATIONS:

Length and Time Phasing of Assistance: Fellowships are held from 6 to 12 months, with payment in quarterly installments. Summer Stipends are held for two consecutive months, with stipends disbursed in one payment. Faculty Graduate Study awards are for 9 to 12 months, with payment in quarterly installments.

POST ASSISTANCE REQUIREMENTS:

Reports: A final report is required within ninety days after the end of the tenure period describing the results of the work done during the period of the award. For Faculty Graduate Study awards, a final report is also required from the appropriate official of the certifying institution.

Audits: Subject to audit by Endowment auditors or their representatives.

FINANCIAL INFORMATION:

Account Identification: 59-0200-0-1-503.

Obligations: (Grants) FY 98 $5,698,474; FY 99 est $6,050,000; and FY 00 est $7,070,000.

Range and Average of Financial Assistance: Fellowships: An award up to $30,000 for a grant period of from 9 to 12 months; an award of $24,000 for a grant period of from 6 to 8 months. Faculty Graduate Study: maximum award of $30,000 for salary replacement and expenses. Summer Stipends: an award of $4,000.

PROGRAM ACCOMPLISHMENTS:

In fiscal year 1998, 2,125 applications were received and 310 awards were made. In fiscal year 1999, it is estimated that 2,206 applications will be received and 308 awards will be made. In fiscal year 2000, it is estimated that 3,550 applications will be received and 682 awards will be made.

REGULATIONS, GUIDELINES, AND LITERATURE:

45 CFR 1100 and 1105. Applications and guidelines as well as a publication entitled "Overview of Endowment Programs" are available upon request from the National Endowment for the Humanities, Room 409, Washington, DC 20506. Available from the Superintendent of Documents, U.S. Government Printing Office, Washington, DC 20402, is the Endowment's official publication, "Humanities" by subscription (six issues annually, $16.00 domestic, $20.00 foreign).

INFORMATION CONTACTS:

Fellowships and Stipends, Division of Research
National Endowment for the Humanities, Room 318
Washington, DC 20506
Telephone: (202) 606-8466

RELATED PROGRAMS:

EXAMPLES OF FUNDED PROJECTS:

(1) Fellowships for University Teachers: Art History and Hegemony in Latin America: Afro-Brazil; (2) Fellowships for College Teachers and Independent Scholars: Studies in Aristotle's Scientific Thinking; (3) Summer Stipends: Citizen Activism for Nuclear Disarmament and Its Impact, 1971-Present; (4) Faculty Graduate Study: A Study of Atlanta's Industrialization and Urbanization, 1879-1929.

CRITERIA FOR SELECTING PROPOSALS:

For Fellowships and Summer Stipends: The significance of the contribution to thought and knowledge in the humanities; the quality or promise of quality of the applicant's work; the quality of the conception, definition, organization, and description of the proposed project; and the likelihood that the applicant will complete the entire project. For Faculty Graduate Study: the significance of the contribution the applicant will make to the humanities upon returning to the employing institution; the quality or promise of quality of the applicant's work; the conception, definition, organization, and description of the proposed study; and the likelihood that the applicant will complete the proposed study successfully by the end of the tenure period.

45.161 Promotion of the Humanities--Research

FEDERAL AGENCY: NATIONAL ENDOWMENT FOR THE HUMANITIES, NATIONAL FOUNDATION ON THE ARTS AND THE HUMANITIES

OBJECTIVES:

To strengthen the intellectual foundations of the humanities through the collaboration of scholars and the support of post- doctoral fellowship programs at independent research institutions.

TYPES OF ASSISTANCE:

Project Grants.

USES AND USE RESTRICTIONS:

Collaborative Research grants support up to three years of research. Awards support direct costs, including salaries, travel, supplies, and appropriate research assistance and consultation. Grants also support fellowships offered through independent research centers and international research organizations.

ELIGIBILITY REQUIREMENTS:

Applicant Eligibility: For collaborative research, institutions of higher education, nonprofit professional associations, scholarly societies, and other nonprofit organizations in the United States may apply. For support of fellowship programs, U.S. independent research centers, scholarly societies, and international research organizations with existing fellowship programs may apply.

Beneficiary Eligibility: U.S. citizens and residents, State and local governments, sponsored organizations, public and private nonprofit institutions/organizations, other public institutions/organizations, Federally recognized Indian tribal governments, Native American organizations, U.S. territories; non-governmental-general; minority organizations, other specialized groups; and quasi-public nonprofit institutions benefit.

APPLICATION AND AWARD PROCESS:

Preapplication Coordination: After application instructions are received, draft applications or brief descriptions of proposed projects may be submitted to determine eligibility and competitiveness at least eight weeks prior to formal application. The standard application forms as furnished by the Federal agency and required by OMB Circular No. A-102 must be used for this program. This program is excluded from coverage under E.O. 12372.

Application Procedure: Direct application to Research, Division of Research and Education Programs, Room 318. NEH application instructions are provided upon receipt of initial inquiry outlining eligible project. This program is subject to the provisions of OMB Circular No. A-110.

Award Procedure: Applications are reviewed by subject area specialists, panels of scholars, and other appropriate individuals outside the agency. Awards are made by the Chairman of the National Endowment for the Humanities after recommendation by the National Council on the Humanities.

Deadlines: For collaborative research, September 1, 1999. For support of fellowship programs offered through independent research centers and international research organizations, September 1, 1999.

Range of Approval/Disapproval Time: For collaborative research, approximately seven months. For research opportunities offered through independent research centers and international research organizations, approximately seven months.

Renewals: Renewal applications are eligible; they are evaluated in competition with new applications.

ASSISTANCE CONSIDERATIONS:

Formula and Matching Requirements: This program has no statutory formula. Cost-sharing by institutional applicants is expected; matching funds are encouraged. Source: Program application instructions. Contact: See Headquarters Office below.

Length and Time Phasing of Assistance: Up to 36 months. Funds are released as required and must be expended during the grant period.

POST ASSISTANCE REQUIREMENTS:

Reports: Progress reports are required at least annually, no more frequently than quarterly. Cash reports are required quarterly. Final progress and expenditure reports are due within 90 days after completion or termination of project support by NEH.

Audits: In accordance with the provisions of OMB Circular No. A-133 (Revised, June 24, 1997), "Audits of States, Local Governments, and Non-Profit Organizations," nonfederal entities that receive financial assistance of $300,000 or more in Federal awards will have a single or a program-specific audit conducted for that year. Nonfederal entities that expend less than $300,000 a year in Federal awards are exempt from Federal audit requirements for that year, except as noted in Circular No. A-133. For nongovernmental recipients, audits are to be carried out in accordance with the provisions set forth in OMB Circular No. A-110, "Grants and Agreements with Institutions of Higher Education, Hospitals, and Other Nonprofit Organizations Uniform Administrative Requirements" and with OMB Circular No. A-133. In addition, grants are subject to inspection and audits by NEH and other Federal officials.

Records: Documentation of expenditures and other fiscal records must be retained for three years following the submission of the final expenditure report.

FINANCIAL INFORMATION:

Account Identification: 59-0200-0-1-503.

Obligations: (Grants) FY 98 $7,737,057; FY 99 est $5,380,000; and FY 00 est $8,620,000.

Range and Average of Financial Assistance: From $18,000 to $277,000; $111,900.

PROGRAM ACCOMPLISHMENTS:

In fiscal year 1998, 151 applications were received; 40 awards were made. In fiscal year 1999, 171 applications were received and 46 grants will be awarded. In fiscal year 2000, 500 applications and 92 awards are anticipated.

INFORMATION CONTACTS:

Division of Research and Education, Room 318

National Endowment for the Humanities

Washington, DC 20506

EXAMPLES OF FUNDED PROJECTS:

(1) A grant was awarded to a university for the preparation of an edition of the papers of Dead Sea Scrolls. (2) A grant was made to a

university to support the preparation of an edition of the papers of Benjamin Franklin. (3) An international team of scholars received a grant to support preparation of published documents and materials on Stalinism in the Soviet countryside. (4) A grant to a university to support the preparation of an edition of the papers of Martin Luther King, Jr. (5) A grant to a university supported excavation of two sites associated with early Khmer culture in the Mekong Delta. (6) A grant was made to a preservation society in support of archaeological investigations of the fort and colonial settlement at Jamestown, Virginia. (7) A grant was made to support research opportunities at an independent research center in San Marino, California. (8) A grant supported fellowships for American scholars at a U.S. research center in Jerusalem.

CRITERIA FOR SELECTING PROPOSALS:

The principal criteria considered by evaluators are: (1) The intellectual significance of the project; (2) the appropriateness of the research questions posed; (3) the quality and expertise of the researchers; (4) the promise of quality and usefulness of the resulting publication or other outcome; (5) the potential for success. For fellowship programs at research centers and international research organizations, evaluators are asked to assess the intrinsic importance of the institution's fellowship programs, the quality of scholarship produced by previous fellows, the relation of this work to the institution's mission and resources, the degree to which the institution promotes collegial exchange, the effectiveness of the administration of the programs, and the equity of the application and selection procedures.

45.201 Arts and Artifacts Indemnity

FEDERAL COUNCIL ON THE ARTS AND THE HUMANITIES, NATIONAL FOUNDATION ON THE ARTS AND THE HUMANITIES

OBJECTIVES:

To provide for indemnification against loss or damage for eligible art works, artifacts, and objects 1) when borrowed from abroad on exhibition in the U.S.; 2) when borrowed from the U.S. for exhibition abroad, preferably when there is an exchange exhibition from a foreign country; and 3) when borrowed from the U.S. for exhibition in the U.S. as part of exhibitions from abroad which include foreign-owned objects.

TYPES OF ASSISTANCE:

Insurance.

USES AND USE RESTRICTIONS:

Certificates of Indemnity will be issued for the following items insuring them against loss or damage: 1) Works of art, including tapestries, paintings, sculpture, folk art, graphics, and craft arts; 2) manuscripts, rare documents, books, and other printed or published materials; 3) other artifacts or objects; and 4) photographs, motion pictures, or audio and video tape; which are of educational, cultural, historical or scientific value; and, the exhibition of which is certified by the United States Information Agency to be in the national interest.

Restrictions: No indemnity agreement for a single exhibition shall exceed $500 million. Deductible amounts are on a sliding scale based on value of certificate, as follows: $15,000 deductible for exhibitions of up to $2 million in value; $25,000 for valuation of $2 million to $10 million; $50,000 for valuation of $10 million to $125 million; $100,000 for valuation of $125 million to $200 million; $200,000 for valuation of $200 million to $300 million; and $400,000 for valuation above $400 million. The total amount of indemnities that can be outstanding at any one time is $5 billion.

ELIGIBILITY REQUIREMENTS:

Applicant Eligibility: Federal, State, and local government entities, nonprofit agencies, institutions, and individuals may apply.

Beneficiary Eligibility: Federal, State, and local government entities, nonprofit agencies, institutions, and individuals will benefit. Audiences of indemnified exhibitions will also benefit.

APPLICATION AND AWARD PROCESS:

Preapplication Coordination: Assistance is available from the Indemnity Administrator, National Endowment for the Arts, Washington, DC 20506. This program is excluded from coverage under OMB Circular No. A- 102; it is also excluded from coverage under E.O. 12372.

Application Procedure: Applicants should request guidelines and   application forms from: The Indemnity Administrator, National Endowment for the Arts, Washington, DC 20506. This program is excluded from coverage under OMB Circular No. A-110.

Award Procedure: The Federal Council on the Arts and the Humanities makes final decisions on all awards based on recommendations from consulting panels of professionals in the field.

Deadlines: April 1 and October 1 of each year.

Range of Approval/Disapproval Time: Dependent on meetings of the Federal Council on the Arts and the Humanities; approximately three months.

Appeals: None.

Renewals: Requests for extensions and renewals must compete against new applications.

ASSISTANCE CONSIDERATIONS:

Formula and Matching Requirements: Coverage does not include the first $15,000, $25,000, $50,000, $100,000, $200,000, $300,000, or $400,000 based on the deductible formula for the value of an exhibition. The applicant must assume the deductible for the exhibition.

Length and Time Phasing of Assistance: The time of assistance varies.

POST ASSISTANCE REQUIREMENTS:

Reports: Reports of loss or damage at termination of exhibit.

Audits: Final audits may be made at the discretion of the Federal Council on the Arts and the Humanities for up to three years after the termination of the indemnity time period.

Records: Applicants are responsible for complete packing, shipping, security and condition reports on all indemnified items.

FINANCIAL INFORMATION:

Account Identification: 59-0100-0-1-503.

Range and Average of Financial Assistance: Coverage: $1,000,000 to $3,000,000,000 in fiscal year 1998; $1,000,000 to $5,000,000,000 in fiscal year 1999; $1,000,000 to $5,000,000,000 in fiscal year 2000.

PROGRAM ACCOMPLISHMENTS:

Thirty-nine certificates of indemnity were issued in fiscal year 1998 for 39 exhibitions insuring $2,985,984,085 out of a $3 billion ceiling. It is anticipated that 35 certificates of indemnity will be issued in fiscal year 1999 for 35 exhibitions insuring $4 billion out of a $5 billion ceiling. It is anticipated that 40 certificates of indemnity will be issued in fiscal year 2000 for 40 exhibitions insuring $4.5 billion out of a $5 billion ceiling.

REGULATIONS, GUIDELINES, AND LITERATURE:

Regulations and guidelines available from: Indemnity Administrator, National Endowment for the Arts, Washington, DC 20506.

INFORMATION CONTACTS:

Indemnity Administrator
National Endowment for the Arts
Washington, DC 20506
Contact: Alice M. Whelihan
Telephone: (202) 682-5452

59.005 Business Development Assistance to Small Business

FEDERAL AGENCY: SMALL BUSINESS ADMINISTRATION

OBJECTIVES:

To help the prospective, as well as the present small business person improve skills to manage and operate a business.

TYPES OF ASSISTANCE:

Advisory Services and Counseling; Dissemination of Technical Information; Training.

USES AND USE RESTRICTIONS:

Advises small business persons of all SBA and other government agency assistance services. This assistance includes the following: (1) Workshops for prospective small business owners; (2) management counseling, including assistance from SCORE (Service Corps of Retired Executives), and other volunteer groups; (3) management courses or conferences and seminars; and (4) educational materials to assist in management of small business.

ELIGIBILITY REQUIREMENTS:

Applicant Eligibility: Existing and potential small business persons, and in some cases, members of community groups are eligible. A small business is one independently owned and operated, and not dominant in its field. Generally for manufacturers, average employment not in excess of 500; wholesalers, average employment not in excess of 100; retail and services concerns, revenues not over $5,000,000, and agricultural enterprises, gross annual sales not over $500,000. Veterans are eligible for all programs.

Beneficiary Eligibility: Small business persons, veterans, community groups.

APPLICATION AND AWARD PROCESS:

Application Procedure: Personal or written application to SBA field offices.

ASSISTANCE CONSIDERATIONS:

Length and Time Phasing of Assistance: As appropriate.

FINANCIAL INFORMATION:

Account Identification: 73-0100-0-1-376.

Obligations: (Salaries and Expenses) FY 98 $1,245,000; FY 99 est $1,280,000; and FY 00 est $1,406,000.

PROGRAM ACCOMPLISHMENTS:

In fiscal year 1998, management counseling was given to approximately 175,000 potential and existing small business entrepreneurs. Management training enrollment was 100,000 for the same period.

REGULATIONS, GUIDELINES, AND LITERATURE:

"The Resource Directory for Small Business Management," from all SBA offices or by calling SBA's answer desk at 1-800-8-ASK-SBA;

FAX: (202) 205-7064; TDD: (202) 205- 7333.

INFORMATION CONTACTS:

Regional or Local Office: Initial contact should be made with the field offices of the SBA. See your phone directory for "Small Business Administration."

Headquarters Office: Associate Administrator for Business Initiatives, Small Business Administration, 409 3rd Street, SW., Washington, DC 20416. Telephone: (202) 205-6665.

For information on SBA's publications, programs and services, SBA's electronic bulletin board system, SBA ON-LINE, can be accessed by calling 1-800-697-4636, 1-900-463-4636, or 202-401-9600 or via Internet at: http://www.sba.gov.

59.006 8(a) Business Development (Section 8(a) Program)

FEDERAL AGENCY: SMALL BUSINESS ADMINISTRATION

OBJECTIVES:

To foster business ownership by individuals who are both socially and economically disadvantaged; and to promote the competitive viability of such firms by providing business development assistance including, but not limited to, management and technical assistance, access to capital and other forms of financial assistance, business training and counseling, and access to sole source and limited competition Federal contract opportunities, to help the firms to achieve competitive viability.

TYPES OF ASSISTANCE:

Provision of Specialized Services.

USES AND USE RESTRICTIONS:

This program utilizes authority provided to SBA under Section 7(j) and 8(a) of the Small Business Act to enter into procurement contracts with other Federal agencies and to subcontract the performance of these contracts to eligible program participants, and to provide access to capital and other forms of financial assistance, and to provide business training and counseling.

ELIGIBILITY REQUIREMENTS:

Applicant Eligibility: Firms applying for 8(a) program participation must meet certain requirements which include, but are not limited to: (a) Status as a small business; (b) at least 51 percent unconditional ownership, control and management of the business by an American citizen(s) determined by SBA to be socially and economically disadvantaged, or by an economically disadvantaged Indian Tribe, Alaska Native Corporation, or Native Hawaiian Organization; and (c) demonstrated potential for success. Absent evidence to the contrary, the following individuals are presumed to be socially disadvantaged: African Americans, Hispanic Americans, Native Americans, Asian Pacific Americans and Subcontinent Asian Americans. Individuals who are not members of the named groups may establish their social disadvantage on the basis of a preponderance of evidence of personal disadvantage stemming from color, national origin, gender, physical handicap, long-term residence in an environment isolated from the American society, or other similar cause beyond the individual's control. Economic disadvantage must be demonstrated on a case-by-case basis.

Beneficiary Eligibility: Socially and economically disadvantaged individuals and businesses owned and operated by such individuals; economically disadvantaged Indian tribes including Alaskan Native Corporations and economically disadvantaged Native Hawaiian organizations.

APPLICATION AND AWARD PROCESS:

Application Procedure: Written application to SBA offices, Division of Program Certification and Eligibility. Application forms, detailed instructions, and if necessary, assistance in completing application is available at SBA District offices and on SBA's home page at http://www.sba.gov.

Award Procedure: Applicant is notified of program participation approval or decline by a letter from the SBA headquarters office. Broad range of business development assistance, including procurement, and access to capital and other forms of financial assistance and business training and counseling is provided to approved program participants.

Deadlines: Applications for program participation are accepted on an ongoing basis.

Range of Approval/Disapproval Time: Approximately 90 days.

Appeals: Within 45 days of the date of decline letter, applicant has right to request that the decision be reconsidered. For applications declined solely on the basis of negative finding with regard to social disadvantage, economic disadvantaged ownership or control of business by socially or economically disadvantaged individuals, the applicant within 45 days of the date of the decline letter or reaffirmation of decline, has a right to appeal the decision to the SBA's Office of Hearing and Appeals.

ASSISTANCE CONSIDERATIONS:

Length and Time Phasing of Assistance: Maximum of 9 years.

POST ASSISTANCE REQUIREMENTS:

Reports: Annual business financial statements; annual business plan update; annual personal financial statements for each disadvantaged owner; annual certification of continuing compliance with program eligibility criteria; records of all payments, compensation and distributions made by the participant firm to each of its owners or to any person or entity affiliated with such owners; and other reports deemed necessary by SBA.

Audits: Program participation audits as needed to evaluate progress. Contract audits as and when required by Federal Acquisition Regulations.

Records: Standard business/accounting records.

FINANCIAL INFORMATION:

Account Identification: 73-0100-0-1-376.

Obligations: (Salaries and Expenses) FY 98 $4,583,000; FY 99 est $4,077,000; and FY 00 est $4,563,000.

PROGRAM ACCOMPLISHMENTS:

In fiscal year 1997, 32,091 contract actions valued at approximately $6.59 billion were awarded to companies participating in the program.

INFORMATION CONTACTS:

Regional or Local Office: Initial contact should be made with the SBA field offices.

Headquarters Office: Associate Administrator for 8(a) Business Development, Small Business Administration, 409 Third Street, SW., Washington, DC 20416. Telephone: (202) 205-6421.

59.007 Management and Technical Assistance for Socially and Economically Disadvantaged Businesses (7(J) Development Assistance Program)

FEDERAL AGENCY: SMALL BUSINESS ADMINISTRATION

OBJECTIVES:

To provide management and technical assistance and access to capital and other forms of financial assistance and business training and counseling through qualified individuals, public or private organizations to 8(a) certified firms and other existing or potential businesses which are economically and socially disadvantaged; businesses operating in areas of high unemployment or low income; firms owned by low-income persons; or participants in activities authorized by Sections 7(i), 7(j) and 8(a) of the Small Business Act.

TYPES OF ASSISTANCE:

Project Grants.

USES AND USE RESTRICTIONS:

Financial assistance under this Section may be given for projects that respond to needs as outlined in each respective program solicitation announcement and services from lending and financial institutions and sureties and business training and counseling. Such assistance must provide a special level of effort or service in the delivery of management and technical assistance, or provide a special level of effort or service in the delivery of access to capital and other forms of financial assistance, and business training and counseling, to socially and economically disadvantaged small businesses in order to provide opportunity for successful and full participation in the free enterprise system. Types of management and technical assistance may include accounting, marketing, proposal preparation workshops and industry specific technical assistance, or access to capital and other forms of financial assistance and business training and counseling.

ELIGIBILITY REQUIREMENTS:

Applicant Eligibility: State and local governments, educational institutions, public or private organizations and businesses, lending and financial institutions and sureties, Indian tribes and individuals that have the capability to provide the necessary assistance, as described in each program solicitation announcement.

Beneficiary Eligibility: Socially and economically disadvantaged persons and businesses owned and operated by participants in the 8(a) program, (59.006) businesses operating in areas of low-income or high-unemployment, and firms owned by low-income individuals.

APPLICATION AND AWARD PROCESS:

Application Procedure: Application proposal forwarded to District Office Director for appropriate geographic area. The standard application forms as furnished by the Federal agency and required by OMB Circular No. A-102 must be used for this program by State and local governments. This program is subject to the provisions of OMB Circular No. A-110.

Award Procedure: Decisions on acceptance are made by the Office of Procurement and Grants Management based upon recommendations of the Associate Administrator for 8(a) Business Development or his/her designee. The Grants Management Officer notifies successful applicants by Notice of Award. Decisions on services from lending and financial institutions and sureties, and business training and counseling will be made by the Associate Administrator for 8(a) Business Development.

Deadlines: As announced within individual "Request for Application Proposals."

Range of Approval/Disapproval Time: Variable.

ASSISTANCE CONSIDERATIONS:

Length and Time Phasing of Assistance: Awards are made for a maximum of 1 year with options as stated in the individual announcements. Disbursements are made within a few days of receipt of request for disbursement. Disbursements are made in partial payments based on work successfully performed. Length and time of services from lending and financial institutions and sureties and business training and counseling will be determined on a case-by-case basis.

POST ASSISTANCE REQUIREMENTS:

Reports: Program and fiscal reports, as described in each award. A final report is also due within 30 days after completion of agreement.

Audits: Pre-award accounting system survey. Final audit by a certified or licensed public accountant. Other audits are required by SBA. In accordance with the provisions of OMB Circular No. A-133 (Revised, June 24, 1997), "Audits of States, Local Governments, and Non- Profit Organizations," nonfederal entities that receive financial assistance of $300,000 or more in Federal awards will have a single or program-specific audit conducted for that year. Nonfederal entities that expend less than $300,000 a year in Federal awards are exempt from Federal audit requirements for that year, except as noted in Circular No. A-133.

Records: Appropriate records as needed for above requirements.

FINANCIAL INFORMATION:

Account Identification: 73-0100-0-1-376.

Obligations: (Cooperative Agreements) FY 98 $2,850,000; FY 99 est $2,600,000 and FY 00 est $5,000,000.

Range and Average of Financial Assistance: Amount subject to negotiation commensurate with management and technical assistance to be provided.

PROGRAM ACCOMPLISHMENTS:

In fiscal year 1997, 153 cooperative agreements were awarded.

INFORMATION CONTACTS:

Regional or Local Office: SBA District Offices

Headquarters Office: Associate Administrator for Minority Enterprise Development, 409 3rd Street, SW., Washington, DC 20416. Telephone: (202) 205-6410.

59.043 Women's Business Ownership Assistance

FEDERAL AGENCY:

SMALL BUSINESS ADMINISTRATION

OBJECTIVES:

To fund nonprofit economic development organizations to assist, through training and counseling, small business concerns owned and controlled by women, and to remove, in so far as possible, the discriminatory barriers that are encountered by women in accessing capital and promoting their businesses.

TYPES OF ASSISTANCE:

Project Grants.

USES AND USE RESTRICTIONS:

To establish women's business centers for the benefit of small business concerns owned and controlled by women. The services and assistance provided by the women's business centers are to include financial, management, procurement, and marketing training and counseling to start-up or established on-going concerns.

ELIGIBILITY REQUIREMENTS:

Applicant Eligibility: Private organizations having experience in training and counseling business women effectively. Public educational institutions and State and local governments are not eligible.

Beneficiary Eligibility: Women entrepreneurs starting their own business or expanding their existing business.

APPLICATION AND AWARD PROCESS:

Application Procedure: Applications are accepted in accordance with and up to the data specified in the Program Announcement issued annually. In addition to properly completed application for Federal Assistance: (Standard Forms 424, 424A and 424B), application procedures require a written proposal addressing all items of the selection criteria published in the Program Announcement. All application/proposals are submitted to the SBA Office of Procurement and Grants Management, 5th Floor, 409 3rd Street, SW., Washington DC 20416.

Award Procedure: SBA Central Office, Office of Procurement and Grants Management enters into a cooperative agreement with every approved applicant.

Deadlines: Applications/proposals must be submitted by the date indicated in the Program Announcement.

Range of Approval/Disapproval Time: Within 120 days from filing deadline.

ASSISTANCE CONSIDERATIONS:

Formula and Matching Requirements: This program has no statutory formula. This program was reauthorized in 1997 to conduct 5-year projects. The recipient organization must obtain cash contributions from nonfederal sources. Matching requirements changed as follows: In the first and second years, one nonfederal dollar for each two Federal dollars; in the third and fourth years, one nonfederal dollar for each Federal dollar; and in the fifth year, two nonfederal dollars for each Federal dollar. Up to one-half of the nonfederal matching assistance May be in the form of in-kind contributions.

Length and Time Phasing of Assistance: Projects funded under the Small Business Reauthorization Act of 1997 do not exceed 5 years. The Administration may disburse up to 25 percent of each year's Federal share awarded to a recipient organization after notice of the award has been issued and before the nonfederal sector matching funds are obtained. Payments are made on a cost reimbursement basis.

POST ASSISTANCE REQUIREMENTS:

Reports: Semi-annual performance and financial status reports are due no later than December 31 and June 30 of each 12-month performance period. A final financial status report is due 90 days after the end of each 12-month performance period. The Administrator must prepare and submit an annual report to the Committees on Small Business of the House of Representatives and the Senate on the effectiveness of all projects. Such report shall provide information concerning: (1) the number of individuals receiving assistance; (2) the number of startup business concerns formed; (3) the gross receipts of assisted concerns; (4) increases or decreases in profits of assisted concerns; and (5) the employment increases or decreases of assisted concerns.

Audits: Under the Small Business Reauthorization Act of 1997, the Agency must conduct an annual programmatic and financial examination of each Women's Business Center.

Records: The awardee shall maintain and submit detailed, complete and accurate client activity records to reflect clearly the nature and variety of services provided. Financial records must be kept until 3 years after the completion and submission of the final report.

FINANCIAL INFORMATION:

Account Identification: 73-0100-0-1-376.

Obligations: (Cooperative Agreements) FY 98 $8,000,000; FY 99 est $9,000,000; and FY 00 est $9,000,000.

Range and Average of Financial Assistance: $75,000 to $150,000; $150,000.

PROGAM ACCOMPLISHMENTS:

At present, training and counseling is being offered at 29 centers across the nation. Project sites received funding to be linked on an Intranet. As of January 1997, all of the sites will participate in the interactive women's business center on the Internet: www.onlinewbc.org.

REGULATIONS, GUIDELINES, AND LITERATURE:

Assistance to individuals or enterprises eligible under the Women's

Business Ownership Act of 1988, Federal Register, 54 FR 50466, Women's Business Development Act of 1991 and the Small Business Reauthorization Act of 1997, P.L. 105-135, 111 Stat. 2592.

INFORMATION CONTACTS:

Regional or Local Office: Women's Business Ownership Representative of the Small Business Administration offices.

Headquarters Office: Small Business Administration, Office of Women's Business Ownership, 409 Third Street, SW., Washington, DC 20416. Telephone: (202) 205-6673. Contact: Sally Murrell.

EXAMPLES OF FUNDED PROJECTS:

A typical project funded was the Women's Economic Self Sufficiency Team in Albuquerque, NM to provide in- depth and quality training and counseling to women entrepreneurs in Albuquerque, Taos, Las Cruces and Farmington, NM.

CRITERIA FOR SELECTING PROPOSALS:

As stated in each solicitation for proposals, but including: (1) Proven experience in conducting programs designed to impact or upgrade business skills of women business owners or potential owners; (2) Ability to undertake the project rapidly; (3) Ability to provide services to a representative number of women who are socially and economically disadvantaged; (4) Proposed location for the women's business center site; (5) Plan to maintain close working relationship with the SBA District Offices and SBA resource partners.

64.116 Vocational Rehabilitation for Disabled Veterans

FEDERAL AGENCY: VETERANS BENEFITS ADMINISTRATION, DEPARTMENT OF VETERANS AFFAIRS

OBJECTIVES:

To provide all services and assistance necessary to enable service-disabled veterans and service persons hospitalized or receiving outpatient medical care services or treatment for a service- connected disability pending discharge to get and keep a suitable job. When employment is not reasonably feasible, the program can provide the needed services and assistance to help the individual learn skills to achieve maximum independence in daily living.

TYPES OF ASSISTANCE:

Direct Payments for Specified Use; Direct Loans; Advisory Services and Counseling.

USES AND USE RESTRICTIONS:

The program offers the services and assistance necessary for an individual to obtain and retain suitable employment. This is employment that matches the individual's aptitudes, interests, and abilities and does not worsen the individual's disabilities. An individual may reach an employment goal directly by receiving employment search and work adjustment services. If direct placement is not possible, the program provides education or training to qualify the individual for employment. If the individual requires education or training, the program provides for direct payment to service providers for the entire cost of tuition, books, fees, supplies, and other services.

As part or all of a rehabilitation program, individuals may receive services and training designed to help them live with a reduced dependency on others in their homes and communities. Counseling services are provided to the individual throughout his or her participation in the program. In addition to disability compensation, the veteran receives a monthly subsistence allowance. Advances of up to $840.90 may be made to veterans to meet unexpected financial difficulties. These advances do not bear interest and are repaid out of future VA or military benefit payments.

Although no set repayment period is established, the monthly rate of repayment may not generally be less than 10 percent. In general, a new advance may not be made until a previous advance has been fully repaid. Usually, the training phase of the rehabilitation program may not exceed 4 years nor may training be provided more than 12 years after the individual becomes eligible to apply for the program.

Following training, or sometimes as the whole of a rehabilitation program, the veteran may also receive up to 18 months of counseling, job placement and post-placement services. The veteran may receive an employment adjustment allowance equal to 2 months of subsistence during this period of services, but only if employability was achieved as a result of services received in a program which included training. Veterans who meet certain requirements may receive an initial supply of goods and commodities to start a small business.

ELIGIBILITY REQUIREMENTS:

Applicant Eligibility: Veterans of World War II and later service with a service-connected disability or disabilities rated at least 20 percent compensable and certain service-disabled servicepersons pending discharge or release from service if VA determines the servicepersons will likely receive at least a 20 percent rating and they need vocational rehabilitation because of an employment handicap. Veterans with a 10 percent service-connected disability may be eligible if they first applied for vocational rehabilitation prior to November 1, 1990, and they have an employment handicap. In addition, veterans with compensable ratings of 10 percent may also be eligible if they are found to have a serious employment handicap.

Beneficiary Eligibility: Veterans of World War II and later service with a service-connected disability or disabilities rated at least 20 percent compensable and certain service-disabled servicepersons pending discharge or release from service if VA determines the servicepersons will likely receive at least a 20 percent rating and they need vocational rehabilitation because of an employment handicap. Veterans with compensable ratings of 10 percent may also be eligible if they are found to have a serious employment handicap.

APPLICATION AND AWARD PROCESS:

Application Procedure: Obtain an application (VA Form 28-1900) from any VA office or regional office and submit it to the nearest VA regional office.

Award Procedure: Awards are authorized at the regional office for direct distribution to beneficiaries.

Deadlines: Generally, vocational rehabilitation must be accomplished within a basic 12-year period of eligibility. The 12-year period of eligibility begins with the date of discharge, notification of establishment of service-connected disability meeting the eligibility requirements, or change in character of discharge, whichever is later.

Range of Approval/Disapproval Time: Average is 88.7 days.

Appeals: Available through special board. Average time to process an appeal is 630 days. In the event of a denial, claimants are advised of appeal rights and procedures at the time of notification.

Renewals: Under certain limited circumstances, a veteran's eligibility period can extend beyond 12 years and entitlement to training and subsistence can be longer than 48 months.

ASSISTANCE CONSIDERATIONS:

POST ASSISTANCE REQUIREMENTS:

Reports: The veteran's progress is monitored throughout the rehabilitation program to assure that goals and objectives of the veteran's rehabilitation plan are carried out. The plan extends throughout the veteran's rehabilitation program to include, when applicable, the securing of and adjusting to employment.

FINANCIAL INFORMATION:

Account Identification: 36-0137-0-1-702; 36-4114-0-3-702; 36-4112-0-3-702.

Obligations: (Direct Payments) FY 98 $405,975,000; FY 99 est $403,206,000; and FY 00 est $405,855,000; (Loan Advances) FY 98

$2,154,000; FY 99 est $2,401,000; and FY 00 est $2,531,000.

Range and Average of Financial Assistance: Full cost of tuition, books, fees, supplies and rehabilitation services. Monthly full-time allowances range from $420.45 for a single veteran to $614.60 for a veteran with two dependents, plus $44.80 for each dependent in excess of two. Non-interest bearing loans of up to $840.90 and a work-study allowance not to exceed the higher of 25 times the Federal or State minimum hourly wage times the number of weeks in the veteran's period of enrollment.

PROGRAM ACCOMPLISHMENTS:

In fiscal year 1998, 53,004 participants received subsistence allowance payments; 4,290 of these received loans. Estimates for subsequent periods are: fiscal year 1999, 51,440 participants and 4,600 loans, and fiscal year 2000, 50,726 participants and 4,600 loans. During fiscal year 1998, 9,289 participants were rehabilitated.

REGULATIONS, GUIDELINES, AND LITERATURE:

38 CFR 21.40-21.47; "Federal Benefits for Veterans and Dependents," VA Pamphlet 80-99-1, $5.00, available from Superintendent of Documents, P.O. Box 371954, Pittsburgh, PA 15250-7954. The stock number is: 051-000-00217-2. "Vocational Rehabilitation - Your Key to an Independent Future," VA Pamphlet 28-82-1, free, available from any VA regional office.

INFORMATION CONTACTS:

Regional or Local Office for Veterans Administration

Headquarters Office: Department of Veterans Affairs, Veterans Benefits Administration, Vocational Rehabilitation and Counseling Service (28), Washington, DC 20420. Telephone: (202) 273-7419.

CRITERIA FOR SELECTING PROPOSALS:

Direct payment for specified use; payments are made directly to the providers of goods or services for program participants; payments include tuition, fees, books, supplies, tutoring, professional services, and medical care if not available in a VA facility; advances are made to program participants to meet unexpected financial obligations which might hinder continued program progress.

82.015 Creative Arts Grants

FEDERAL AGENCY: UNITED STATES INFORMATION AGENCY

OBJECTIVES:

The Creative Arts Exchanges program works with nonprofit organizations to develop cooperative international group projects that introduce American and foreign participants to each other's cultural and artistic life and traditions. Our projects emphasize the relationship between the arts and broader social and diplomacy issues. We seek organizations that have a disciplinary expertise in the arts as well as broad outreach and networking capabilities with American artists.

TYPES OF ASSISTANCE:

Project Grants.

USES AND USE RESTRICTIONS:

International projects in the United States or overseas may involve an international exchange of composers, choreographers, playwrights, theater designers, writers and poets, filmmakers, arts administrators and visual artists. Projects should involve U.S. Information Service posts worldwide to carry out activities supportive of the USIA mission to increase mutual understanding between the United States and other countries and to promote international cooperation in educational and cultural fields. Ineligible proposals would include those focusing on: youth or youth related activities, speaking tours, research projects, the exchange of amateurs or semi- professionals, community-level arts presentations or vocational and technical long-term academic study programs.

ELIGIBILITY REQUIREMENTS:

Applicant Eligibility: Applicants must be public or nonprofit organizations that demonstrate disciplinary expertise in the arts and meet the provisions described in IRS regulation 501 (C) (3). Organizations must have 4 years of experience in exchange to qualify for grants of more than $60,000. In 1998, USIA held an open competition for Creative Arts Exchanges grant awards. Six grants ranging between $30,000-$75,000 were awarded for projects in AF, AR, WEU and EEN. A grant was also awarded to the City of Chicago Department of Cultural Affairs, to conduct another cycle of the Chicago Artists International Program. Whether USIA will hold another open grant competition for Creative Arts Exchange projects in 1999 has yet to be determined.

Beneficiary Eligibility: Individual participants must be professional artists and arts administrators over the age of 25. There is no age-limit for participants. Some exchanges require participants to have a minimum level of English language ability.

APPLICATION AND AWARD PROCESS:

Application Procedure: For renewals of projects such as those conducted by the American Association of Museums and American Dance Festival a letter of solicitation is used. For open competitions, the request for proposals is published in the Federal Register.

Award Procedure: Funding decisions are at the discretion of the USIA Associate Director for Educational And Cultural Affairs and are based on the advice of a panel of USIA reviewers and various USIA officers. Final technical authority resides with the USIA Office of Contracts.

Deadlines: Deadlines for submission of proposals are established in the request for proposals or letters of solicitation.

Range of Approval/Disapproval Time: Decisions are generally made within 3 months of the submission of proposals, subject to the availability and timing of funding.

Renewals: Renewal grants for several of our long-term projects have been awarded in the past, in order to build on existing successful projects.

ASSISTANCE CONSIDERATIONS:

Formula and Matching Requirements: Usually a 30 percent cost-share is requested from grantee organizations.

Length and Time Phasing of Assistance: Awards range in length from 12 to 36 months.

FINANCIAL INFORMATION:

Account Identification: 67-0209-0-1-154.

Range and Average of Financial Assistance: $60,000 to $300,000.

PROGRAM ACCOMPLISHMENTS:

By fiscal year 1998, seven grants were awarded.

REGULATIONS, GUIDELINES, AND LITERATURE:

USIA regulations governing exchange visitor (J-1) programs. Guidelines for grants are distributed in conjunction with the request for proposals/letter of solicitation.

INFORMATION CONTACTS:

Jill Johansen

Creative Arts Exchanges Program, Office of Citizen Exchanges

Bureau of Educational and Cultural Affairs, USIA

301 4th Street SW

Washington DC 20547

Telephone: (202) 205-2209

Fax (202) 619-5311.

CRITERIA FOR SELECTING PROPOSALS:

Programmatic planning, project objectives and quality; organization's capacity and track record; support for diversity; expertise; cost-effectiveness; project evaluation plan; value to US-partner country relations; cost-sharing; and multiplier effect.

82.032 Cultural Exchange (Visual Arts) Fund for U.S. Artists at International Festivals and Exhibitions (Visual Arts)

FEDERAL AGENCY: UNITED STATES INFORMATION AGENCY

OBJECTIVES:

To help ensure that the excellence, diversity and vitality of the arts in the United States are represented at international visual and performing arts festivals.

TYPES OF ASSISTANCE:

Project Grants.

USES AND USE RESTRICTIONS:

The Fund makes grants to independent curators and nonprofit museums and galleries that have been recommended by a peer committee following a competitive solicitation nationwide from some 400 curators of contemporary art. Curators and artists must be mindful of the diplomatic context under which U.S. exhibitions are presented given their sponsorship by the U.S. Embassy. All exhibitions and accompanying publications should advance mutual understanding and respect between the U.S. and the host country.

ELIGIBILITY REQUIREMENTS:

Applicant Eligibility: Applications are accepted from nonprofit museums, galleries, artists cooperatives, or independent curators. Applications are not accepted from commercial galleries. Applicants should not have kinship or close personal ties to proposed artists.

Beneficiary Eligibility: Proposed artists must be working at a professional level as painters, sculptors, photographers, printmakers, or working with electronic media, installations or traditional arts.

APPLICATION AND AWARD PROCESS:

Preapplication Coordination: Curators are invited to contact project coordinator Rex Moser. Telephone: (202) 619-4806, Fax: (202) 619-6315, email: RMOSER@USIA.GOV, to discuss planned project and clarify details of venues, on-site coordination, budget, publication, etc.

Application Procedure: Curators wishing to submit a proposal for an international visual arts festivals should contact the project coordinator described in 091 Preapplication Coordination, or request an application from: The Fund for U. S. Artists, Arts International, Institute of International Education, 809 United Nations Plaza, New York, NY 10017. Telephone: (212) 984-5370. Fax: (212) 984-5574. Website: WWW.IIE.ORG.

Award Procedure: Letters are sent periodically to curators describing upcoming festivals for which an official U.S. representation is sought. The event is described, giving parameters of media, scale, format, etc. required by event organizers. The letters also describe the application process, required format, theme, budget and deadlines. After receipt, the proposals are reviewed by the Federal Advisory Committee for International Exhibitions (FACIE), a standing committee of the National Endowment for the Arts consisting of seven curators and directors of contemporary art museums and galleries. The committee recommends the proposal it thinks would best represent the U.S. at a particular event.

Deadlines: Deadlines vary depending on receipt of information from event organizers concerning opening dates and themes. There are normally two deadlines each year, usually in the Spring and Fall.

Range of Approval/Disapproval Time: Six weeks.

ASSISTANCE CONSIDERATIONS:

Formula and Matching Requirements: The Fund is supported by two Federal agencies -- the U. S. Information Agency and the National Endowment for the Arts -- and two foundations -- the Rockefeller Foundation and The Pew Charitable Trusts. There is no matching requirement. However applications which exceed the amount budgeted for that project by the Fund must describe how additional funds will be raised. The Fund looks for evidence of an institution's commitment in terms of contributed salaries and infrastructure support.

Length and Time Phasing of Assistance: Variable.

POST ASSISTANCE REQUIREMENTS:

Reports: Reports are required from grantees of the Fund within 90 days after artworks have been returned to lenders and bills have been paid.

Audits: Subject to audit.

Records: As prescribed by grant terms.

FINANCIAL INFORMATION:

Account Identification: 67-0209-0-1-154.

Obligations: (Grants) FY 98 $450,000; FY 99 est $450,000; and FY 00 est $450,000.

Range and Average of Financial Assistance: Each project is budgeted by the Fund at a different level, depending on the scale of the event, expected local costs, etc. These range from $40,000 for a print exhibition to the Ljubljana Graphics Biennial, to $300,000 for the Venice Biennale.

PROGRAM ACCOMPLISHMENTS:

The Festivals Fund supports a number of official U.S. artists at from three to five international biennials each year. In addition, another three to five self-curated biennials receive grant support.

REGULATIONS, GUIDELINES, AND LITERATURE:

Consult websites of USIA at WWW.USIA.GOV or Arts International at WWW.IIE.ORG; or write or phone Arts International at the Institute of International Education, 809 United Nations Plaza, New York, NY 10017. Telephone: (212) 984-5370. Fax: (212) 984-5574.

INFORMATION CONTACTS:

Office of Citizens Exchanges, USIA

Washington, DC 20547

Contact: Rex Moser

Telephone: (202) 619-4806.

EXAMPLES OF FUNDED PROJECTS:

1998: Judy Pfaff created a site- specific installation in Sao Paulo, and Nancy Spero created an installation in Cairo, winning the jury's 2nd cash prize. The U.S. exhibition at Cuenca was a group exhibition of computer-generated paintings. Carrie Mae Weems represented the U.S. at the Dakar Biennale, and a grant was provided the Sydney Biennale. 1999: Ann Hamilton is to create a site-specific installation in the U.S. pavilion at the 1999 Venice Biennale, and a grant is to be provided the Istanbul Biennial. 2000: Anticipated events include grants to the Saaremaa Bienaal in Riga, Latvia, the Havana Bienal, the Johannesburg Biennale, and the Sydney Biennale. Official U.S. representation will take place in Cuenca and Cairo.

CRITERIA FOR SELECTING PROPOSALS:

Eligible proposals are reviewed based on the following criteria: (A) artistic excellence; (B) extent to which proposal represents the vitality and diversity of contemporary U.S. visual arts; (C) suitability of the exhibition for the specific venue; (D) ability of applicant to carry out the proposed exhibition; (E) record of professional activity and achievement by individuals/organizations involved.

84.170 Javits Fellowships

FEDERAL AGENCY: OFFICE OF THE ASSISTANT SECRETARY FOR POSTSECONDARY EDUCATION, DEPARTMENT OF EDUCATION

OBJECTIVES:

To provide fellowships for graduate study in the arts, humanities, and social sciences to individuals of superior ability selected on the basis of demonstrated achievement, financial need, and exceptional promise. Fellowships are awarded to students intending to pursue a doctoral degree and may be awarded to students pursuing a master's degree in those fields in which the master's degree is commonly accepted as the terminal degree.

TYPES OF ASSISTANCE:

Project Grants.

USES AND USE RESTRICTIONS:

A recipient is entitled to use the fellowship in a graduate program at any accredited institution of higher education in which the recipient may decide to enroll. For each fellowship awarded, the institution receives an institutional allowance determined in accordance with the statutory formula in Section 703 of the Higher Education Act of 1965, as amended. The student receives a stipend set at the level of support based on that provided by the National Science Foundation graduate fellowships. No stipend may exceed the Fellow's demonstrated level of need according to measurements of need set forth in Part F of Title IV of the Higher Education Act. An individual receives payments only during the periods that he or she maintains satisfactory progress in his or her program of study and devotes essentially full time to study or research in the field in which the fellowship was awarded.

ELIGIBILITY REQUIREMENTS:

Applicant Eligibility: Eligibility is limited to U.S. citizens or nationals, permanent residents of the United States, and citizens of any one of the Freely Associated States. An individual who is enrolled or plans to enroll in a terminal degree program is eligible only if he or she is a citizen of the United States. Applicants must be enrolled or eligible to be enrolled in a graduate program in an approved field of study at an accredited institution of higher education. In fiscal year 1999 sixty percent of new awards shall be available for fellowships to otherwise eligible applicants who have earned no graduate credit hours. The remaining forty percent of new awards shall be available for fellowships to all otherwise eligible applicants who are within the first year of graduate study. In each of these two categories, a minimum of sixty percent of these new fellowships shall be awarded to applicants in the humanities, twenty percent to applicants in the social sciences, and twenty percent to applicants in the arts.

Beneficiary Eligibility: Citizens and nationals of the United States, permanent residents of the United States, and citizens of any one of the Freely Associated States.

APPLICATION AND AWARD PROCESS:

Application Procedure: Applications must be submitted in accordance with the notice of closing date published in the Federal

Register. This program is excluded from coverage under OMB Circular No. A-110.

Award Procedure: The Education Department will make awards in accordance with the criteria established by the Javits Fellowship Board. Contact the program office for additional information.

Deadlines: Published in the Federal Register. Contact the program office for more information.

Range of Approval/Disapproval Time: Approximately 120 days.

Renewals: Requests for continuation of support are made on an annual basis by the institution at which the fellow is pursuing graduate study, but may not exceed 48 months. Continuation awards are subject to the availability of funds.

ASSISTANCE CONSIDERATIONS:

Formula and Matching Requirements: None.

Length and Time Phasing of Assistance: The length of the grant is one year, but renewable for up to a total of 48 months, subject to the availability of funds.

POST ASSISTANCE REQUIREMENTS:

Reports: Certification from an appropriate official at an institution of higher education approved by the Secretary, stating that the fellow is making satisfactory progress and has devoted essentially full time to study or research in the field in which the fellowship was awarded.

Audits: Fiscal records of institutions administering funds are subject to audit by the Education Department at any time within 5 years after the close of the fiscal year in which expenditures are liquidated.

Records: All records bearing on the receipt and expenditure of funds under this program must be available for inspection by the Education Department. Records must be held for three years after the fiscal year in which expenditures are liquidated, or five years after the grant, or until resolution of any audit questions.

FINANCIAL INFORMATION:

Account Identification: 91-0201-0-1-502.

Obligations: (Grants) FY 98 $6,075,000; FY 99 est $7,148,000; and FY 00 est $8,200,000. (Note: Funds are provided under the Graduate Assistance in Areas of National Need program).

Range and Average of Financial Assistance: In fiscal year 1999, the fellowship stipend awards averaged $15,000. The institutional allowance covering tuition and fees was $10,375.

PROGRAM ACCOMPLISHMENTS:

In fiscal year 1998, approximately 267 new and continuing fellowships were awarded.

REGULATIONS, GUIDELINES, AND LITERATURE:

Javits Fellowship Program, U.S. Department of Education, Washington, DC 20202-5247.

INFORMATION CONTACTS:

International Education and Graduate Programs

Office of Postsecondary Education, Department of Education

Washington, DC 20202-5247

Contact: Melissa Burton

Telephone: (202) 260-3574

EXAMPLES OF FUNDED PROJECTS:

Awards are made in the following areas: arts, humanities, and social sciences.

CRITERIA FOR SELECTING PROPOSALS:

Criteria are established by the Fellowship Board. Fellowship applications are evaluated based on scholarly achievements, including Graduate Record Examination (GRE) scores on the general test only if applying in the humanities, social sciences, multi-or interdisciplinary fields of art history or creative writing; awards; honors; narratives describing personal goals; and three letters of recommendation.

President's Committee on the Arts and Humanities to Award *Coming Up Taller* Awards for Youth

This program is not listed in the *Catalog of Federal Domestic Assistance* programs but is an outreach of the National Endowment for the Arts.

The *Coming Up Taller* Awards, an annual awards program of the National Endowment for the Arts recognizes outstanding programs that foster the creative and intellectual development of America's youth through education and practical experience in the arts and humanities.

To be considered, projects must be community-based and incorporate one or more disciplines in the arts or humanities as the core content of their work with at-risk children and youth. Each of the ten honorees will receive a $10,000 award.

Contact:

Coming Up Taller Awards

President's Committee on the Arts and the Humanities

1100 Pennsylvania Avenue, NW Suite 526

Washington, DC 20506

Web site: http://www.cominguptaller.org/awards.html

National Forest Service, U.S. Department of Agriculture

This program is not listed in the *Catalog of Federal Domestic Assistance*. The NEA has joined with the US Department of Agriculture's Forest Service for the fourth round of Arts and Rural Community Assistance Grants for arts-based rural community development projects eligible under the Forest Service's Economic Action Program guidelines.

Funding is available for projects that demonstrate the importance of the arts in economic development, community development, or a community's heritage. In general, projects must take place in communities that are within 100 miles of a National Forest or Grassland.

The NEA and the Forest Service have awarded 55 grants in 24 states and Puerto Rico. Contact:

Anthony J. Tighe
Intergovernmental Affairs Specialist
National Endowment for the Arts
1100 Pennsylvania Avenue NW
Washington, DC 20506
tighet@arts.endow.gov
(202) 682-5616

Steve Yaddof
Cooperative Forestry
Forest Service
Auditors Building
201-14th Street SW
Washington, DC 20250
(202) 205-1386

U.S. Department of Agriculture

The Department of Agriculture has several grant and loan programs for fostering development of rural businesses like arts and crafts.

The delivery of programs is accomplished through three National Office Divisions and a nationwide field staff serving the 50 States, the Virgin Islands, Puerto Rico, and Western Pacific Territories.

All USDA Rural Development mission area programs, including Rural Business-Cooperative Service programs, are administered by Rural Development field staff.

In Fiscal Year 1999, a total of 941 loans and 453 grants totalling $1,365,246,287 were disbursed. This resulted in 79,839 jobs either being created or saved, and 3,742 businesses assisted in rural America.

Rural Business Enterprise Grants

The Rural Business-Cooperative Service (RBS) makes grants under the Rural Business Enterprise Grants (RBEG) Program to public bodies, nonprofit corporations, and Federally-recognized Indian Tribal groups to finance and facilitate development of small and emerging private business enterprises located in areas outside the boundary of a city or unincorporated areas of 50,000 or more and its immediately adjacent urbanized or urbanizing area.

Costs that may be paid from grant funds include the acquisition and development of land and the construction of buildings, plants, equipment, access streets and roads, parking areas, and utility and service extensions; refinancing; fees for professional services; technical assistance and related training for adults; startup operating costs and working capital, providing financial assistance to a third party; production of television programs to provide information to rural residents; and to create, expand, and operate rural distance learning networks. Grants may also be made to establish or fund revolving loan programs.

Who is Eligible?

Eligibility is limited to public bodies, private nonprofit corporations, and Federally-recognized Indian Tribal groups. Public bodies include incorporated towns and villages, boroughs, townships, counties, States, authorities, districts, Indian Tribes on Federal and State reservations, and other Federally-recognized Indian Tribal groups in rural areas. Small and emerging businesses with less than 50 new employees and less than $1 million in gross annual revenues are eligible for assistance.

How May Funds be Used?

Funds may be used to facilitate the development of small and emerging private business enterprises. Costs that may be paid from grant funds include the acquisition and development of land and the construction of buildings, plants, equipment, access streets and roads, parking areas, and utility and service extensions; refinancing; fees for professional services; technical assistance and adult training associated with technical assistance; startup operating costs and working capital, providing financial assistance to a third party; production of television programs to provide information to rural residents; and to create, expand, and operate rural distance learning networks.

Limitations:

Grants cannot be used for:

1. Production of agricultural products through growing, cultivating, and harvesting either directly or through horizontally integrated livestock operations except for commercial nurseries or timber operations or

limited agricultural production related to technical assistance.

2.Comprehensive areawide planning.

3.Loans by grantees when the rates, terms, and charges for those loans are not reasonable or would be for purposes not eligible under RBEG regulations.

4.Development of a proposal that may result in the transfer of jobs or business activity from one area to another. This provision does not prohibit establishment of a new branch or subsidiary.

5.Development of a proposal which may result in an increase of goods, materials, commodities, services, or facilities in an area when there is not sufficient demand.

6.For programs operated by cable television systems.

7.To fund part of a project which is dependent on other funding, unless there is a firm commitment of the other funding to ensure completion of the project.

All applications are considered without regard to race, color, religion, sex, national origin, age marital status, or physical or mental handicap (provided applications have the capacity to enter into a legal contract) of the members of the groups applying for assistance. Service must be extended on the same basis.

How are Applications Processed?

Applicants are required to submit supporting data before formal application is made. After determining the order of funding priorities, RBS will tentatively determine eligibility and request applicants to assemble and submit formal applications.

How are Grants Closed?

After determining that applicable administrative actions and the required work of the applicant have been completed, RBS will deliver the grant funds by Treasury check.

Where Should Applications be Filed?

Forms are available from and may be filed in any USDA Rural Development State Office, check your telephone directory under "Federal Government" or call the RBS National Office Specialty Lenders Division, (202) 720-1400.

Other Conditions

Applicants for grants to help develop private business enterprises must file written notice of intent with the State single point of contact consistent with Intergovernmental Review requirements. Federally-recognized Indian Tribes are exempt from this requirement.

Applicants for grants to establish a revolving loan program must include detail on the applicant's experience operating a revolving loan program, proposed projects, applicant's financial ability to administer a revolving fund, the need for a revolving fund, and other funds proposed to leverage funds made available under this program.

Rural Business Opportunity Grants

Rural Business Opportunity Grant funds provide for technical assistance, training, and planning activities that improve economic conditions in rural areas. Applicants must be located in rural areas (this includes all areas other than cities of more than 10,000 people).

Nonprofit corporations, cooperatives and public bodies are eligible. A maximum of $1.5 million per grant is authorized by the legislation. RBS is designing the program to promote sustainable economic development in rural communities with exceptional needs.

These grant programs are listed here because you may live in an area where a community organization or local government is eligible for these types of funding. There are two programs listed that follow:

Program Name: **Rural Business Opportunity Grant Program**

Web Address: http://www.rurdev.usda.gov/rbs/busp/bpdir.htm

Office\Agency: US Department of Agriculture Rural Business-Cooperative Service Business Programs Specialty Lenders Division

Address: Room 6867 - South, Stop 1521, 1400 Independence Ave., S.W., Washington, DC 20250-1521

Program Contact: Donald E. Scruggs, Division Director or Wayne Stansberry, Loan Specialist

Phone: (202) 720-1400   (202) 720-6819

E-Mail: wstansbe@rus.usda.gov

Eligible Applicants: Public bodies, non-profits, Indian Tribes, and cooperatives with members that are primarily rural residents.

Type of Assistance: Provide technical assistance for rural business economic planning for rural communities or training for rural entrepreneurs or economic development officials.

Application Process: USDA Rural Development programs are administered through the State Office in each State. All applications must be submitted through the appropriate State Office.

Target Population: Areas outside the boundaries of a city of 50,000 or more and its immediate adjacent urbanized area.

Types of Services Provided to Target Population by Grantees\Recipients:

Loans and loan guarantees

Business Training & Technical Assistance

Grant assistance for economic development in the form of technical assistance and training.

Available Funding: 1999 $500,000

Program Name: **Rural Business Enterprise Grant Program**

Web Address: http://www.rurdev.usda.gov/rbs/busp/bpdir.htm

Office\Agency: US Department of Agriculture Rural Business-Cooperative Service Business Programs Specialty Lenders Division

Address: Room 6867-South, MC 1521, 1400 Independence Ave., S.W. Washington, DC 20250-1521

Program Contact: Donald E. Scruggs, Division Director Carole Boyko, Loan Specialist Phone (202) 720-1400 or (202) 720-0661

E-Mail: cboyko@rurdev.usda.gov

Eligible Applicants: Public bodies, private nonprofits, and Indian Tribes.

Type of Assistance: Establish revolving loan program to provide loans for working capital, equipment, real estate; technical assistance and training to adult students; construct, modernize, or repair buildings; purchase and develop land; and refinancing.

Application Process: USDA Rural Development programs are administered through the State Office in each State. All applications must be submitted through the appropriate State Office.

Target Population: Areas outside the boundaries of a city of 50,000 or more and its immediately adjacent urbanized area.

Types of Services Provided to Target Population by Grantees\Recipients:

Loans and loan guarantees

Business Training & Technical Assistance

Grant assistance for small emerging business development

Available Funding: Fiscal Year 1999; $37.193 Million

Business and Industry Direct Loans

The Business and Industry (B&I) Direct Loan Program provides loans to public entities and private parties who cannot obtain credit from other sources. Loans to private parties can be made for improving, developing, or financing business and industry, creating jobs, and improving the economic and environmental climate in rural communities.

This type of assistance is available in rural areas (this includes all areas other than cities or unincorporated areas of more than 50,000 people and their immediately adjacent urban or urbanizing areas).

Eligible applicants include any legally organized entity, including cooperatives, corporations, partnerships, trusts or other profit or nonprofit entities, Indian tribes or Federally recognized tribal groups, municipalities, counties, any other political subdivision of a State, or individuals. Loans are available to those who cannot obtain credit elsewhere and for public bodies. The maximum aggregate B&I Direct Loan amount to any one borrower is $10 million.

Program Name: **Business and Industry Direct Loan Program**
Web Address: http://www.rurdev.usda.gov/rbs/busp/bpdir.htm
Office\Agency: US Department of Agriculture Rural Business-Cooperative Service Business Programs Processing Division
Address: Room 5050 - South 1400 Independence Ave., S.W. Washington, DC 20250-3200
Program Contact: Dwight Cannon, Division Director
Phone #: (202) 690-4100
E-Mail: dcarmon@rurdev.usda.gov
Eligible Applicants: Most legal entities engaged in rural business and industry.
Type of Assistance: For real estate, buildings, equipment, supplies, working capital, and some debt refinancing.
Application Process: USDA Rural Development programs are administered through the State Office in each State. All applications must be submitted through the appropriate State Office.
Target Population: Areas outside the boundaries of a city of 50,000 or more and its immediately adjacent urbanized area.
Types of Services Provided to Target Population by Grantees\Recipients:
Loans only, not loan guarantees
Business Training & Technical Assistance
Available Funding: Fiscal Year 1999; $50 Million

Business and Industry Guaranteed Loans

The Business and Industry (B&I) Guaranteed Loan Program helps create jobs and stimulates rural economies by providing financial backing for rural businesses. This program provides guarantees up to 90 percent of a loan made by a commercial lender. Loan proceeds may be used for working capital, machinery and equipment, buildings and real estate, and certain types of debt refinancing.

The primary purpose is to create and maintain employment and improve the economic climate in rural communities. This is achieved by expanding the lending capability of private lenders in rural areas, helping them make and service quality loans that provide lasting community benefits. This program represents a true private- public partnership.

B&I loan guarantees can be extended to loans made by recognized commercial lenders or other authorized lenders in rural areas (this includes all areas other than cities or unincorporated areas of more than 50,000 people and their immediately adjacent urban or urbanizing areas).

Generally, recognized lenders include Federal or State chartered banks, credit unions, insurance companies, savings and loan associations, Farm Credit Banks or other Farm Credit System institutions with direct lending authority, a mortgage company that is part of a bank holding company, and the National Rural Utilities Finance Corporation.

Assistance under the B&I Guaranteed Loan Program is available to virtually any legally organized entity, including a cooperative, corporation, partnership, trust or other profit or nonprofit entity, Indian tribe or Federally recognized tribal group, municipality, county, or other political subdivision of a State.

Program Web Address: http://www.rurdev.usda.gov/rbs/busp/bpdir.htm

Office\Agency: US Department of Agriculture Rural Business-Cooperative Service Business Programs Processing Division

Address: Room 5050 - South 1400 Independence Ave., S.W. Washington, DC 20250-3200

Program Contact: Dwight Carmon, Division Director

Phone #: (202) 690-4100

E-Mail: dcarmon@rurdev.usda.gov

Eligible Applicants: Most legal entities engaged in rural business and industry.

Type of Assistance: For real estate, buildings, equipment, supplies, working capital, and some debt refinancing.

Application Process: USDA Rural Development programs are administered through the State Office in each State. All applications must be submitted through the, appropriate State Office.

Target Population: Areas outside the boundaries of a city of 50,000 or more and its~ immediately adjacent urbanized area.

Types of Services Provided to Target Population by Grantees\Recipients:

Loans and loan guarantees
Business Training/ Technical Assistance
Available Funding: Fiscal Year 1999; $1 billion

Appendix V Funding for International Arts/Crafts Projects

Federal sources for artists and craft persons seeking to work or study abroad are the National Endowment for the Arts and the United States Information Agency (USIA). Both government agencies sponsor American artistic expression in other countries.

In addition to their funding programs, the Arts Endowment and USIA have become important resources for information and contacts abroad because of the wealth of knowledge they each possess about international arts and crafts activities.

Other federal agencies may also be able to provide assistance. For example, the Smithsonian Institution has a separate Office of International Relations that has, in the past, conducted artistic and cultural exchanges. The Department of Housing and Urban Development may also serve as an resource for referrals for architects and design artists.

The best starting place may be in your own neighborhood. Contact state and local arts agencies because many agencies work internationally through *Sister Cities International* or *Partners of the Americas*. Approximately half of state arts agencies support international activities.

International Partnerships Office

The International Partnerships Office of the National Endowment of the Arts help increase worldwide recognition of the arts of the U.S.. This office helps American artists and arts organizations develop international ties that strengthen the many art forms of the United State.

The International Partnerships Office brings the benefits of international exchange to arts organizations, artists, and audiences nationwide through its collaborative initiative with other funders.

For more information contact:
International Partnerships Office
Room 726
The Nancy Hanks Center
1100 Pennsylvania Avenue NW
Washington, DC 20506-0001
(202) 682-5249
(202) 682-5602 fax

The Fund for U.S. Artists at International Festivals & Exhibitions

Established to ensure that the excellence, diversity and vitality of the arts in the United States are represented at international performing and visual arts events around the world. Contact:

Arts International
809 United Nations Plaza
New York, NY 10017
Tel: 212/984-5370
Fax: 212/984-5574
Email: artsinternational@iie.org
Web site: http://iserver.iie.org/ai/

The US/Japan Creative Artists' Program

Each year leading contemporary and traditional artists from the United States spend six months in Japan as part of the United States/Japan Creative Artists' Program. They go as seekers and as living liaisons to the traditional and contemporary cultural life of Japan. The outlook they bring home provides an opportunity to promote cultural understanding between the United States and Japan.

This program provides funds for up to five artists to complete the residency in Japan. Artists are free to live anywhere in the country to pursue activities of greatest relevance to their creative process. While artists will be predominantly on their own upon their arrival in Tokyo, International House of Japan provides in-depth orientation materials, expert advice and professional contacts, as well as logistical support during the residency period.

The Japan-US Friendship Commission works cooperatively with the National Endowment for the Arts to sponsor this program.

Grant Award:

• a monthly stipend of 400,000 yen for living expenses, 100,000 yen a month as a housing supplement, and up to 100,000 yen a month for professional support services.

• up to $6,000 for round-trip transportation for the artist, domestic partner and / or unmarried children (up to age 18), and a baggage/storage allowance

• a stipend for pre-departure Japanese language study in the United States.

Contact:
Japan-United States Friendship Commission
1120 Vermont Avenue, NW, Suite 925
Washington, DC 20005
Tel: (202) 418-9800
Fax: (202) 418-9802
Web site: http://www.jusfc.gov/commissn/commissn.html

United States Information Agency

The USIA is an independent foreign affairs agency within the U.S. Government. USIA's educational and cultural activities are conducted to advance its mission of promoting mutual understanding between the United States and other nations.

For artists and craft persons, your major point of contact at USIA will be the Bureau of Educational and Cultural Affairs, which oversees numerous programs and services for arts and cultural exchange.

Bureau of Educational and Cultural Affairs
United States Information Agency
301 4th Street SW
Washington, DC 20547
(202) 619-4779
(202) 619-6315 fax

Appendix VI Directory of Arts Agencies

Local arts agencies vary in function according to the community and resources. Arts agencies offer the artist and craft person several types of programs and services. They often produce arts programs in various disciplines. LAA's support arts education through classes for children and adults, artist-in-school residencies, curriculum development, cultural trips and tours, and teacher and artist training.

Some LAA's provide grant funds raised from united arts fundraising to support community crafts, public art, artists and arts organization. They may also manage theaters, galleries, arts centers, artist studios, office space for community arts organizations, retail shops, and community centers.

Other services to artists, craft people and arts organizations include producing newsletters, grants information, arts management workshops, events and promotion calendars, artist directories, and slide banks; offering consultations and referrals.

Following is a list of state and jurisdictional arts agencies and regional arts organizations working with arts endowments utilizing funds mandated by the Congress as well as funds from state governments and other sources. Contact these state agencies to learn of their programs and to learn about local arts agencies near you. You can also find arts agencies listed in your Yellow Pages under the subject titles "Arts Agencies" or "Arts Councils" or Commission for the Arts."

National arts agencies

National Assembly of State Arts Agencies
1029 Vermont Avenue, NW, 2nd Floor
Washington, DC 20005
202/347-6352
nasaa@nasaa-arts.org

Americans for the Arts
1000 Vermont Avenue, N.W., 12th Floor
Washington, DC 20005
Ph: 202/371-2830

Statewide Assemblies of Arts Agencies

These state organizations can put you in touch with local arts agencies in your community for grant funding and other forms of assistance.

Alabama Federation for the Arts
c/o The Arts Council
700 Monroe Street
Huntsville, AL 35801
phone: (205) 533-6565

Alabama State Council on the Arts
One Dexter Avenue
Montgomery, AL 36130
Ph: 334/242-4076

Alliance of Alaskan Local Arts
Agencies
c/o Ketchican Area Arts & Humanities
338 Main Street
Ketchikan, AK 99901-
phone: (907) 225-2211

Alaska State Council on the Arts
411 West 4th Avenue, Suite 1E
Anchorage, AK 99501-2343
907/269-6610
asca@alaska.net

American Samoa Council on Arts,
Culture & Humanities
P.O. Box 1540
Pago Pago, American Samoa 96799
Ph: 011-684-633-4347

Arizona Commission on the Arts
417 West Roosevelt
Phoenix, AZ 85003
Ph: 602/255-5882
general@ArizonaArts.org

Arkansas Arts Council
1500 Tower Building
323 Center Street
Little Rock, AR 72201
Ph: 501/324-9766
info@dah.state.ar.us

California Assembly of Local Arts
Agencies
693 Sutter Street, Third Floor
San Francisco, CA 94102
Ph: (415) 441-5900
eMail: calaa@calaa.net

California Arts Council
1300 I Street, #930
Sacramento, CA 95814
Ph: 916/322-6555
cac@cwo.com

Colorado Arts Consortium
1940 South Locust Street
Denver, CO 80224
phone: (303) 722-8689
fax: (303) 733-0733
cac@artstozoo.org

Colorado Council on the Arts
750 Pennsylvania Street
Denver, CO 80203-3699
Ph: 303/894-2617
coloarts@artswire.org

Connecticut Statewide Assembly
c/o Middletown Comm on Arts
P.O. Box 1300
Middletown, CT 06457
phone: (203) 344-3520

Connecticut Commission on the Arts
Gold Building 755 Main Street
Hartford, CT 06103
Ph: 860-566-4770

Delaware Division of the Arts
State Office Building
820 North French Street
Wilmington, DE 19801
Ph: 302/577-3540

Cultural Alliance of Greater
Washington
1436 U Street, NW Suite 103
Washington, DC 20009-3997
phone: (202) 638-2406
Ph: (202) 638-3388
staff@cultural-alliance.org

District of Columbia Commission on
the Arts & Humanities
410 8th Street, NW
Washington, DC 20004
Ph: 202/724-5613
carrien@tmn.com

Florida Association of Local Arts
Agencies
2725 Judge Fran Jameson Way
Building C2
Viera, FL 32940-6605
phone: (407) 690-6817
fax: (407) 690-6818

Division of Cultural Affairs
Florida Department of State
The Capitol
Tallahassee, FL 32399-0250
Ph: 904/487-2980

Georgia Assembly of Community Arts
Agencies
P.O.Box 318
Conyers, GA 30207
phone: (770) 483-4841
fax: (770) 760-0475
gasue@aol.com

Georgia Council for the Arts
530 Means Street, NW, Suite 115
Atlanta, GA 30318-5730
Ph: 404/651-7920
gca@gwins.campus.mci.net

Guam Council on the Arts &
Humanities
Office of the Governor
P.O. Box 2950
Agana, GU 96910
Ph: 011-671-647-2242
arts@ns.gov.nu

State Foundation on Culture & the Arts
44 Merchant Street
Honolulu, HI 96813
Ph: 808/586-0300
sfca@sfca.state.hi.us

Arts in Rural Towns Network of Idaho
c/o Idaho Arts Commission
304 West State Street
Boise, ID 83720
phone: (208) 334-2807
fax: (208) 334-2488

Idaho Commission on the Arts
P.O. Box 83720
Boise, ID 83720-0008
Ph: 208/334-2119
idarts@artswire.org

Assembly of Illinois Community Arts
Organizations
724 N Bruns Ln #B
Springfield, IL 62702
phone: (217) 698-4301

Illinois Arts Council
State of Illinois Center
100 West Randolph, Suite 10-500
Chicago, IL 60601
Ph: 312/814-6750
ilarts@artswire.org

Indiana Assembly of Local Arts
Agencies
4907 North Kenwood Avenue
Indianapolis, IN 46208-
phone: (317) 259-7696
fax: (317) 638-3540

Indiana Arts Commission
402 West Washington Street, #072
Indianapolis, IN 46204-2741
Ph: 317/232-1268
inarts@aol.com

Iowa Assembly of Local Arts Agencies
40690 Dogwood Road
Carson, IA 51525-4154
phone: (712) 484-2218
cnilsson@netins.net

Iowa Arts Council
600 East Locust
State Capitol Complex
Des Moines, IA 50319
Ph: 515/281-4451

Association of Community Arts
Agencies of Kansas
P.O. Box 1363
Salina, KS 67402-1363
phone: (913) 825-2700
fax: (913) 823-1992

Kansas Arts Commission
Jayhawk Tower
700 Jackson, Suite 1004
Topeka, KS 66603
Ph: 785/296-3335

Arts Kentucky
624 W Main St
Louisville KY 40202
phone: 502-561-0701
www.artsky.org
connect@artsky.org

Kentucky Arts Council
31 Fountain Place
Frankfort, KY 40601
Ph: 502/564-3757

Louisiana Partnership for the Arts
P.O. Box 205
Shreveport, LA 71162-0205
phone: (504) 646-4375
fax: (504) 646-4231

Division of the Arts
Louisiana Department of Culture,
Recreation, & Tourism
1051 North 3rd Street
P.O. Box 44247
Baton Rouge, LA 70804
Ph: 504/342-8180
arts@crt.state.la.us

Maine Arts Sponsors Association
P.O. Box 2352
Augusta, ME 04338-
phone: (207) 626-3277
fax: (207) 626-3277
masa@mint.net

Maine Arts Commission
55 Capitol Street
State House Station 25
Augusta, ME 04333
Ph: 207/287-2724

Community Arts Alliance of Maryland
135 East Main Street
Elkton, MD 21921-
phone: (410) 392-5740
fax: (410) 392-5740

Maryland State Arts Council
601 North Howard Street, 1st Floor
Baltimore, MD 21201
Ph: 410/333-8232
msac@digex.net

M'Assembly
c/o Dedham Cultural Council
15 Worthington Street
Dedham, MA 02026-
phone: (617) 329-5691
fax: (617) 357-5369
ivalsk@aol.com

Massachusetts Cultural Council
120 Boylston Street, 2nd Floor
Boston, MA 02116-4600
617/727-3668
TT: 617/338-9153

Michigan Association of Community
Arts Agencies
32330 West 12 Mile Rd Suite 10
Farmington Hills, MI 48334
phone: (248) 848-9911

Michigan Council for Arts and Cultural
Affairs
525 West Ottawa Street
P.O. Box 30705
Lansing, MI 48909-8205
Ph: 517/241-4011

Arts Midwest
528 Hennepin Avenue Suite 310
Minneapolis, MN 55403-1899
phone: (612) 341-0755

Minnesota State Arts Board
Park Square Court
400 Sibley Street, Suite 200
St. Paul, MN 55101-1949
Ph: 612/215-1600
msab@tc.umn.edu

Arts Alliance of Jackson & Hinds
County
P.O. Box 17
255 E Pascagoula
Jackson, MS 39205
phone: (601) 960-1557

Mississippi Arts Commission
239 North Lamar Street, Second Floor
Jackson, MS 39201
Ph: 601/359-6030

Missouri Association of Community
Arts Agencies
c/o Office of Cultural Affairs
P.O. Box N
Columbia, MO 65205
phone: (573) 874-7519

Missouri State Council on the Arts
Wainwright Office Complex
111 North Seventh Street, Suite 105
St. Louis, MO 63101
314/340-6845
mac@state.mt.us

Montana Arts Council
316 North Park Avenue
Room 252
Helena, MT 59620
406/444-6430
TT/Relay: 1-800-833-8503
mac@state.mt.us

Nebraska Arts Council
The Joslyn Castle Carriage House
3838 Davenport Street
Omaha, NE 68131-2329
Ph: 402/595-2122
nacart@synergy.net

Nevada Statewide Arts Assembly
5 South Main Street
Yerington, NV 89447
phone: (702) 463-3066

Nevada Arts Council
Capitol Complex
602 North Curry Street
Carson City, NV 89710
Ph: 702/687-6680

New Hampshire Assembly
c/o Federated Arts
P.O. Box 36
Manchester, NH 03105
phone: (603) 688-6186

New Hampshire State Council on the
Arts
Phenix Hall
40 North Main Street
Concord, NH 03301
Ph: 603/271-2789

Camden County Cultural and Heritage
Commission
250 South Park Dr & Shady Lane
Haddon Township, NJ 08108
phone: (609) 858-0040
fax: (609) 869-3548

New Jersey State Council on the Arts
20 West State Street, # 306
Trenton, NJ 08625-0306
Ph: 609/292-6130

Arts New Mexico
P.O. Box 4234
Santa Fe, NM 87502-4234
phone: (505) 984-2787
fax: (505) 986-8134

New Mexico Arts Division
228 East Palace Avenue
Santa Fe, NM 87501
Ph: 505/827-6490
artadmin@oca.state.nm.us

Alliance of New York State Arts
Organizations
P.O. Box 96
245 Love Lane
Mattituck, NY 11952-1101
phone: (516) 298-1234
fax: (516) 298-1101
anysac@artswire.org

New York State Council on the Arts
915 Broadway
New York, NY 10010
Ph: 212/387-7000
nysca@artswire.org

Arts North Carolina
P.O. Box 1366
Raleigh, NC 27602-
phone: (919) 834-1411
fax: (919) 828-3056
artsnc@aol.com

North Carolina Arts Council
Department of Cultural Resources
Raleigh, NC 27601-2807
Ph: 919/733-2821

North Dakota Arts Alliance
1514 Cheyenne Street
West Fargo, ND 58708
phone: (701) 241-8667

North Dakota Council on the Arts
418 East Broadway Ave., Suite 70
Bismarck, ND 58501-4086
701/328-3954
thompson@pioneer.state.nd.us

Alliance of Ohio Community Arts
Agencies
77 South High Street
Vern Riffe Center, 2nd Floor
Columbus, OH 43215-
phone: (614) 241-5327
fax: (614) 241-5329

Ohio Arts Council
727 East Main Street
Columbus, OH 43205
Ph: 614/466-2613
bfisher@mail.oac.ohio.gov

Assembly of Community Arts Councils
of Oklahoma
428 West California Suite 200
Oklahoma City, OK 73102-
phone: (405) 236-1446
fax: (405) 235-1327
acaco@aol.com

Oklahoma Arts Council
P.O. Box 52001-2001
Oklahoma City, OK 73152-2001
Ph: 405/521-2931
okarts@tmn.com

Oregon Advocates for the Arts
707 - 13th Street, S.E., #275
Salem, OR 97301-
phone: (503) 588-2787
fax: (503) 362-6393

Oregon Arts Commission
775 Summer Street, NE
Salem, OR 97310
Ph: 503/986-0082
oregon.artscomm@State.OR.US

Pennsylvania Arts Alliance
1500 North Second Street
Second Floor
Harrisburg, PA 17102
phone: (717) 234-0587
fax: (717) 234-1501

Commonwealth of Pennsylvania
Council on the Arts
Finance Building, Room 216A
Harrisburg, PA 17120
Ph: 717/787-6883

Institute of Puerto Rican Culture
Cultural Centers Program
P.O.Box 902-4184
San Juan, PR 00902-4184
phone: (809) 725-1986
fax: (787) 724-4305

Institute of Puerto Rican Culture
Apartado Postal 4184
San Juan, PR 00902-4184
Ph: 809/723-2115

Rhode Island Consortium of Local Arts
Agencies
c/o RI St Council on the Arts
95 Cedar Street, Ste 103
Providence, RI 02903-
phone: (401) 277-3880

Rhode Island State Council on the Arts
95 Cedar Street, Suite 103
Providence, RI 02903
Ph: 401/277-3880
ride0600@ride.ri.net

South Carolina Arts Alliance
858 Eden Terrace
Rock Hill, SC 29730-
phone: (803) 324-8296
fax: (803) 324-4860
bjpSCAA@InfoAve.net

South Carolina Arts Commission
1800 Gervais Street
Columbia, SC 29201
803/734-8696
kenmay@scsn.net

South Dakotans for the Arts
P.O. BOX 472
Deadwood, SD 57732
phone: (605) 578-1783
fax: (605) 578-3789
jbsoda@blackhills.com

South Dakota Arts Council
Office of Arts
800 Governors Drive
Pierre, SD 57501-2294
Ph: 605/773-3131
sdac@stlib.state.sd.us

Tennessee Arts Commission
Citizens Plaza
401 Charlotte Avenue
Nashville, TN 37243-0780
Ph: 615/741-1701
btarleton@mail.state.tn.us

Texas Alliance for Education and the
Arts
3939 Beecave Road
Suite 203
Austin, TX 78746
phone: (512) 327-5282
fax: (512) 327-1993

Texas Commission on the Arts
P.O. Box 13406
Austin, TX 78711-3406
Ph: 512/463-5535
front.desk@arts.state.tx.us

Utah Community Arts Council Network
1163 Windsor Street
Salt Lake City, UT 84105

Utah Arts Council
617 East South Temple Street
Salt Lake City, UT 84102
Ph: 801/533-5895
dadamson@email.st.ut.us

Vermont Arts Council
136 State Street
Montpelier, VT 05633-6001
Ph: 802/828-3291
info@arts.vca.state.vt.us

Community Arts Agencies of Virginia
Arlington City Cultural Affairs
2100 Clarendon Blvd
Arlington, VA 22201-
phone: (703) 358-3315
fax: (703) 358-3328

Virginia Commission for the Arts
223 Governor Street
Richmond, VA 23219
Ph: 804/225-3132
vacomm@artswire.org

Virgin Islands Council on the Arts
41-42 Norre Gade, 2nd Floor
P.O. Box 103
St. Thomas, VI 00802
Ph: 340/774-5984

Arts Network of Washington State
P.O. Box 1548
Olympia, WA 98507-1548
phone: (360) 705-1183
fax: (360) 705-1183
nlaaws@artswire.org

Washington State Arts Commission
234 East 8th Avenue
P.O. Box 42675
Olympia, WA 98504-2675
Ph: 360/753-3860
wsac@artswire.org

Arts & Humanities Section
West Virginia Division of Culture &
History
1900 Kanawha Blvd. East
Capitol Complex
Charleston, WV 25305-0300
Ph: 304/558-0220

Wisconsin Assembly of Local Arts
Agencies
P.O. Box 1054
Madison, WI 53701-1054
phone: (608) 255-8316
fax: (608) 256-2386
walaa@itis.com

Wisconsin Arts Board
101 East Wilson Street, 1st Floor
Madison, WI 53702
Ph: 608/266-0190

Wyoming Arts Alliance
P.O. Box 3951
University Station
Laramie, WY 82071
phone: (307) 766-5139

Wyoming Arts Council
2320 Capitol Avenue
Cheyenne, WY 82002
Ph: 307/777-7742
wyoarts@artswire.org

Appendix VII Public Art/Craft Programs

Federal public art program

The U.S. government General Services Administration maintains the Art-in-Architecture Program to provide an opportunity to include art in or around government buildings. To learn when and where the GSA solicits proposals for such projects, contact the GSA office in your local area. For more general information on this program contact Susan Harrison by email at: susan.harrison@gsa.gov.

Other national programs:
Art in the Public Interest *(national organization)*
P.O. Box 68
Saxapahaw, NC 27340
Ph: 336-376-8404
email: highperf@artswire.org

Arts for the Parks
PO Box 608
Jackson Hole, WY 83001
Ph: 800.553.ARTS (2787)
Web: http://www.artsfortheparks.com

The Center for Land Use Interpretation
9331 Venice Boulevard
Culver City, CA 90232
Telephone: (310) 839-5722
Web site: http://www.clui.org/

State public art programs

Several states have either a "Percent for Art" or "Art in Public Places" program, which allocates a portion of the capital construction dollars for public buildings toward the creation and maintenance of public art. Below is a list of contacts for these public art programs which you may be able to participate in.

| Arkansas | Sally Williams | 501.324.9348 |
| Colorado | Roberta Kaserman | 303.894.2617 |

Connecticut	Linda Dente	860.566.4770
D.C.	Matt Radford	202.724.5613
Florida	Lee Modica	850.487.2980
Hawaii	Ronald Yamakawa	808.586.0304
Illinois	Mike Dunbar	217.782.9561
Iowa	Bruce Williams	515.281.4451
Louisiana	Ann Russo	225.342.8180
Maine	Paul Faria	207.287.2724
Minnesota	Mason Riddle	
	Melissa Stephens	651.215.1600
Montana	Lori Ryker	406.994.4240
Nebraska	Suzanne Wise	402.595.2122
New Hampshire	Audrey Sylvester	603.271.2789
New Jersey	Tom Moran	609.292.6130
New Mexico	Kathryn Minette	
	Carla Sanders	
	Michelle Barela	505.827.6490
North Carolina	Beverly Ayscue	919.733.2111
Ohio	Irene Finck	614.466.2613
Oregon	Leah Wiebe	503.986.0084
Rhode Island	Randy Rosenbaum	401.222.3880
South Dakota	Jocelyn Hanson	605.773.3131
Utah	Jim Glenn	801.533.4039
Vermont	Michelle Bailey	802.828.3291
Washington	Beverly Watt	
	Lorin Doyle	360.586.2423
Wisconsin	Chris Manke	608.266.9737
Wyoming	Lillian Francuz	307.777.7742

Local public art programs

The following are a few examples of community public art programs. To learn if your city or community has a public art program, contact your city's arts council which will be listed in your Yellow Pages under "Arts Councils" or "Arts Agencies". Most public art money comes from large national grants disbursed to local arts agencies.

Albuquerque, NM area
City of Albuquerque Public Art Program
PO Box 1293
Albuquerque, NM 87103
Ph: 505-768-3829
Web site: http://www.collectorsguide.com/ab/abfa04.html?

Austin TX area
Parks and Recreation Department, Cultural Affairs Division
1110 Barton Springs Road, #201
Austin, TX 78704
Ph: 512-397-1455
Web site: http://www.ci.austin.tx.us/aipp/

Cambridge MA area
Cambridge Arts Council, Public Art Program
57 Inman Street
Cambridge, MA 02139
Web site: http://www.ci.cambridge.ma.us/~CAC/publicart/
pubart.html

Dallas TX area
City of Dallas Public Art Program
Dallas Office of Cultural Affairs, Majestic Theatre
1925 Elm Street, Suite 500
Dallas, TX 75201
Ph: 214-670-3687)

Houston, TX area
Public Art Director, CACHH/PASTA
3201 Allen Parkway
Houston, TX 77019
Ph: 713/527-9330 x32
Web site: http://www.cachh.org/PASTA.html

Los Angeles area
Community Redevelopment Agency (CRA)
Percent for Art Program
354 S. Spring St, Suite 700
Los Angeles, CA 90013

City of Los Angeles Cultural Affairs Department
Public Art Program
433 S. Spring St, 10th Floor
Los Angeles, CA 900134

Social and Public Arts Resource Center (SPARC)
685 Venice Blvd.
Venice, CA 90291
Ph: (310) 822-9560

Miami FL area
Art in Public Places
111 NW 1 St, Ste 610
Miami, FL 33128
Ph: 305-375-5362
Web site: http://www.co.miami-dade.fl.us/publicart/

New York NY area
Percent for Art Program
New York City Department of Cultural Affairs
330 West 42nd Street, 14th Floor
New York, New York 10036
Ph: 212.643.7770
Web site: http://www.ci.nyc.ny.us/html/dcla/html/pahome.html

Palo Alto CA area
Palo Alto's Art in Public Places Program
c/o Gerald Brett
873 Newell Place 94303
Ph: (650) 322-6166
Web site: http://www.city.palo-alto.ca.us

Phoenix AZ area
Phoenix Arts Commission
Ph: (602) 495-0188
Web site: http://www.ci.phoenix.az.us/ARTS/artgrant.html

Portland OR area
Arts Council of Portland
Public Art Program
620 SW Main Street, Suite 420
Portland, Oregon 97205
Ph: 503-823-5111
Web site: http://www.racc.org/

Tampa FL area
Administrator, Tampa Public Art Program
600 North Ashley Drive
Tampa, Florida 33611
Web site: http://www.ci.tampa.fl.us/

Seattle WA area
Call-To-Artists, King County Public Art Program
506 Second Avenue, Ste 200
Seattle, WA 98104-2307
Ph: 206-296-8676
Web site: http://www.metrokc.gov/exec/culture/publicart/index.htm

Also see the chapter on Internet resources for online web links to public art programs.

Appendix VIII Craft Artist in Residency Programs

Craft schools with residency, work/study or scholarship programs

There are many artist in residency programs for fine arts. However, not all programs will be suitable for craft persons. The following schools accept craft artists in residency or on scholarship.

Appalachian Center for Crafts
1560 Craft Center Drive
Smithville, TN 37166
Phone: (931) 372-3051 (in Cookeville)
(615) 597-6801 (outside of Cookeville)
Web site: http://plato.ess.tntech.edu/acc/Default.htm

Arrowmont School of Arts and Crafts
556 Parkway
Gatlinburg, TN 37738
Phone: 865-436-5860   Fax: 865-430-4101
Web site: http://www.arrowmont.org/

Brookfield Craft Center
P.O. Box 122
Brookfield, CT 06804-0122
phone: 203-775-4526   fax: 203-740-7815
Web site: http://www.craftweb.com/org/brookfld/brookfld.shtml

Coupeville Arts Center
15 NW Birch St
Coupeville WA
Ph: 360-678-3396   Fax: 360-678-7420
Web site: http://www.coupevillearts.org/index.html

Frog Hollow - Vermont State Craft Center
One Mill Street
Middlebury, Vermont
Ph: 802.388.3177
Web site: http://www.froghollow.org
Community Services Education

Glendale Community College
1122 East Garfield Avenue
Glendale, California 91205
Ph: (818) 548-0864, ext.5015
Fax (818) 548-6216
Web site: http://www.glendale.cc.ca.us/cse/index.htm

Great Divide Weaving School
PO Box 100
Divide, CO 80814
Ph: (719) 687~3249
Email: gad@chaffee.net
Web site: http://www.vtinet.com/tapestry/

Guilford Handcraft Center
411 Church St
Guildord, CT 06437
Phone: 203-453-5947   fax: 203-453-6237
Web site: http://pages.cthome.net/guilfordhandcrftctr/

Haystack Mountain School of Crafts
PO Box 518
Deer Isle, Maine 04627
Telephone: (207) 348-2306   Fax: (207) 348-2307
Web site: http://www.haystack-mtn.org

John C. Campbell Folk School
One Folk School Road
Brasstown, NC 28902
Phone: 1-800-365-5724 or 828-837-2775
Fax - 828-837-8637
Web site: http://www.folkschool.com/

Mendocino Art Center
45200 Little Lake Street
PO Box 765
Mendocino CA, 95460 USA
Email mendoart@mcn.org
Phone 800-653-3328 or 707-937-5818
Fax 707-937-1764
Web site: http://www.mendocinoartcenter.org/

Oregon School of Arts & Crafts
8245 SW Barnes Rd.
Portland, OR 97225
Ph: 503-297-5544
Web site: http://www.ohwy.com/or/o/orschart.htm

Peninsula Art School
3906 Cty. Rd. F
PO Box 304
Fish Creek, WI 54212-0304
Ph: 920-868-3455
Web site: http://www.peninsulaartschool.com

Penland School of Crafts
P.O. Box 37
Penland, NC 28765
Ph: 828-765-2359   Fax 828-765-7389
Email: office@penland.org
Web site: http://www.penland.org/

Peters Valley Craft Center
19 Kuhn Rd.
Layton, NJ 07851
Ph: 973 948-5200
Fax 973 948-0011
Web site: http://www.pvcrafts.org/

Michael Wilson, Sagamore
Kiwassa Rd
Saranac Lake, NY 12983
Ph: 315-354-5311 or 518-891-1718
Web site: http://www.sagamore.org/

Worcester Center for Crafts
25 Sagamore Road
Worcester, MA 01605
Ph: (508) 753-8183   Fax: (508) 797-5626
Web site: http://www.craftcenter.worcester.org/school/

Organizations

Alliance of Artists' Communities is a national service organization that supports the field of artists' communities and residency programs. It does this by encouraging collaboration among members of the field on field issues, raising the visibility of artists' communities, promoting philanthropy in the field, and generally encouraging programs that support the creation of art. Currently made up of about 80 leading, nonprofit artists' communities and 65 individuals.

Alliance of Artists Communities
2311 East Burnside
Portland, Oregon 97214 U.S.A.
Telephone: (503) 797-6988
Fax: (503) 797-9560
Email: aac@teleport.com

In addition to the listings here, see the chapter on using the Internet for online links to directories of artist in residencies programs.

Appendix IX The Foundation Center Cooperating Collections

The Foundation Center

The Foundation Center is an independent nonprofit information clearinghouse established in 1956. The Center's mission is to foster public understanding of the foundation field by collecting, organizing, analyzing, and disseminating information on foundations, corporate giving, and related subjects. The audiences that call on the Center's resources include grantseekers, grantmakers, researchers, policymakers, the media, and the general public.

The Foundation Center operates libraries at five central locations and through a network of cooperating collections around the U.S.. Center libraries provide access to materials on philanthropy and are open to the public free of charge. Professional reference librarians are on hand to show library users how to research funding information using Center publications and other materials and resources.

Here are the locations of the central locations:

The Foundation Center
79 Fifth Avenue
New York, NY 10003
Tel: (212) 620-4230   Fax: (212) 691-1828
Hours: Monday and Wednesday 10:00 a.m. - 8:00 p.m.
Tuesday, Thursday, and Friday 10:00 a.m. - 5:00 p.m.

The Foundation Center
1001 Connecticut Avenue at K Street Suite #938
Washington, D.C. 20036
Tel: (202) 331-1400   Fax: (202) 331-1739
Hours: Monday 10:00 a.m. - 7:00 p.m.
Tuesday - Friday 10:00 a.m. - 5:00 p.m.

The Foundation Center
50 Hurt Plaza, Suite 150
Atlanta, GA 30303
Tel: (404) 880-0094   Fax: (404) 880-0097
Hours: Monday - Friday 10:00 a.m. - 5:00 p.m.

The Foundation Center
1422 Euclid Avenue Suite 1356
Cleveland, OH 44115-2001
Tel: (216) 861-1933   Fax: (216) 861-1936
Hours: Monday - Friday 9:30 a.m. - 4:30 p.m.
Open until 8:00 p.m. the first Monday of each month

The Foundation Center
312 Sutter Street
San Francisco, CA 94108-4314
Tel: (415) 397-0902   Fax: (415) 397-7670
Hours: Monday -Friday 10:00 a.m. - 5:00 p.m.
Wednesday 10:00 a.m. - 8:00 p.m.

The Foundation Center's Database is available for sale on a CD-ROM. The expense, around $1,000 makes it a tool for nonprofit organizations more than individuals. However, the database can be searched for free at any of the cooperating collections listed below. The program to ask for is called *FC Search*. *FC Search* is a fully searchable fundraising database that catalogs close to 50,000 U.S. foundations and corporate givers.

Center staff also provide custom services ranging from photocopying to telephone reference to database searching. Staff consult with customers to identify their needs and determine the most cost-effective and timely way of obtaining the information they require.

Center staff can perform database searches for grantmakers to assess philanthropic giving in a specific region or state, map funding patterns, or locate grantmakers active in a particular field. There is a charge for this service based on the data requested and staff time required. You can learn to use the *FC Search* program easily, so it would be worth your while to spend a little time studying the program rather than spend money on search fees.

When people wish to conduct their own research, they often call or visit the Center for advice on how to proceed. Center staff can recommend the best online and other sources of regional and national information, offering assistance in performing a variety of searches.

Cooperating Collections are free funding information centers in libraries, community foundations, and other nonprofit resource centers that provide a core collection of Foundation Center publications and a variety of supplementary materials and services in areas useful to grantseekers. See the bibliography of this book for a list of Foundation

Center directories.

It is recommended that you call the collection in advance of a visit to determine hours and availability of *FC Search*. Participants in the Foundation Center's Cooperating Collections network are libraries or nonprofit information centers that provide fundraising information and other funding-related technical assistance in their communities.

Cooperating Collections agree to provide free public access to a basic collection of Foundation Center publications during a regular schedule of hours, offering free funding research guidance to all visitors. Many also provide a variety of services for local nonprofit organizations, using staff or volunteers to prepare special materials, organize workshops, or conduct orientations.

Here is a listing of The Foundation Center's Cooperating Collections.

Alabama
BIRMINGHAM PUBLIC LIBRARY
Government Documents
2100 Park Place
Birmingham 35203
(205) 226-3620

HUNTSVILLE PUBLIC LIBRARY
915 Monroe St.
Huntsville 35801
(256) 532-5940
UNIVERSITY OF SOUTH
ALABAMA
Library Building
Mobile 36688
(334) 460-7025

AUBURN UNIVERSITY AT
MONTGOMERY LIBRARY
7300 University Drive
Montgomery 36124-4023
(334) 244-3200

Alaska
UNIVERSITY OF ALASKA AT
ANCHORAGE LIBRARY
3211 Providence Drive
Anchorage 99508
(907) 786-1846

JUNEAU PUBLIC LIBRARY
Reference
292 Marine Way
Juneau 99801
(907) 586-5267

Arizona
FLAGSTAFF CITY-COCONINO
COUNTY PUBLIC LIBRARY
300 West Aspen Ave.
Flagstaff AZ 86001
(520) 779-7670

PHOENIX PUBLIC LIBRARY
Information Services Dept.
1221 N. Central
Phoenix 85004
(602) 262-4636

TUCSON-PIMA LIBRARY
101 N. Stone Ave.
Tucson 87501
(520) 791-4010

Arkansas
WESTARK COMMUNITY
COLLEGE - BORHAM LIBRARY
5210 Grand Avenue
Ft. Smith 72913
(501) 788-7200

CENTRAL ARKANSAS LIBRARY
SYSTEM
100 Rock St.
Little Rock 72201
(501) 918-3000

PINE BLUFF-JEFFERSON
COUNTY LIBRARY SYSTEM
200 E. Eighth
Pine Bluff 71601
870) 534-2159

California
HUMBOLDT AREA FOUNDATION
P.O. Box 99
Bayside 95524
(707) 442-2993

VENTURA COUNTY
COMMUNITY FOUNDATION
Resource Center for Nonprofit
Organizations
1317 Del Norte Road, Suite 150
Camarillo 93010-8504
(805) 988-0196

FRESNO REGIONAL
FOUNDATION
Nonprofit Advancement Center
1999 Tuolumne Street, Suite 650
Fresno 93720
(559) 498-3929

CENTER FOR NONPROFIT
MANAGEMENT IN SOUTHERN
CALIFORNIA
Nonprofit Resource Library
315 West 9th Street, Suite 1100
Los Angeles 90015
(213) 623-7080

FLINTRIDGE FOUNDATION
Philanthropy Resource Library
1040 Lincoln Avenue, Suite 100
Pasadena 91103
(626) 449-0839

GRANT & RESOURCE CENTER
OF NORTHERN CALIFORNIA
Building C, Suite A
2280 Benton Dr.
Redding 96003
(530) 244-1219

LOS ANGELES PUBLIC LIBRARY
West Valley Regional Branch
Library
19036 Van Owen St.
Reseda 91335
(818) 345-4393

RIVERSIDE PUBLIC LIBRARY
3581 Mission Inn Ave.
Riverside 92501
(909) 782-5202

NONPROFIT RESOURCE
CENTER
Sacramento Public Library
828 I Street, 2nd Floor
Sacramento 95814
(916) 264-2772

SAN DIEGO FOUNDATION
Funding Information Center
1420 Kettner Boulevard, Suite 500
San Diego 92101
(619) 239-8815

SAN FRANCISCO FIELD OFFICE
AND LIBRARY
312 Sutter Street, Rm. 312
San Francisco 94108
(415) 397-0902

NONPROFIT DEVELOPMENT
CENTER
Library
1922 The Alameda, Suite 212
San Jose 95126
(408) 248-9505

PENINSULA COMMUNITY
FOUNDATION
Peninsula Nonprofit Center
1700 S. El Camino Real, #300
San Mateo 94402-3049
(650) 358-9392

LOS ANGELES PUBLIC LIBRARY
San Pedro Regional Branch
9131 S. Gaffey St.
San Pedro 90731
(310) 548-7779

VOLUNTEER CENTER OF
ORANGE COUNTY
Nonprofit Management Assistance
Center
1901 East 4th Street, Suite 100
Santa Ana 92705
(714) 953-5757

SANTA BARBARA PUBLIC
LIBRARY
40 E. Anapamu St.
Santa Barbara 93101-1019
(805) 564-5633

SANTA MONICA PUBLIC
LIBRARY
1343 Sixth St.
Santa Monica 90401-1603
(310) 458-8600

SONOMA COUNTY LIBRARY
3rd & E Streets
Santa Rosa 95404
(707) 545-0831

SEASIDE BRANCH LIBRARY
550 Harcourt St.
Seaside 93955
(831) 899-8131

SONORA AREA FOUNDATION
20100 Cedar Road, N.
Sonora 95370
(209) 533-2596

Colorado
EL POMAR NONPROFIT
RESOURCE LIBRARY
1661 Mesa Ave.
Colorado Springs 80906
(719) 577-7000

DENVER PUBLIC LIBRARY
General Reference
10 West 14th Avenue Parkway
Denver 80204
(303) 640-6200

Connecticut
DANBURY PUBLIC LIBRARY
170 Main St.
Danbury 06810
(203) 797-4527

GREENWICH PUBLIC LIBRARY
101 West Putnam Ave.
Greenwich 06830
(203) 622-7900

HARTFORD PUBLIC LIBRARY
500 Main St.
Hartford 06103
(860) 543-8656

NEW HAVEN FREE PUBLIC
LIBRARY
Reference Dept.
133 Elm St.
New Haven 06510-2057
(203) 946-8130

Delaware
UNIVERSITY OF DELAWARE
Hugh Morris Library
Newark 19717-5267
(302) 831-2432

District of Columbia
FOUNDATION CENTER OFFICE
AND LIBRARY
1001 Connecticut Avenue, NW
Suite 938
Washington, DC 20036
(202) 331-1400

Florida
VOLUSIA COUNTY LIBRARY
CENTER
City Island
105 E. Magnolia Ave.
Daytona Beach 32114-4484
(904) 257-6036

NOVA SOUTHEASTERN
UNIVERSITY
Einstein Library
3301 College Ave.
Fort Lauderdale 33314
(954) 262-4601INDIAN RIVER

COMMUNITY COLLEGE
Learning Resources Center
3209 Virginia Ave.
Fort Pierce 34981-5596
(561) 462-4757

JACKSONVILLE PUBLIC
LIBRARIES
Grants Resource Center
122 N. Ocean St.
Jacksonville 32202
(904) 630-2665

MIAMI-DADE PUBLIC LIBRARY
101 W. Flagler St.
Miami 33130
(305) 375-5575

ORANGE COUNTY LIBRARY
SYSTEM
Social Sciences Department
101 E. Central Blvd.
Orlando 32801
(407) 425-4694

SELBY PUBLIC LIBRARY
Reference
1331 First St.
Sarasota 34236
(941) 316-1183

TAMPA-HILLSBOROUGH
COUNTY PUBLIC LIBRARY
900 N. Ashley Drive
Tampa 33602
(813) 273-3652

COMMUNITY FDN. OF PALM
BEACH & MARTIN COUNTIES
324 Datura St., Suite 340
West Palm Beach 33401
(561) 659-6800

Georgia
ATLANTA FIELD OFFICE AND
LIBRARY
Suite 150, Grand Lobby
Hurt Building, 50 Hurt Plaza
Atlanta 30303-2914
(404) 880-0094

ATLANTA-FULTON PUBLIC
LIBRARY
Foundation Collection
1 Margaret Mitchell Square
Atlanta 30303-1089
(404) 730-1900

UNITED WAY OF CENTRAL
GEORGIA
Community Resource Center
277 Martin Luther King Jr. Blvd.,
Suite 301
Macon 31201
(912) 745-4732

SAVANNAH STATE UNIVERSITY
Asa Gordon Library
P.O. Box 20394
Savannah 31404
(912) 356-2185

THOMAS COUNTY PUBLIC
LIBRARY
201 N. Madison St.
Thomasville 31792
(912) 225-5252

Hawaii
UNIVERSITY OF HAWAII
Hamilton Library
2550 The Mall
Honolulu 96822
(808) 956-7214

HAWAII COMMUNITY
FOUNDATION FUNDING
RESOURCE LIBRARY
900 Fort St., Suite 1300
Honolulu 96813
(808) 537-6333

Idaho
BOISE PUBLIC LIBRARY
715 S. Capitol Blvd.
Boise 83702
(208) 384-4024

CALDWELL PUBLIC LIBRARY
1010 Dearborn St.
Caldwell 83605
(208) 459-3242

Illinois
DONORS FORUM OF CHICAGO
208 South LaSalle, Suite 735
Chicago 60604
(312) 578-0175

EVANSTON PUBLIC LIBRARY
1703 Orrington Ave.
Evanston 60201
(847) 866-0305

ROCK ISLAND PUBLIC LIBRARY
401 - 19th St.
Rock Island 61201
(309) 788-7627

UNIVERSITY OF ILLINOIS AT
SPRINGFIELD
Brookens Library
P.O. Box 19243
Springfield 62794-9243
(217) 206-6633

Indiana
EVANSVILLE-VANDERBURGH
COUNTY PUBLIC LIBRARY
22 Southeast Fifth St.
Evansville 47708
(812) 428-8200

ALLEN COUNTY PUBLIC
LIBRARY
900 Webster St.
Ft. Wayne 46802
(219) 421-1200

INDIANAPOLIS-MARION
COUNTY PUBLIC LIBRARY
Social Sciences
P.O. Box 211
40 E. St. Clair
Indianapolis 46206
(317) 269-1733

VIGO COUNTY PUBLIC LIBRARY
1 Library Square
Terre Haute 47807
(812) 232-1113

Iowa
PUBLIC LIBRARY OF DES
MOINES
100 Locust
Des Moines 50309-1791
(515) 283-4295

SIOUX CITY PUBLIC LIBRARY
529 Pierce St.
Sioux City 51101-1202
(712) 252-5669

Kansas
DODGE CITY PUBLIC LIBRARY
1001 2nd Ave.
Dodge City 67801
(316) 225-0248

TOPEKA AND SHAWNEE
COUNTY PUBLIC LIBRARY
1515 SW 10th Ave.
Topeka 66604-1374
(785) 233-2040

WICHITA PUBLIC LIBRARY
223 S. Main St.
Wichita 67202
(316) 261-8500

Kentucky
WESTERN KENTUCKY
UNIVERSITY
Helm-Cravens Library
Bowling Green 42101-3576
(502) 745-6125

LEXINGTON PUBLIC LIBRARY
140 East Main Street
Lexington 40507-1376
(606) 231-5520

LOUISVILLE FREE PUBLIC
LIBRARY
301 York Street
Louisville 40203
(502) 574-1611

Louisiana
E BATON ROUGE LIBRARY
120 St. Louis
Baton Rouge 70802
(225) 389-4967

BEAUREGARD PARISH
LIBRARY
205 S. Washington Ave.
De Ridder 70634
(318) 463-6217

OUACHITA PARISH PUBLIC
LIBRARY
1800 Stubbs Avenue
Monroe 71201
(318) 327-1490

NEW ORLEANS PUBLIC
LIBRARY
Business & Science Division
219 Loyola Ave.
New Orleans 70140
(504) 596-2580

SHREVE MEMORIAL LIBRARY
424 Texas St.
Shreveport 71120-1523
(318) 226-5894

Maine
MAINE GRANTS INFORMATION
CENTER
University of Southern Maine
Library
314 Forrest Ave.
Portland 04104-9301
(207) 780-5039

Maryland
ENOCH PRATT FREE LIBRARY
Social Science & History
400 Cathedral St.
Baltimore 21201
(410) 396-5430

Massachusetts
ASSOCIATED GRANTMAKERS
OF MASSACHUSETTS
294 Washington St., Suite 840
Boston 02108
(617) 426-2606

BOSTON PUBLIC LIBRARY
700 Boylston Street
Boston 02117
(617) 536-5400

WESTERN MASSACHUSETTS
FUNDING RESOURCE CENTER
65 Elliot St.
Springfield 01101-1730
(413) 452-0615

WORCESTER PUBLIC LIBRARY
Grants Resource Center
60 Fremont St.
Worcester 01603
(508) 799-1655

Michigan
ALPENA COUNTY LIBRARY
211 N. First St.
Alpena 49707
(517) 356-6188

UNIVERSITY OF MICHIGAN
Graduate Library
Reference & Research Services
Department
Ann Arbor 48109-1205
(313) 764-9373

WILLARD PUBLIC LIBRARY
Nonprofit and Funding Resource
Collections
7 West Van Buren St.
Battle Creek 49017
(616) 968-8166

HENRY FORD CENTENNIAL
LIBRARY
Adult Services
16301 Michigan Ave.
Dearborn 48124
(313) 943-2330

WAYNE STATE UNIVERSITY
Purdy/Kresge Library
5265 Cass Avenue
Detroit 48202
(313) 577-6424

MICHIGAN STATE UNIVERSITY
LIBRARIES
Reference
100 Library
East Lansing 48824-1048
(517) 355-2344

FARMINGTON COMMUNITY
LIBRARY
32737 West 12 Mile Rd.
Farmington Hills 48334
(248) 553-0300

UNIVERSITY OF MICHIGAN-
FLINT
Library
Flint 48502-2186
(810) 762-3408

GRAND RAPIDS PUBLIC
LIBRARY
Business Dept., 3rd Floor
60 Library Plaza NE
Grand Rapids 49503-3093
(616) 456-3600

MICHIGAN TECHNOLOGICAL
UNIVERSITY
Van Pelt Library
1400 Townsend Dr.
Houghton 49931
(906) 487-2507

MAUD PRESTON PALENSKE
MEMORIAL LIBRARY
500 Market St.
St. Joseph 49085
(616) 983-7167

NORTHWESTERN MICHIGAN
COLLEGE
Mark & Helen Osterin Library
1701 E. Front St.
Traverse City 49684
(616) 922-1060

Minnesota
DULUTH PUBLIC LIBRARY
520 W. Superior St.
Duluth 55802
(218) 723-3802

SOUTHWEST STATE
UNIVERSITY
University Library
North Highway 23
Marshall 56253
(507) 537-6176

MINNEAPOLIS PUBLIC LIBRARY
Sociology Department
300 Nicollet Mall
Minneapolis 55401
(612) 630-6300

ROCHESTER PUBLIC LIBRARY
101 2nd Street, SE
Rochester 55904-3777
(507) 285-8002

ST. PAUL PUBLIC LIBRARY
90 W. Fourth St.
St. Paul 55102
(651) 266-7000

Mississippi
JACKSON/HINDS LIBRARY
SYSTEM
300 N. State St.
Jackson 39201
(601) 968-5803

Missouri
CLEARINGHOUSE FOR
MIDCONTINENT FOUNDATIONS
University of Missouri
5110 Cherry, Suite 310
Kansas City 64110
(816) 235-1176

KANSAS CITY PUBLIC LIBRARY
311 E. 12th St.
Kansas City 64106
(816) 701-3541

METROPOLITAN ASSOCIATION
FOR PHILANTHROPY, INC.
One Metropolitan Square, #1295
211 North Broadway, Suite 1200
St. Louis 63102
(314) 621-6220

SPRINGFIELD-GREENE COUNTY
LIBRARY
397 E. Central
Springfield 65802
(417) 837-5000

Montana
MONTANA STATE UNIVERSITY -
BILLINGS
Library - Special Collections
1500 North 30th St.
Billings 59101-0298
(406) 657-2046

BOZEMAN PUBLIC LIBRARY
220 E. Lamme
Bozeman 59715
(406) 582-2402

MONTANA STATE LIBRARY
Library Services
1515 E. 6th Ave.
Helena 59620
(406) 444-3004

UNIVERSITY OF MONTANA
Maureen & Mike Mansfield Library
Missoula 59812-1195
(406) 243-6800

Nebraska
UNIVERSITY OF NEBRASKA-
LINCOLN
Love Library
14th & R Streets
Lincoln 68588-0410
(402) 472-2848

W. DALE CLARK LIBRARY
Social Sciences Department
215 S. 15th St.
Omaha 68102
(402) 444-4826

Nevada
CLARK COUNTY LIBRARY
1401 E. Flamingo
Las Vegas 89119
(702) 733-3642

WASHOE COUNTY LIBRARY
301 S. Center St.
Reno 89505
(775) 785-4190

New Hampshire
CONCORD PUBLIC LIBRARY
45 Green Street
Concord 03301
(603) 225-8670

PLYMOUTH STATE COLLEGE
Herbert H. Lamson Library
Plymouth 03264
(603) 535-2258

New Jersey
CUMBERLAND COUNTY
LIBRARY
800 E. Commerce St.
Bridgeton 08302
(609) 453-2210

FREE PUBLIC LIBRARY OF
ELIZABETH
11 S. Broad St.
Elizabeth 07202
(908) 354-6060

NEW JERSEY STATE LIBRARY
Governmental Reference Services
185 West State St.
Trenton 08625-0520
(609) 292-6220

New Mexico
ALBUQUERQUE COMMUNITY
FOUNDATION
3301 Menaul NE, Suite 30
Albuquerque 87176-6960
(505) 883-6240

NEW MEXICO STATE LIBRARY
Information Services
1209 Camino Carlos Rey
Santa Fe 87505-9860
(505) 476-9714

New York
NEW YORK STATE LIBRARY
Humanities Reference
Cultural Education Center, 6th floor
Empire State Plaza
Albany 12230
(518) 474-5355

SUFFOLK COOPERATIVE
LIBRARY SYSTEM
627 N. Sunrise Service Rd.
Bellport 11713
(516) 286-1600

NEW YORK PUBLIC LIBRARY
Bronx Reference Center
2556 Bainbridge Ave.
Bronx 10458-4698
(718) 579-4257

THE NONPROFIT CONNECTION,
INC.
One Hanson Place, Room 2504
Brooklyn 11243
(718) 230-3200

BROOKLYN PUBLIC LIBRARY
Social Sciences/Philosophy Division
Grand Army Plaza
Brooklyn 11238
(718) 230-2100

BUFFALO & ERIE COUNTY
PUBLIC LIBRARY
Business, Science, and Technology
Dept.
1 Lafayette Square
Buffalo 14203
(716) 858-7097

HUNTINGTON PUBLIC LIBRARY
338 Main St.
Huntington 11743
(516) 427-5165

QUEENS BOROUGH PUBLIC
LIBRARY
Social Sciences Division
89-11 Merrick Blvd.
Jamaica 11432
(718) 990-0700

LEVITTOWN PUBLIC LIBRARY
1 Bluegrass Lane
Levittown 11756
(516) 731-5728

FOUNDATION CENTER OFFICE
AND LIBRARY
79 Fifth Avenue
2nd Floor New York 10003-3076
(212) 620-4230

NEW YORK PUBLIC LIBRARY
Countee Cullen Branch Library
104 W. 136th St.
New York 10030
(212) 491-2070

ADRIANCE MEMORIAL
LIBRARY
Special Services Department
93 Market St.
Poughkeepsie 12601
(914) 485-3445

ROCHESTER PUBLIC LIBRARY
Social Sciences
115 South Avenue
Rochester 14604
(716) 428-8120

ONONDAGA COUNTY PUBLIC
LIBRARY
447 S. Salina St.
Syracuse 13202-2494
(315) 435-1818

UTICA PUBLIC LIBRARY
303 Genesee St.
Utica 13501
(315) 735-2279

WHITE PLAINS PUBLIC
LIBRARY
100 Martine Ave.
White Plains 10601
(914) 422-1480

YONKERS PUBLIC LIBRARY
Reference Department, Getty
Square Branch
7 Main St.
Yonkers, NY 10701
(914) 476-1255

North Carolina
COMMUNITY FDN. OF WESTERN
NORTH CAROLINA
Nonprofit Resources Center
16 Biltmore Avenue, Suite 201
P.O. Box 1888
Asheville 28802
(828) 254-4960

THE DUKE ENDOWMENT
100 N. Tryon St., Suite 3500
Charlotte 28202
(704) 376-0291

DURHAM COUNTY PUBLIC
LIBRARY
301 North Roxboro
Durham 27702
(919) 560-0110

STATE LIBRARY OF NORTH
CAROLINA
Government and Business Services
Archives Bldg., 109 E. Jones St.
Raleigh 27601
(919) 733-3270

FORSYTH COUNTY PUBLIC
LIBRARY
660 W. 5th St.
Winston-Salem 27101
(336) 727-2680

North Dakota
BISMARCK PUBLIC LIBRARY
515 North Fifth St.
Bismarck 58501
(701) 222-6410

FARGO PUBLIC LIBRARY
102 N. 3rd St.
Fargo 58102
(701) 241-1491

Ohio
STARK COUNTY DISTRICT
LIBRARY
715 Market Ave. N.
Canton 44702
(330) 452-0665

FOUNDATION CENTER OFFICE
AND LIBRARY
Kent H. Smith Library
1422 Euclid Avenue, Suite 1356
Cleveland, OH 44115
(216) 861-1933

PUBLIC LIBRARY OF
CINCINNATI & HAMILTON CTY
Grants Resource Center
800 Vine St., Library Square
Cincinnati 45202-2071
(513) 369-6940

COLUMBUS METROPOLITAN
LIBRARY
Business and Technology Dept.
96 S. Grant Ave.
Columbus 43215
(614) 645-2590

DAYTON & MONTGOMERY
COUNTY PUBLIC LIBRARY
Grants Resource Center
215 E. Third St.
Dayton 45402
(937) 227-9500 x211

MANSFIELD/RICHLAND
COUNTY PUBLIC LIBRARY
42 West 3rd Street
Mansfield 44902
(419) 521-3110

TOLEDO-LUCAS COUNTY
PUBLIC LIBRARY
Social Sciences Department
325 Michigan St.
Toledo 43624-1614
(419) 259-5245

LIBRARY OF YOUNGSTOWN &
MAHONING CTY
305 Wick Ave.
Youngstown 44503
(330) 744-8636

MUSKINGUM COUNTY LIBRARY
220 N. 5th St.
Zanesville 43701
(614) 453-0391

Oklahoma
OKLAHOMA CITY UNIVERSITY
Dulaney Browne Library
2501 N. Blackwelder
Oklahoma City 73106
(405) 521-5822

TULSA CITY-COUNTY LIBRARY
400 Civic Center
Tulsa 74103
(918) 596-7940

Oregon
OREGON INSTITUTE OF
TECHNOLOGY Library
3201 Campus Dr.
Klamath Falls 97601-8801
(541) 885-1780

PACIFIC NON-PROFIT
NETWORK
Grantsmanship Resource Library
33 N. Central, Suite 211
Medford 97501
(541) 779-6044

MULTNOMAH COUNTY
LIBRARY
Government Documents
801 SW Tenth Ave.
Portland 97205
(503) 248-5123

OREGON STATE LIBRARY
State Library Building
Salem 97310
(503) 378-4277

Pennsylvania
NORTHAMPTON COMMUNITY
COLLEGE
Learning Resources Center
3835 Green Pond Rd.
Bethlehem 18017
(610) 861-5360

ERIE COUNTY LIBRARY
160 East Front St.
Erie 16507
(814) 451-6927

DAUPHIN COUNTY LIBRARY
SYSTEM
Central Library
101 Walnut St.
Harrisburg 17101
(717) 234-4976

LANCASTER COUNTY PUBLIC
LIBRARY
125 N. Duke St.
Lancaster 17602
(717) 394-2651

FREE LIBRARY OF
PHILADELPHIA
Regional Foundation Center
Logan Square
Philadelphia 19103
(215) 686-5423

CARNEGIE LIBRARY OF
PITTSBURGH
Foundation Collection
4400 Forbes Ave.
Pittsburgh 15213-4080
(412) 622-1917

POCONO NORTHEAST
DEVELOPMENT FUND
James Pettinger Memorial Library
1151 Oak St.
Pittston 18640-3795
(570) 655-5581

READING PUBLIC LIBRARY
100 South Fifth St.
Reading 19475
(610) 655-6355

MARTIN LIBRARY
159 Market St.
York 17401
(717) 846-5300

Rhode Island
PROVIDENCE PUBLIC LIBRARY
225 Washington St.
Providence 02903
(401) 455-8000

South Carolina
ANDERSON COUNTY LIBRARY
202 East Greenville St.
Anderson 29621
(864) 260-4500

CHARLESTON COUNTY
LIBRARY
68 Calhoun St.
Charleston 29401
(843) 805-6950

SOUTH CAROLINA STATE
LIBRARY
1500 Senate St.
Columbia 29211-1469
(803) 734-8666

COMMUNITY FOUNDATION OF
GREATER GREENVILLE
27 Cleveland Stree, Suite 101
P.O. Box 6909
Greenville 29606
(864) 233-5925

South Dakota
SOUTH DAKOTA STATE
LIBRARY
800 Governors Drive
Pierre 57501-5070
(605) 773-3131
(800) 592-1841 (SD residents)

DAKOTA STATE UNIVERSITY
Nonprofit Grants Assistance 132 S.
Dakota Ave.
Sioux Falls 57104
(605) 367-5380

SIOUXLAND LIBRARIES
201 N. Main Ave.
Sioux Falls 57104
(605) 367-7081

Tennessee
KNOX COUNTY PUBLIC
LIBRARY
500 W. Church Ave.
Knoxville 37902
(423) 544-5750

MEMPHIS & SHELBY COUNTY
PUBLIC LIBRARY
1850 Peabody Ave.
Memphis 38104
(901) 725-8877

NASHVILLE PUBLIC LIBRARY
225 Polk Ave.
Nashville 37203
(615) 862-5842

Texas
NONPROFIT RESOURCE
CENTER
500 N. Chestnut, Suite 1511
P.O. Box 3322
Abilene 79604
(915) 677-8166

AMARILLO AREA FOUNDATION
Funding Research and Nonprofit
Management Library
Nonprofit Services Center
700 First National Place, Ste. 700
801 S. Fillmore
Amarillo 79101
(806) 376-4521

HOGG FOUNDATION FOR
MENTAL HEALTH
3001 Lake Austin Blvd.
Austin 78703
(512) 471-5041

BEAUMONT PUBLIC LIBRARY
801 Pearl Street
Beaumont 77704-3827
(409) 838-6606

CORPUS CHRISTI PUBLIC
LIBRARY
Funding Information Center
805 Comanche Street
Corpus Christi 78401
(361) 880-7000

DALLAS PUBLIC LIBRARY
Urban Information
1515 Young St.
Dallas 75201
(214) 670-1487

SOUTHWEST BORDER
NONPROFIT RESOURCE
CENTER
1201 W. University Drive
Edinburgh 78539
(956) 384-5900

CENTER FOR VOLUNTEERISM &
NONPROFIT MANAGEMENT
1918 Texas Avenue
El Paso 79901
(915) 532-5377

FUNDING INFORMATION
CENTER OF FORT WORTH
329 S. Henderson
Fort Worth 76104
(817) 334-0228

HOUSTON PUBLIC LIBRARY
Bibliographic Information Center
500 McKinney
Houston 77002
(713) 236-1313

NONPROFIT MANAGEMENT
AND VOLUNTEER CENTER
Laredo Public Library
1120 East Calton Road
Laredo 78041
(956) 795-2400

LONGVIEW PUBLIC LIBRARY
222 W. Cotton St.
Longview 75601
(903) 237-1352

LUBBOCK AREA FOUNDATION,
INC.
1655 Main St., Suite 209
Lubbock 79401
(806) 762-8061

NONPROFIT RESOURCE
CENTER OF TEXAS
111 Soledad, Suite 200
San Antonio 78205
(210) 227-4333

WACO-McLENNAN COUNTY
LIBRARY
1717 Austin Ave.
Waco 76701
(254) 750-5975

NORTH TEXAS CENTER FOR
NONPROFIT MANAGEMENT
624 Indiana, Suite 307
Wichita Falls 76301
(940) 322-4961

Utah
SALT LAKE CITY PUBLIC
LIBRARY
209 East 500 South
Salt Lake City 84111
(801) 524-8200

Vermont
VERMONT DEPT. OF LIBRARIES
Reference & Law Info. Services
109 State St.
Montpelier 05609
(802) 828-3268

Virginia
HAMPTON PUBLIC LIBRARY
4207 Victoria Blvd.
Hampton 23669
(757) 727-1312

RICHMOND PUBLIC LIBRARY
Business, Science & Technology
101 East Franklin St.
Richmond 23219
(804) 780-8223

ROANOKE CITY PUBLIC
LIBRARY SYSTEM
Main Library
706 S. Jefferson St.
Roanoke 24016
(540) 853-2477

Washington
MID-COLUMBIA LIBRARY
405 South Dayton
Kennewick 99336
(509) 586-3156

SEATTLE PUBLIC LIBRARY
Fundraising Resource Center
1000 Fourth Ave.
Seattle 98104-1193
(206) 386-4620

SPOKANE PUBLIC LIBRARY
Funding Information Center
West 811 Main Ave.
Spokane 99201
(509) 444-5336

UNITED WAY OF PIERCE
COUNTY
Center for Nonprofit Development
1501 Pacific Ave., Suite 400
P.O. Box 2215
Tacoma 98401
(253) 597-7496

GREATER WENATCHEE
COMMUNITY FOUNDATION AT
THE WENATCHEE PUBLIC
LIBRARY
310 Douglas St.
Wenatchee 98807
(509) 662-5021

West Virginia
KANAWHA COUNTY PUBLIC
LIBRARY
123 Capitol St.
Charleston 25301
(304) 343-4646

Wisconsin
UNIVERSITY OF WISCONSIN-
MADISON
Memorial Library, Grants
Information Center
728 State St., Room 276
Madison 53706
(608) 262-3242

MARQUETTE UNIVERSITY
MEMORIAL LIBRARY
Funding Information Center
1415 W. Wisconsin Ave.
Milwaukee 53201-3141
(414) 288-1515

UNIVERSITY OF WISCONSIN-
STEVENS POINT
Library - Foundation Collection
900 Reserve St.
Stevens Point 54481-3897
(715) 346-4204

Wyoming
NATRONA COUNTY PUBLIC
LIBRARY
307 E. 2nd St.
Casper 82601-2598
(307) 237-4935

LARAMIE COUNTY COMMUNITY
COLLEGE
Instructional Resource Center
1400 E. College Dr.
Cheyenne 82007-3299
(307) 778-1206

CAMPBELL COUNTY PUBLIC
LIBRARY
2101 4-J Road
Gillette 82718
(307) 687-0115

TETON COUNTY LIBRARY
125 Virginia Lane
Jackson 83001
(307) 733-2164

ROCK SPRINGS LIBRARY
400 C St.
Rock Springs 82901
(307) 362-6669

Puerto Rico
UNIVERSIDAD DEL SAGRADO
CORAZON
M.M.T. Guevara Library
Santurce 00914
(809) 728-1515 x 4357

The Foundation Center directories

The Foundation Center directories are a vehicle for compiling an initial list of foundations or grant-making organizations that may be interested in your project. You can access these directories free of charge at any of the main branch locations of The Foundation Center or the cooperating collections just listed.

No single directory covers every conceivable source of funding. Some focus only on the largest national foundations; others on corporate foundations or corporate giving programs; others attempt to cover all three. Some specialize according to topic; others by location or recipient categories.

Be sure to check through all the pertinent types to identify an appropriate number of potential funding sources. Then research each one carefully to make sure you qualify. The following sources are good starting points for such a search.

National Directories of Corporate Foundations or Direct Giving Programs National Directories

FOUNDATION DIRECTORY. New York, N.Y. : Foundation Center, annual. [AS911 .A2 F65]

The Foundation Directory is one of the oldest and most widely used directories covering American private foundations having assets of $2 million or that awarded $200,000 or more in grants during the preceeding reporting period. Each foundation listing provides the latest fiscal data plus updates on addresses and phone numbers, officers and trustees, purpose and activities, giving restrictions, types of support, contact person, application guidelines and deadlines, publication listings, and IRS number.

FOUNDATION DIRECTORY, PART 2. New York, N.Y. : Foundation Center, annual. [AS911 .A2 F65 Pt. 2]

A companion volume to the Foundation Directory focusing on mid-sized foundations — those with total grants between $50,000 — $200,000. Each entry includes contact information, relevant financial data, giving priorities and limitations, and statement of purpose. Most entries also feature sample descriptions of recently awarded grants. Information is indexed in five ways : alphabetically by foundation name, geographically, subject, type of support provided, and donors, officers, and trustees.

DIRECTORY OF CORPORATE AND FOUNDATION GIVERS : A NATIONAL LISTING OF THE 8,000 MAJOR FUNDING SOURCES FOR NONPROFITS. Rockville, Md. : Taft Group, annual. In two volumes. [HV97 .A3 F62]

Profiles approximately 8000 leading funders in America, including private foundations, corporate foundations, and corporate direct giving programs. Includes contact information, program descriptions, officers and directors (including biographical information), grant types, application information, and the top ten foundation grants. Nine different indexes are provided for access purposes : by headquarters state, by operating location, by grant type, by nonmonetary support type, by recipient type, by major products/industry, by name of officers and directors, by state of grant recipients, and in alphabetic order by name of the corporation or foundation.

GUIDE TO U.S. FOUNDATIONS, THEIR TRUSTEES, OFFICERS, AND DONORS. New York, N.Y. : Foundation Center, annual. [AS911 .A2 F645]

Provides fundraisers with current, accurate information on all 35,000+ active grantmaking foundations in the U.S. The two-volume set also includes a master list of the names of the people who establish, oversee, and manage those institutions. With access to this information, fundraisers can facilitate their funding prospect research by discovering the philanthropic connections of their current donors, board members, volunteers, and prominent families in their geographic area. Each entry includes asset and giving amounts as well as geographic limitations, so fundraisers can quickly determine whether or not to pursue a particular grant source. The only source for information on some of the smaller, local foundations.

NATIONAL DIRECTORY OF GRANTMAKING PUBLIC CHARITIES. New York, N.Y. :Foundation Center, 1998. 2nd edition, 435pp. [HV89 .N37 Ed. 2]

Many public charities, like foundations, award grants to nonprofit organizations. This publication covers 1050 public charities, featuring data-packed entries that include the facts you need when seeking new grant prospects : current fiscal information, purpose and activities statements, giving interests and limitations, information on formal giving programs, descriptions of recently awarded grants, application information, names of key officials, and chapter locations.

Directories of Corporate Foundations and Corporate Giving Programs

CORPORATE FOUNDATION PROFILES. New York, N.Y. : Foundation Center, biennial. [HV97 .A3 C64]

Contains comprehensive, detailed analyses of 228 of the largest company-sponsored foundations in the U.S, grantmakers that each give at least $1.25 million annually. Foundation portraits feature the essential facts you need to write a proposal, such as the grantmaker's name, address, and contact person; purpose and giving limitation statements, application guidelines, and a list of key officials; and an analysis of the sponsoring company. By studying the in-depth profile, you should be able to deduce the subject areas favored by the foundation, the kinds of recipient organizations that have received grants, tne the type of population groups a grantmaker targets for support. An appendix provides quick-reference data on an additional 1,000 smaller corporate grantmakers.

CORPORATE GIVING DIRECTORY. Rockville, Md. : Taft Group, annual. [HV97 .A3 T32]

Provides detailed descriptive profiles of 1,000 of the largest and most important corporate charitable giving programs in the U.S. Approximately 60% of these profiles cover corporate giving programs, the rest corporate foundations. Each profile describes the funder's priorities, geographic preferences, as well as providing background information on the decision-makers within the companies and giving programs, application procedures, nonmonetary and in-kind support, and recent grants. Eight indexes help identify prospects. These include indexes by headquarters state, operating location, grant type, nonmonetary support, recipient type, individuals by name, individuals by place of birth, and individuals by alma mater.

CORPORATE GIVING YELLOW PAGES : GUIDE TO CORPORATE GIVING CONTACTS. Rockville, Md. : Taft Group, 1995. 349pp. [HV89 .C683]

Consists of a main section listing over 3800 corporate direct giving programs and company-sponsored foundations, arranged alphabetically by the sponsoring company name. Three indexes follow the main section : geographic by headquarters and operating locations, and by major products/industry.

DIRECTORY OF CORPORATE AND FOUNDATION GIVERS : A NATIONAL LISTING OF THE 8,050 MAJOR FUNDING SOURCES FOR NONPROFITS. Rockville, Md. : Taft Group, annual.

Profiles 8050 leading funders in America, including private foundtions, corporate foundations, and corporate direct giving programs. Includes contact information, program descriptions, officers and directors (including biographical information), grant types, application information, and the top ten foundation grants. Nine different indexes are provided for access purposes : by headquarters state, by operating location, by grant type, by nonmonetary support type, by recipient type, by major products/ industry, by name of officers and directors, by state of grant recipients, and in alphabetic order by name of the corporation or foundation.

NATIONAL DIRECTORY OF CORPORATE GIVING. New York, N.Y. : Foundation Center,

The most comprehensive directory on corporate giving available. The fifth edition profiles over 2,532 companies making contributions to nonprofit organizations, including 1905 corporate foundations and 990 direct giving programs, as well as including those of 363 Fortune 500 and 457 Forbes 500 companies. Entries provide a general description of the company and its activities and specific information on giving programs and foundations, including: name, address, phone number, contact person, financial data (with assets, high and low gifts, and amount and number of employee matching gifts), purpose and activities, limitations, types of support, application information, and sample grants. Includes guidelines for grantseekers, a glossary, and a bibliography.

Guides to individual donors

Approximately 90 percent of the philanthropic dollar actually comes from individuals. Attached is a list of possible sources of information on individual donors, including guides to some of the nation's wealthiest individuals as well as persons in foundation and corporate positions who have influence on who gets funded in their organizations.

FUNDING DECISION MAKERS : A GUIDE TO PHILANTHROPIC CONNECTIONS. Rockville, Md. : Taft Group.

Lists more than 15,000 officers, directors, and trustees from approximately 4000 grant-making organizations. They support a wide range of activities, from arts and humanities to social services, from the environment to volunteerism. Through their funding affiliations, they make decisions on various types of charitable contributions, from cash grants to nonmonetary donations to planned giving. Each individual affiliation of an individual is provided.

GUIDE TO PRIVATE FORTUNES : The Taft Group.

Provides detailed profiles of individuals with a minimum net worth of $25 million and an established history of charitable giving—either directly or through private foundations. In some cases, individuals have been included whose net worth is less than $25 million, or whose wealth cannot be accurately described, but who have strong connections to philanthropic institutions in the U.S. Individuals as well as wealthy and philanthropic families are represented, as are non-U.S. millionaires and billionaires who have charitable and/or corporate ties to this country.

MAJOR DONORS. Rockville, Md. : The Taft Group.

Lists more than 8,000 individuals who have recently donated major gifts to America's largest nonprofit organizations.

WHERE THE MONEY IS : A FUND RAISER'S GUIDE TO THE RICH. Alexandria, Va. : BioGuide Press.

A definitive guide to prospect and donor research, including information on how to locate wealthy individuals, how to use over 200 biographical reference sources, how to find a person's financial net worth, how to research corporations and their executives, how politicians raise funds through networking, how to solicit large contributions from the rich, and how to use computer technology for prospect research.

WHO'S WEALTHY IN AMERICA: The Taft Group.

A directory of the 50,000 richest people in America, who have a net worth of over $1 million, including information such as phone numbers, addresses, age, educational background, personal interests, stock holdings, political contributions, and references to additional sources of information. Company name, geographic area, alma mater, and political contribution indexes are also provided.

Appendix X Access Points to *Catalog of Federal Domestic Assistance* Programs

Arkansas
Tracy L. Copeland, Manager
State Clearinghouse
Office of Intergovernmental Services
Department of Finance and Administration
1515 W. 7th St., Room 412
Little Rock, AR 72203
Ph: (501) 682-1074

California
Grants Coordination
Office of Planning and Research
1400 Tenth Street, Room 222
Sacramento, CA 95812-3044
Ph: (916) 445-0613

Delaware
Francine Booth, State Single Point of Contact
Executive Department, Office of the Budget
540 S. Dupont Highway, Suite 5
Dover, DE 19901
Ph: (302) 739-3326

District of Columbia
Charles Nichols, State Single Point of Contact
Office of Grants Management and Development
717 14th Street, N.W. Suite 1200
Washington, DC 20005
Ph: (202) 727-1700

Florida
Cherie L. Trainor, Florida State Clearinghouse
Department of Community Affairs
2555 Shumard Oak Blvd.
Tallahassee, FL 32399-2100
Ph: (850) 414-5495

Georgia
Z. J. Curry, Coordinator
Georgia State Clearinghouse
270 Washington Street, SW
Atlanta, GA 30334
Ph: (404) 656-3855

Illinois
Virginia Bova
Department of Commerce and Community Affairs
James R. Thompson Center
100 West Randolph, Suite 3-400
Chicago, IL 60601
Ph: (312) 814-6028

Indiana
Renee Miller, State Budget Agency
212 State House
Indianapolis, IN 46204-2796
Ph: (317) 232-2971

Iowa
Steven R. McCann
Division of Community and Rural Development
Iowa Department of Economic Development
200 East Grand Avenue
Des Moines, Iowa 50309
Ph: (515) 242-4719

Kentucky
Kevin J. Goldsmith, Director Intergovernmental Affairs
Office of the Governor
700 Capitol Avenue
Frankfort, Kentucky 40601
Ph: (502) 564-2611

Maine
Joyce Benson, State Planning Office
184 State Street
38 State House Station
Augusta, Maine 04333
Ph: (207) 287-3261

Maryland
Linda Janey, Manager, Plan and Project Review
Maryland Office of Planning
301 West Preston Street - Room 1104
Baltimore, Maryland 21201-2305
Ph: (410) 767-4490

Michigan
Richard W. Pfaff
Southeast Michigan Council of Governments
660 Plaza Drive - Suite 1900
Detroit, Michigan 48226
Ph: (313) 961-4266

Mississippi
Cathy Mallette, Clearinghouse Officer
Department of Finance and Administration
550 High Street
303 Walters Sillers Building
Jackson, Mississippi 39201-3087
Ph: (601) 359-6762

Missouri
Lois Pohl, Coordinator
Federal Assistance Clearinghouse
Office of Administration
P.O. Box 809
Room 915, Jefferson Building
Jefferson City, Missouri 65102
Ph: (573) 751-4834

Nevada
Department of Administration
State Clearinghouse
209 E. Musser Street, Room 200
Carson City, Nevada 89701
Ph: (775) 684-0222

New Hampshire
Jeffrey H. Taylor, Director
New Hampshire Office of State Planning
Attn: Intergovernmental Review Process, Mike Blake
2 1/2 Beacon Street
Concord, New Hampshire 03301
Ph: (603) 271-2155

New Mexico
Nick Mandell
Local Government Division
Room 201 Bataan Memorial Building
Santa Fe, New Mexico 87503
Ph: (505) 827-3640

North Carolina
Jeanette Furney
North Carolina State Clearinghouse
Office of the Secretary of Administration
116 West Jones Street, Suite 5106
Raleigh, North Carolina 27603-8003
Ph: (919) 733-7232

North Dakota
North Dakota Single Point of Contact
Office of Intergovernmental Assistance
600 East Boulevard Ave, Dept 105
Bismarck, North Dakota 58505-0170
Ph: (701) 224-2094

Puerto Rico
Jose Caballero-Mercado, Chairman
Puerto Rico Planning Board
Federal Proposals Review Office
Minillas Government Center
P.O. Box 41119
San Juan, Puerto Rico 00940-1119
Ph: (787) 727-4444/723-6190

Rhode Island
Kevin Nelson, Review Coordinator
Department of Administration
Division of Planning
One Capitol Hill, 4th Floor
Providence, Rhode Island 02908-5870
Ph: (401) 277-2656

South Carolina
Omeagia Burgess
State Single Point of Contact
Budget and Control Board
Office of State Budget
1122 Ladies Street - 12th Floor
Columbia, South Carolina 29201
Ph: (803) 734-0494

Texas
Tom Adams
Governors Office
Director, Intergovernmental Coordination
P.O. Box 12428
Austin, Texas 78711
Ph: (512) 463-1771

Utah
Carolyn Wright
Utah State Clearinghouse
Office of Planning and Budget
Room 116, State Capitol
Salt Lake City, Utah 84114
Ph: (801) 538-1027

West Virginia
Fred Cutlip, Director
Community Development Division
West Virginia Development Office
Building #6, Room 553
State Capitol
Charleston, West Virginia 25305
Ph: (304) 558-4010

Wisconsin
Jeff Smith, Section Chief
Federal/State Relations
Wisconsin Department of Administration
101 East Wilson Street - 6th Floor
Madison, Wisconsin 53707
Ph: (608) 266-0267

Wyoming
Sandy Ross, State Single Point of Contact
Department of Administration and Information
2001 Capitol Avenue, Room 214
Cheyenne, WY* 82002
Ph: (307) 777-5492

Appendix XI Miscellaneous Resources

Helpful organizations

Americans for the Arts
One East 53rd Street
New York, NY 10022
phone : 212.223.2787
Web site: http://www.artsusa.org

The Grantsmanship Center
1125 W. Sixth Street, Fifth Floor
Los Angeles, CA 90017
Phone: (213) 482-9860
Web site: http://www.tgci.com

National Assembly of State Arts Agencies
1029 Vermont Avenue, NW, 2nd Floor
Washington, DC 20005
Ph: 202/347-6352
nasaa@nasaa-arts.org

National Council for the Traditional Arts
1320 Fenwick, Suite 200
Silver Spring, MD 20910
phone 301/565-0654, fax 301/565-0472
Web site: http://www.ncta.net

National Society of Mural Painters
c/o American Fine Arts Society
215 West 57th Street
New York, NY 10019

Volunteer Lawyers for the Arts
One East 53rd St
New York NY 10022
Ph: 212-319-2787
Web site: http://www.artswire.org/artlaw/info.html
Also see the list of state and regional arts agencies listed earlier
in the appendix.

Periodicals

The Crafts Report
300 Water St. Wilmington, DE 09801
phone: 1-800-777-7098
fax 302-656-4894
email: editor@craftsreport.com

Craft News
1001 Connecticut Ave. N.W. 1138
Washington, D.C. 20036
Phone: 202-728-9603
E-mail: craftsdc@fmn.com

Competitions *(artist announcements of public art programs)*
P.O. Box 20445
Louisville, KY 40250
Web site: http://www.competitions.org/

Bibliography

• *Artists Communities: Directory of Residencies in the U.S. Offering Time and Space for Creativity,* by Tricia Snell, Allworth Press, 1996
• *Artists and Writers Colonies : Retreats, Residencies, and Respites for the Creative Mind,* by Gail Hellund Bowler, Blue Heron Publishing, 1995
• *Arts Funding : A Report on Foundation and Corporate Grantmaking Trends,* by Renz, Loren, Mirande Dupuy, Steven Lawrence, Nathan Weber, Foundation Center, 1993
• *Born to Raise,* by Jerold Panas, Precept Press, 1998
• *The Complete Book of Model Fundraising Letters,* by Roland Kuniholm, Prentice Hall, 1995
• *The Complete Guide to Getting a Grant: How to Turn Your Ideas into Dollars,* by Laurie Blum, John Wiley & Sons, 1996
• *Don't Just Applaud-Send Money!: The Most Successful Strategies for Funding and Marketing the Arts,* by Alvin H. Reiss, Theatre Communications Group, 1995
• *Free Money from the Federal Government for Small Businesses and Entrepreneurs,* by Laurie Blum, John Wiley & Sons, 1996
• *Free Money to Change Your Life,* by Matthew Lesko, Information USA, 1997
• *The Fund Raiser's Guide to the Internet,* by Michael Johnston, John Wiley and Sons, 1998
• *Foundation Grants to Individuals,* by Phyllis Edelson, Foundation Center, 1999
• *Government Giveaways for Entrepreneurs III,* by Mathew Lesko, Information USA, 1996
• *Grant Application Writers Handbook,* by Liane Reif-Lehrer Ph.D., Jones & Bartlett Publishers
• *Grant Proposals That Succeeded,* by Virginia White (Editor), Plenum Publishing, 1983
• *Grants for Arts, Culture and the Humanities,* Foundation Center, 1999
• *The Grants Register 2000,* by Ruth Austin (Editor), St. Martins Press, 1999
• *The 'How To' Grants Manual : Successful Grantseeking Techniques for Obtaining Public and Private Grants,* by David G. Bauer, Oryx Press, 1999

Glossary

Annual report: A foundation or corporation provides a summary of financial data of the grants it gives every year in the form of a report.

Application: The formal document submitted by a potential Grantee seeking funds. The application is the most complete presentation of the project and is often the basis for the Grant Agreement.

Audit (Financial): A examination of an agency's accounting documents by an outside expert for the purpose of rendering an opinion as to fairness, consistency, and conformity with Generally Accepted Accounting Principals. Audits are generally conducted after the end of the fiscal year. Some grant programs require an audit of grant funds at the end of the project.

Audit (Program): A review of the accomplishments of a grant funded program by the staff of the funding agency. A program audit may be mandatory or random. Also know as Monitoring.

Authorization: Authorization is the legal authority upon which a program is based. Sometimes known as Enabling Legislation.

Beneficiary: A member of the target population for whom the grant was prepared. For example, a student attending adult literacy classes would be the beneficiary of a grant, while the school district would be the grantee.

Bricks and mortar: An informal term for capital funds generally used for building renovation or construction.

Cash contributions: The grantee's cash outlay for budgeted project activities, including the outlay of money contributed to the grantee by third parties.

Capital support: Money that goes toward operations, maintenance or new building construction, or equipment.

Cash flow: In general terms, money flowing in from sales or funding minus money flowing out for expenses. A positive cash flow is essential for a business to survive.

Challenge grant: See Matching funds

Community foundation: Usually considered public charities, these organizations fund grants in local communities or areas. Community foundations get their funding from larger foundation grants.

Corporate foundation: A foundation whose assets are donated by a for-profit business.

Drawdown: A drawdown is the method by which a successful grantee requests payment from the funding agency. Frequency of drawdowns, also known as draws, range from weekly electronic wire-transfers to a single lump sum payment at the end of the project.

Endowment: Funds invested in perpetuity to provide income for continued support of a nonprofit organization.

Family foundation: A private foundation whose funds come from donations by members of a single family.

Federated giving program: A fundraising effort that distributes contributed funds from a larger funder (like a government grant) to several nonprofit agencies like arts councils.

Federally recognized Indian tribal government: The governing body or a governmental agency of any Indian tribe, band, nation, or other organized group or community certified by the Secretary of the Interior as eligible for the special programs and services provided through the Bureau of Indian Affairs.

Fiscal year: A 12-month accounting period at the end of which the books are closed for an agency or governmental unit. Financial audits are conducted after the end of the fiscal year.

Funder: See Grantor

Funding cycle: The schedule of events starting with the announcement of the availability of funds, followed by the deadline for submission of applications, review of applications, award of grants, issuance of contract documents and release of funds.

Grant: A legal instrument that provides financial assistance in the form of money or property to an eligible recipient.

Grantee: The recipient of grant funds. Also known as Recipient.

Grantor: The agency, foundation, or governmental unit that awards grants. Also known as Funder or Funding Agency.

Grant period: The period established in the grant award during which support begins and ends.

Grantee: The organization to which a grant is awarded and which is accountable for the use of the funds provided.

Guidelines: Instructions for applying for funds set forth by a funder that grantseekers should follow when approaching a grantmaker.

In-kind contributions: The value of noncash contributions provided by third parties. In-kind contributions may be in the form of charges for real property and equipment or the value of goods and services directly benefiting and specifically identifiable to the project.

Institutional grant administrator: The member of the grantee organization who has the official responsibility for administering the grant, e.g., negotiating budget revisions, overseeing the submission of required reports, ensuring compliance with the terms and conditions of the grant.

Letter of intent: A letter of intent expresses a grantor's willingness to commit funds to a project if other conditions are met. This letter allows the grantee to seek other funds without firmly committing the grantor to the project.

Local government: A county, municipality, city, town, township, local public authority, school district, special district, intrastate district, council of government, any other regional or interstate government entity, or any agency or instrumentality of a local government.

Matching funds: Many funding sources will pay only a percentage of the cost of a project. The grantee is required to pay the difference with money or noncash donations from other sources. The non-grant funds are known as Matching Funds or the Match.

Obligation: The amounts of orders placed, contracts and grants awarded, goods and services received, and similar transactions during the grant period that will require payment.

Nonprofit or not-for-profit: An incorporated organization in which stockholders and trustees do not share in profits. Nonprofits are usually established to accomplish some charitable, humanitarian, or educational purpose. See also 501(c)(3).

Pass through: The act of a grantee receiving grant funds and dispersing those same funds to a sub-grantee. It is common for the Grantee to perform the Program Audit of the Sub-Grantee. A portion of the grant funds are often retained by the Grantee to cover the cost of administration.

Pipeline: An informal term for grant applications that score well, but fall just short of being awarded. If additional money is allocated to the program, or if funded projects do not materialize, a grant application "in the pipeline" may be funded.

Pre-application: A condensed version of an application. A pre-application is submitted before a full application is prepared. It is often used by Grantors to determine which applicants will be invited to submit a full application.

Program income: Money that is earned or received by a grantee or a subrecipient from the activities supported by grant funds or from products resulting from grant activities. It includes, but is not limited to, income from fees for services performed and from the sale of items fabricated under a grant; usage or rental fees for equipment or property acquired under a grant; admission fees; broadcast or distribution rights; and royalties on patents and copyrights.

Pro forma: Latin for "as a matter of form". A pro forma is a projected, proposed or hypothetical set of numbers for a project, typically the budget.

Project funds: Both the federal and non-federal funds that are used to cover the cost of budgeted project activities.

Proposal: A written document used as an application to a foundation or giving program in requesting a grant.

Public charity: Nonprofit organization that qualifies for tax-exempt status under section 501(c)(3) of the IRS code.

Query letter: Short letter of inquiry written to a funder to learn if the funding organization is willing to accept a full proposal for a project.

Recipient: See Grantee

Request for proposals (RFP): A solicitation by a grantor seeking applications from potential grantees. Also used by grantees to hire professional services.

Sponsorship: Associating with a nonprofit organization in order to receive grant funding.

Subgrant: An award of financial assistance in the form of money or property, made under a grant by a grantee to an eligible subrecipient or by a subrecipient to a lower-tier subrecipient.

Subrecipient: The legal entity to which a subgrant is awarded and which is accountable to the grantee for the use of the funds provided.

Supplies: All personal property excluding equipment and intangible property.

Tax-exempt: Organizations that are not required to pay taxes such as federal or state income tax or state sales tax.

Termination: Cancellation of sponsorship of a project.

Trustee: An officer or foundation board member with the legal authority to make decisions about how money is spent.

501(c)(3): The section of the tax code that defines non-profit, charitable (as broadly defined), tax-exempt organizations.

990-PF: The public record information return that all private foundations are required by law to submit annually to the Internal Revenue Service.

Index

Symbols

501(c)(3) 203
990-PF 203

A

AboutCom Guide 48
ACCION International 14
Aid to Artisans 14, 15
Alliance of Artists Communities 48, 169
American Association of Fund-Raising Counsel 44
American Association of Fundraising Consultants 31
American Philanthropy Review 45
Americans for the Arts 45, 160, 196
annual report 199
Appalachian Center for Crafts 166
application 8, 16, 20, 24, 29, 34, 36, 199
Arrowmont School of Arts and Crafts 166
art & craft grants to individuals 50
art in public places 7, 16, 161
Art-in-Architecture Program 161
artist in residency programs 13, 48, 166, 198
arts agencies 9, 18, 21, 30, 151, 159
Arts and Artifacts Indemnity 118
Arts and Rural Community Assistance Grants 148
arts councils 9, 12, 17, 18, 44
Arts Edge 47
Arts Grants Deadlines Newsletter 45

B

Basic Guide to Selling Arts & Crafts 212
beneficiary 199
Best of the Web for Grant Seekers 45
Brookfield Craft Center 166
budget 17, 38, 42
Bureau of Educational and Cultural Affairs 141, 153
Bureau of Indian Affairs, Department of the Interior 106
Business and Industry Direct Loans 145

Business and Industry Guaranteed Loans 146
Business and Legal Forms for Crafts 213
Business Development Assistance to Small Business 120
business plan 8

C

Canadian community foundations 47
Canadian government grants 47
capital support 199
cash flow 199
Catalog of Federal Domestic Assistance 10, 32, 34, 46, 96,
charities 9, 11
Coming Up Taller Awards 140
Common Grant Application 20, 23, 24, 28
community foundations 9, 12, 18, 44, 95, 200
cooperating collections (The Foundation Center) 177
corporate foundation 12, 200
costs projection 23
Coupeville Arts Center 166
cover letter 22, 23, 28
craft and photography grant winners 18
Craft News 197
craft schools 166
craftmarketer.com 44
Creative Arts Exchanges program 140
Creative Arts Grants 132
Criteria For Selecting Proposals 41
Cultural Exchange (Visual Arts) Fund for Artists 135

D

database 8, 43
Department of Agriculture 141-147
Department of Commerce 11
Department of Education 47, 145, 147
Department of Veterans Affairs 139
direct loans 33
Direct Payments for Specified Use 33
Direct Payments with Unrestricted Use 33
directory of art & craft grants to individuals 50
directory of grants to art/craft organizations 97
Directory of U.S. Microenterprise Programs 15
drawdown 200

E

education 7, 11
eligibility requirements 36
emergency funds 7
endowment 200
evaluation 41

F

face-to-face contact 36
family foundation 200
FC Search 147, 171, 172
Federal Budget 36
federal depository libraries 42
federal government 9, 11, 33
federal grant 10, 38, 47
Federal Register 45, 47
Federal Web Locator 47
federally recognized Indian tribal government 200
federated giving program 7, 200
FedWorld 47
fellowships 7, 11, 17, 97
FileMaker Pro 43
fiscal year 200
folk & traditional arts 7, 96, 97
Forest Service 148
formula grants 32
Foundation Center (The) 16, 18, 30, 44, 45, 97, 146, 177
Foundation Center cooperating collection library 18
Foundation Center directories 186
Foundation Center's Cooperating Collections 172
Foundation Center's Database 147
Foundation Center's Guide to Proposal Writing 147
Foundation Directory 147
Foundation Grants Index 147
foundation grants to art/craft organizations 97
foundations 7, 17, 18, 20, 21, 23, 29, 44, 50, 97
Frog Hollow - Vermont State Craft Center 166
Fund for U.S.Artists at International Festivals 152
funding cycle 200

G

government 47
government agencies 20

government grant applications 20, 34
government grants 10, 21, 44, 46, 96, 143
government web pages 47
grant period 201
grant proposal *(see proposal)*
grant winners in arts and crafts 18
grant writing 45, 48
grantee 201
grantor 201
Grants for Arts, Culture and the Humanities 65
grants from individuals 13
grants to art/craft organizations 97, 99
grants to individuals 7, 12, 50
Grants Web 47
Grantsmanship Center (The) 30, 45, 196
grantsmanship workshops 29, 30
GrantsNet 47
guaranteed/insured loans 33
guidelines 17, 20, 21, 28, 201
GuideStar 44, 45
Guilford Handcraft Center 167

H

Haystack Mountain School of Crafts 167

I

Idealist 45
in-kind contributions 201
Indian Arts and Crafts Development 103
individuals who give money 13
information contacts 36
institutional grant administrator 201
insurance 33, 128
international education and graduate programs 147
International Partnerships Office 151
Internet 18, 43, 44
Internet Prospector 46
internships 7
introduction (proposal) 38
Ironworker Training Program 102
IRS information 44

J

Japan-US Friendship Commission 152

Javits Fellowships 137-140
John C. Campbell Folk School 167

L

letter of intent 201
letter of request 28
local government 201

M

Maktrix Internet 44
matching grants 7, 201
Mendocino Art Center 168
micro-loans 14
microenterprise loans 14
microenterprise program 14, 15
Microsoft Access 43
Microsoft Word 43
minorities 7, 16
Minority Business Development 97
Minority Business Development Agency (MBDA) 96, 97, 99
Minority Business Development Centers (MBDC) 16
mission statement 21

N

National Assembly of State Arts Agencies 159, 196
National Council for the Traditional Arts 196
National Endowment for the Arts (NEA) 10, 11, 30, 46,
      106-111, 112, 115, 148, 151, 152
National Endowment for the Humanities 30, 47, 113, 115
National Forest Service 141
National Foundation for Advancement in the Arts 60
National Grant Writers Association 31
National Heritage Fellowship Award 10, 96, 97
National Heritage Fellowships in the Folk Arts 96, 98
National Network of Grantmakers 24
National Society of Fund Raising Executives 31, 46
Native American Program 96
Native Americans 7, 16, 97
nonprofit 9, 11, 13, 15, 35, 44, 45, 97, 202
Nonprofit Management Development Center 30

O

Objectives and Uses 36

obligation 202
Office of Citizens Exchanges, USIA 141, 144
Oregon School of Arts & Crafts 168

P

Partners of the Americas 151
pass through 202
patrons of the arts 13
peer lending 14
Peninsula Art School 168
Penland School of Crafts 168
Percent for Art 161
Peters Valley Craft Center 168
PhilanthropySearch 46
pipeline 202
Polaris Grants Central 29
pre-application 202
preservation 12
President's Committee on the Arts 140
private foundations 9, 11, 12, 17, 21
pro forma 202
problem statement 39
professional grant writers 30
program evaluation 41
program income 202
program methods 40
project evaluation 38
project funds 202
project grants 32
project objectives 38, 40
Promotion of the Arts--Grants to Organizations 111
Promotion of the Humanities--Fellowships 121
Promotion of the Humanities--Research 124
proposal 8, 9, 17, 20, 21, 22, 23, 24, 28, 29, 32, 34, 43, 46
proposal budget 42
proposal summary 24, 35, 38
Provision of Specialized Services 33
public art programs 47, 165
public charity 203

Q

query letter 203

R

recipient 203
request for proposals 203
Res Artis 48
research grants 11
residency programs 169
restoration 12
resume 22
reviewers 21, 24
Rural Business Enterprise Grant Program 142
Rural Business Opportunity Grant 144

S

scholarship programs 7, 11, 166
seed money 7
Service Corps of Retired Executives (SCORE) 16, 131
Sister Cities International 151
small business 7, 11, 16
Small Business Administration (SBA) 11, 16, 120-122, 124, 126
Small Business Development Centers (SBDC) 16
sponsors 13, 203
state and local access points 191
state arts councils 11
state government 9
state grant programs 11
statement of purpose 21, 22
subgrant 203
subrecipient 203
summary (proposal) 24, 38

T

tax exempt 9, 12, 203
technical and educational support 14
technical assistance 9, 151
termination 203
testimonials 22
The Crafts Report 197
The Law (In Plain English) for Crafts People 213
The Learning Annex 30
timeline plan 23
training 34
trustee 12, 203

U

United States Information Agency (USIA) 132-137
US/Japan Creative Artists' Program 152
USDA Rural Development 149
Use of Property, Facilities, and Equipment 33
use restrictions 36

V

visual arts 7, 16
vitae 22
Vocational Rehabilitation for Disabled Veterans 129
Volunteer Lawyers for the Arts 196

W

women 7, 16
Women's Business Centers (WBC) 16
Women's Business Ownership Assistance 126
Worcester Center for Crafts 169
word processor 43
WordPerfect 43
work/study 166

Y

youth development 7

About the Author

James Dillehay began creating and selling his fiber art in 1984. In 1991, he published the first marketing guide ever written for fiber artisans called Weaving Profits, hailed as *"the blueprint for success in the crafts industry"* by The Crafts Report.

Author of seven books, Dillehay's craft marketing articles have reached readers of *Family Circle, The National Examiner, The Crafts Report, Better Homes & Gardens: Crafting for Profit, Sunshine Artist, Ceramics Monthly, Florida Retirement Lifestyles* and many more publications. He was a featured guest on The Carol Duvall Show, HGTV.

His book, *The Basic Guide to Selling Arts and Crafts*, was included in the training program of the Association of Creative Craft Industries (ACCI).

James is a member of the advisory board to the National Craft Association and was listed in the 1998 *Who's Who of American Entrepreneurs*.

He published the first book ever written to help craft artists understand how to successfully sell their work online in, *The Basic Guide to Selling Crafts on the Internet*.

James lives in the Manzano Mountains of New Mexico. He teaches and speaks nationally on how to achieve craft business success.

For a free email newsletter with tips and news about craft business, visit www.craftmarketer.com